PRAISE FOR *CHINA SAFARI*

"A remarkable look at an urgent problem. Worth reading immediately!" —*Associated Press*

"The question is whether ordinary Africans will draw lasting benefit from this new association. . . . Accompanied by photographer Paolo Woods, Swiss journalists Serge Michel and Michel Beuret put in extensive legwork trying to provide an answer. . . . Michel and Beuret are admirably even-handed." —*Washington Post*

"The strength of this book is the legwork. These guys go to places Americans have never heard of. They are nosy, sneaky and persistent." —*Seattle Times*

"Through a witty narrative that at times becomes a first-person travelogue, the authors entertain while educating, revealing in the process the absurdities that come with reporting on the ground in Africa . . . [A]n admirable contribution to a story with broad geopolitical implications." —*USA Today*

"A significant book that insightfully examines China's role in Africa, *China Safari* reveals not only the complexities of Chinese immigration to Africa, but also the political rivalries that result from it. . . . Recommended for all interested readers." —*Library Journal*

"*China Safari* is a fascinating, provocative work of firsthand reporting that illuminates an important global economic story." —*New York Times*

"*China Safari* tackles an important and largely underreported topic with an engaging and lively verve. . . . Mr. Michel and Mr. Beuret make an important contribution, without passing judgment, toward our understanding of China's intentions in Africa." —*Washington Times*

"The authors of *China Safari* describe the ingredients that contribute to China's success in Africa . . . they bring their protagonists to life, describe their enthusiasm, their ardor for work, their discipline. And let's remember, by the way, that if economic power plays a role, it is the human factor that makes the difference."   —*Le Soir*

"An exceptional investigation!"   —*Le Monde*

"[*China Safari*] forces us to come face to face with reality."
—*Non Fiction*

"This impressive investigation . . . allows us to get a glimpse of the phenomenon . . . precise facts, eyewitness accounts, characters and testimonies."   —*Le Point*

"The authors of *China Safari* chose the best method for these circumstances; they went to observe in person. . . . The result is a fascinating book, a fusion of reportage, analysis, and historical narrative."   —*Amina*

"The result is remarkable. This should be widely read—especially by the elite Africans who are, almost as much as the Chinese, the subject of this book."   —*Les Afriques*

"The information *China Safari* offers about the Chinese exploitation of African (and Chinese) workers is a hefty wake up call for those in the pursuit of global fair trade and environmental and human rights. . . . The authors leave no stone unturned. The amount of research they did for this book is staggering."
—*Feminist Review*

"The authors of *China Safari* are the first to show all the constructive seeds and destructive weeds currently working in the soil of this strange new union."
—*Curled Up With A Good Book*

CHINA SAFARI

ALSO BY THE AUTHORS

Serge Michel

Bondy Blog: Des journalistes suisses dans le 93, avec la rédaction de l'Hebdo, Seuil, 2006

Serge Michel and Paolo Woods

American Chaos: Retour en Afghanistan et an Irak, 2002–2004, Seuil, 2004

Un Monde de Brut: Sur les routes de l'or noir (with Serge Enderlin), Seuil, 2003

Michel Beuret

Désirs de France: Quinze correspondants de la presse internationale nous regardent, ouvrage collectif, Michalon, 2007.

SERGE MICHEL AND MICHEL BEURET

CHINA SAFARI

On the Trail of Beijing's Expansion in Africa

PHOTOGRAPHS BY PAOLO WOODS

TRANSLATED BY RAYMOND VALLEY

NATION
BOOKS

New York

**The authors wish to acknowledge the vital contribution of James Pryor
as development editor of this book.**

Set in 11.5 point Minion by the Perseus Books Group

Library of Congress Cataloging-in-Publication Data
Michel, Serge.
    [Chinafrique. English]
    China safari : on the trail of China's expansion in Africa / Serge Michel
and Michel Beuret ; photography by Paolo Woods.
        p.   cm.
    ISBN 978-1-56858-426-3 (alk. paper)
    1. Africa—Foreign economic relations—China. 2. China—Foreign
economic relations—Africa. I. Beuret, Michel. II. Woods, Paolo. III.
Title. IV. Title: On the trail of China's expansion in Africa.
HF1611.Z4C65 2009
337.5106—dc22   2009009754

International ISBN: 978-1-56858-606-9
Paperback ISBN: 978-1-56858-614-4

10 9 8 7 6 5 4 3 2 1

Cover photo: *Some 400 yellow-helmeted Chinese technicians supervise 1,000 blue-helmeted Congolese workers a the Imboulou Dam, a China National Mechanical and Equipment Corporation project. The 120-megawatt dam will double the country's entire current electrical output.* (Congo-Brazzaville, June 2007)

CONTENTS

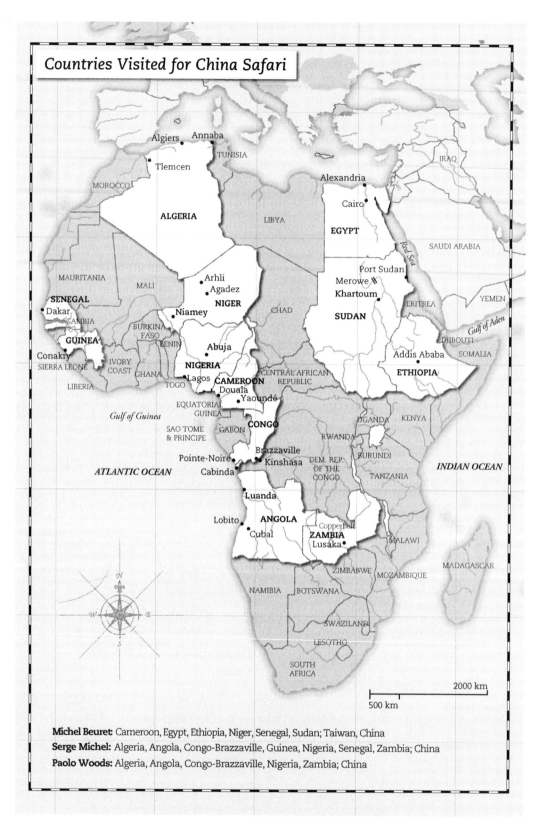

Countries Visited for China Safari

Michel Beuret: Cameroon, Egypt, Ethiopia, Niger, Senegal, Sudan; Taiwan, China
Serge Michel: Algeria, Angola, Congo-Brazzaville, Guinea, Nigeria, Senegal, Zambia; China
Paolo Woods: Algeria, Angola, Congo-Brazzaville, Nigeria, Zambia; China

Prologue

"People can't eat democracy."
—*Serge Mombouli, adviser to
Congolese President Denis Sassou N'Guesso*

While walking along a street in Brazzaville we are met by a lively group of Congolese children who have stopped their ball game to greet us. Whites in Africa are used to hearing "Hello mista!" "Salut toubab!" or "Monsieur Monsieur!" but these smiling children, lined up single file on the edge of the street, shout, "Ni hao, ni hao"—"Hello" in Chinese—before going back to their game. These days Congolese kids assume that all foreigners are Chinese, and for good reason.

Fourteen hundred miles northwest, in a suburb of Lagos, Nigeria, the Newbisco factory sits like a scar on the landscape. The biscuit factory, British-built before independence in 1960, has had a succession of owners. In a country where oil-related inflation and corruption dampen other economic activity, the factory had always operated at a loss. By 2000, production had stalled, machinery was broken, and the storerooms had run out of ingredients. But then, on one April morning in 2007, the sweet smell of baking biscuits filled the air. Thousands of little cookies were pouring from four brand-new ovens onto conveyor belts and into boxes that were immediately sealed by a

1

dozen female workers. This transformation is the result of the factory's sale to Chinese businessman Y. T. Chu. Newbisco now employs seven hundred people working shifts around the clock, producing 2,100 tons[1] of biscuits per month. Chu's smiling announcement that "we barely meet 1 percent of Nigerian market demand" hints at his ambitious expansion plans. The pristine new machinery and a large, well-stocked storeroom make it clear that for the first time in its history the factory is turning a profit.

Reporters often return from Africa with haunting images of starving children, interethnic conflicts, and meaningless violence. We have seen all this, but the images that stayed with us after intense trips to ten different nations are of a changing Africa, an Africa undergoing a transformation as momentous as decolonization: the children of Brazzaville cheering us in Chinese, Lagos's successful biscuit factory, or the new Chinese-built highway running across Sudan along which we traveled in the summer of 2007.

The highway was to have been a present from Osama Bin Laden, who was granted safe haven in Sudan after calling for a holy war against the Americans at home in his native Saudi Arabia in 1993.[2] His plan was to replace the old, winding road between the capital and Port Sudan (stretching over 745 miles) with a new 520-mile highway. Following the U.S. embassy bombings in Kenya and Tanzania in 1998, Osama Bin Laden abandoned this grand project and left Khartoum for Afghanistan to pursue interests outside civil engineering. The Chinese came to the rescue, completing the road in record time, even adding a railroad track alongside the highway. Since the early 1990s Chinese companies have invested over $20 billion in oil wells, a refinery, and a pipeline that carries crude oil to Port Sudan, where Chinese tankers load up with 8 percent of China's annual oil imports.

For almost two years, we have traveled thousands of miles, from Beijing to Khartoum, Algiers to Brazzaville, to tell the story of what China is doing in Africa. The idea took form during at an impromptu meeting with Guinea's late president Lansana Conté in October 2006.[3] At that point Conté had not spoken to a foreign journalist for twelve years. Our meeting was his opportunity to prove—despite rumors that he was dying and that his country was sliding into chaos—that he was still a political force to be reckoned with. The conversation was gloomy. The president labeled most of his ministers "thieves," berated the whites "who have never stopped acting like colonizers," and was despondent about the discovery of oil off Guinea's coast, which would, in his opinion, fan the country's already rampant corruption. However, at the mention of the Chinese the president's face lit up.

"There's no one like the Chinese!" exclaimed the old general. "At least they work. They live with us in the mud. Some of them grow rice like me. I gave them a worn-out piece of land. You should see what they have done with it!"

China's presence in Africa is hardly a recent development. Reporting on events in Angola, Senegal, Ivory Coast, and Sierra Leone since the early part of the century, we have seen the Chinese advance their pawns throughout the continent. But the scale of their activities is growing at an astonishing rate. As their projects balloon, the Chinese are penetrating the imagination of an entire continent, from the old president of Guinea who used to leave his country only to go to Switzerland for medical treatment, to the children of Brazzaville, too young to distinguish a European from an Asian.

Between 2004 and 2006, China's presence in Africa went from being a topic of debate for dedicated Africa watchers to a central theme in international relations and everyday African life.[4] Bilateral trade between the two regions multiplied fiftyfold from 1980 to 2005, quintupling between 2000 and 2006 from $10 billion to $55 billion, and is expected to reach $100 billion by 2010. It is estimated that in 2006 there were nine hundred Chinese companies operating on African soil, with an overall investment of $6 billion. China has taken France's place as Africa's second largest business partner and is hot on the heels of number one, the United States.

These figures do not take into account the investments of the Chinese migrants and entrepreneurs. The South African Migration Project, a seminar organized in South Africa in late 2006, estimated that 750,000 Chinese are resident across the entire continent, while much of the African press already refers to "millions" of Chinese. The highest official Chinese estimate comes from the vice chairman of the Chinese-African People's Friendship Association, Huang Zequan, who has visited thirty-three of the fifty-three African nations. In an interview in the *China Business Journal*,[5] he estimated that some 500,000 of his fellow Chinese live in Africa (compared to 250,000 Lebanese and under 100,000 French expats).

The West, of course, is watching keenly. China's investments in Africa, especially in Sudan, are under increasing scrutiny. Yet journals and newspapers do not give these Chinese migrants a name, a face, or a voice. Journalists complain that they cannot gain access to the Chinese, but the tone of recent articles has been anxious, even alarmist, as though the arrival in Africa of this new power is one more calamity for a continent whose misery is already proverbial.

However, for China, success in Africa has reinforced its status as a global superpower. It has proved itself capable of economic miracles both at home and in some of the least developed corners of the planet. For many Africans, China offers a long-awaited opportunity for growth. It brings hope not just to the Guinean president, but to 900 million other Africans, too.

To Western eyes the Chinese appear incongruous arrivals on the African scene, like the red and yellow high-rises built in the Algerian desert by their construction companies. Yet, in the light of recent developments in China, their presence does not seem so out of place. In 1978, as the Celestial Empire emerged from the throes of the Cultural Revolution, Deng Xiaoping launched China's economic boom with the revolutionary slogan "To get rich is glorious." It has become the motto of over a billion Chinese, and for a lucky few, the reality. For the rest, especially those living in rural China, reality has not kept pace with rising expectations. For ambitious young men and women an already tough life has become unbearable. For centuries enterprising Chinese have left their homeland to make their fortune abroad. Estimates suggest that the Chinese diaspora is one of the richest and biggest in the world, consisting as it does of over 100 million people. From the beginning of the Christian era, the Chinese had migrated across Southeast Asia, but it wasn't until the end of the nineteenth century that the diaspora population exploded.[6] Following the abolition of the slave trade, European traders forced their way into Chinese ports looking for poorly paid "coolies" (derived from the Chinese word *ku-li*, meaning "hard work") to fill the labor shortage. According to sources, between 2 and 8 million Chinese laborers were hired to do the dirty work on the major construction projects of the day: Australian mines, the Panama Canal, railroads in the Belgian Congo and Mozambique, the Trans-Siberian Railway, and the Central Pacific Railway in the United States. By 1870, there were already 50,000 Chinese in San Francisco, and emigration continued during the communist era, mostly to Europe and North America, where some 10 million Chinese have settled.

Until the late 1990s the ruling Chinese Communist Party, embarrassed by the exodus, attempted to limit emigration, but today China encourages its brave citizens to try their luck in Africa. Chinese leaders, especially President Hu Jintao (who is sometimes referred to as "the African"), see emigration as a good way to lower demographic pressure, economic overheating, and pollution in mainland China.

"We have six hundred rivers in China, four hundred of which have been killed by pollution," said a Chinese scientist[7] who asked not to be named. "We will have to send at least 300 million people to Africa before we begin to see the end of our problems."

Hundreds of thousands of Chinese have made the trip, and nations across Africa have witnessed the encounter of two of the Earth's most disparate cultures. In their new Wild West, Chinese arrivals are discovering flamboyant lifestyles, precious natural resources, chaos, confusion, and opportunity on a previously unimaginable scale. They understand that the world is more complex than the *People's Daily* would have them believe. All they see contrasts strongly with the ordered Confucian existence that they have left behind, with its emphasis on hard work and self-sacrifice. The Chinese we visited tended to keep to themselves and eat as they did at home. They made little effort to learn local languages or adopt local customs, much less intermarry with their African hosts. They are, however, happy to live in camps and set up shops in small towns and villages where no Westerner would consider working. Julia Lovell suggests[8] that the Chinese, having been cloistered for thousands of years behind their Great Wall, have not been forced to adapt to other civilizations or to cohabit with them. Yet all of them will be changed by their African experience, and their discoveries will rock the boat of China's isolation, just as its conversion to capitalism did in the 1980s.

Since China expanded its presence in Africa, the Chinese government has undergone deep changes. Very proud of its "noninterference" policy in the domestic affairs of others countries, China is gradually realizing that its visible support of certain dictators may eventually backfire. Having been Khartoum's and Harare's most staunch ally, it is now backtracking, putting pressure on the Sudanese government to end the hostilities in Darfur, and reducing aid to Robert Mugabe.

While the mood shifts in Beijing, the Chinese are making waves across much of what was long considered a stagnating continent. The predations of the colonial era and Western governments' support of brutal postcolonial regimes left much of Africa struggling. Aid, which has totaled $400 billion since 1960 (equivalent only to the GDP of Turkey in 2007 or the amount of cash African leaders have deposited abroad, according to a recent UN report),[9] has brought its own problems. After forty years, the West has grown frustrated with a continent that defeats the efforts of development agencies and stubbornly remains the victim of dictators, genocides, wars, epidemics, and encroaching deserts. French anthropologist Stephen Smith cruelly declared that "since independence, Africa has been working at its recolonization. In any case, even if this was not the intention, it couldn't have done a better job. The continent is doomed to failure. No one is ready to take it on."[10]

But the Chinese are taking it on. The People's Republic desperately needs Africa's copious raw materials to fuel its colossal growth, materials such as oil and minerals, wood, fish, and agricultural produce. China is not apparently bothered by the absence of democracy or the abundant corruption. Its foot soldiers are used to sleeping on mats on the floor and going without meat. Where others only see discomfort or chaos, the Chinese see opportunities. They are willing to make long-term investments in infrastructure projects and industry where Western investors would want quick returns. China has a lasting vision for Africa, and its goals far exceed the limited scope of the former colonial powers. Some critics believe that China is motivated purely by a strategy based on the teachings of Sun Tzu: "To defeat your enemy, first offer him help so that he slackens his vigilance; to take, one must first give." Conversely, others see the arrival of a new power in Africa as a "win-win" relationship. China unloads its cheap consumer goods on the African market; rebuilds roads, railroads, and official buildings; builds dams in Congo-Brazzaville, Sudan, and Ethiopia; and is about to help Egypt boost its civilian nuclear energy program. It has spread its wireless networks across Africa, and when host governments ask for help, the Chinese are happy to build hospitals, clinics, and orphanages. Against a backdrop of "colonial arrogance," Chinese discretion and humility have impressed many of the Africans the Chinese encounter, thousands of whom already speak or are learning Chinese. Many more praise their perseverance, courage, and efficiency. Africa welcomes any competition that shakes up the Western, Lebanese, and Indian business monopolies.

Day after day, from friendship pacts to cooperation agreements, from interest-free loans to operating contracts, Beijing is replacing

Paris, London, Washington, and Taipei both in the African ministries and in the African heart. The repeated visits of President Hu Jintao and his diplomatic armada work wonders. Drawing on cold war rhetoric, he offers his African brothers in the nonaligned movement a Chinese development model that seeks to banish the ghost of colonialism and replace the bitter Washington consensus (privatization, democratization, governance) with a much sweeter Beijing consensus. Meanwhile he helps himself to Africa as if it were a supermarket, filling his shopping basket with whatsoever he chooses.

China's move into Africa is not just a product of globalization but is its ultimate realization: a landslide in the international balance of power and a geopolitical earthquake. What the West needs to know is whether it will lose out as China expands in Africa, if China will help Africa direct its own fate and finally bring light to what was once called the "dark continent."

At the end of the interview President Lansana Conté arranged for us to speak with a few of his ministers in Conakry the next day. In fact, the Guinean policymakers were so keen to unburden themselves that we sat like father confessors as almost the entire Guinean government filed through our room in the presidential palace.

Ousmane Sylla, then the minister of mines, had been at a conference in Düsseldorf discussing the immense potential of his country's bauxite reserves, the largest in the world. All of the multinational mining companies were there to court him, not surprisingly given the skyrocketing prices of aluminum, refined from bauxite. The minister could only sigh with despair. Forty years of Western companies' mining bauxite in Guinea have brought minimal benefit to its citizens. The average monthly salary in 2007 bought the equivalent of a sack of rice, enough to feed a family of five for two weeks. For the last two weeks of the month, and for anything beyond rice, the Guineans are left to fend for themselves. The American giant Alcoa, the world's leading producer of aluminum, with earnings of $2.6 billion in 2006 (double those of the previous year), claims on its Web site to have "refined the refining process to an art" (under the entry "It all starts with dirt"). Four tons of bauxite are refined to two tons of alumina, which is smelted down into one ton of aluminum, "enough to produce 60,000 cans of Coke, Pepsi or Bud," Alcoa explains. "Enough to make the space frames for seven full-size cars or 40,000 computer memory disks, capable of storing all the books ever published. All from a truckload of dirt. It's almost magical. And we're proud to have the magicians who can pull it off!"

Guinea produces 20 million tons of bauxite a year, enough to produce 300 billion beer cans or the space frames for 35 million cars. But the ore is exported before it is processed. It generates few jobs and adds minimal value to Guinea. Few Guineans could afford a beer, let alone a car, and that's why they no doubt count themselves so lucky to have very few roads that cars can actually drive down. As for the 200 billion memory disks that their bauxite could produce, Guineans have neither computers nor the electricity to power them. Before their exams, students in Conakry spend the whole night cramming in the airport parking lot, the only place in the capital that has electricity at night.

Mining giants like Alcoa and Alcan repeatedly state that Guinea generates too little electricity to support a refinery, a claim that many find ludicrous in a country where experts have identified 122 possible sites for hydroelectric dams. But there is hope.

"The Chinese," sighed Ousmane Sylla. "They are the only ones who offer us 'package' deals or turnkey contracts: a mine, a hydroelectric dam, a railroad, and a refinery—all financed by the China Exim Bank, which is paid in alumina. The operation doesn't cost us anything but generates tax revenues, jobs, infrastructure, and energy. When we ask Alcoa for the same thing, they say that their business is aluminum, not hydroelectric dams," said the minister of mines indignantly.

The minister of public works seemed depressed. Six years before, the European Union had cut off aid to Guinea, citing a lack of good governance and democracy. There are $325 million just sitting in a bank in Brussels while the holes in Guinea's roads—and in its national budget—gape open. A particularly violent rainy season had stripped the asphalt from a section of the Nzérékoré road, leaving the Guinea Forest Region cut off from the rest of the country. The price of goods had risen sharply, and rumors of revolt were rampant. The Chinese, once again, saved the day. The minister outlined with enthusiasm how "they work faster and cheaper than everyone else. They wrote off $45 million of our debt and loaned us money again."

Next came the minister of foreign affairs, a certain Mamadi Condé, who seemed to be in more of a hurry than the others. "The Chinese are bulldozing over European efforts in Africa. They have no political ambitions; they just want prosperity for them and for us, a 'win-win' partnership. I was ambassador to Beijing in the 1990s and I went back three months ago to discuss a billion-dollar investment in Guinea. Can we please finish this interview quickly? I'm leaving for Beijing in an hour for the China-Africa Summit, which starts on November 3."

Like other Western journalists, we had been keeping a keen eye out for the precise dates of this summit. In what seemed to be an attempt to reserve the event for African heads of state and official Communist Party journalists, the organizers had kept the dates under wraps until the last minute. It was already October 31. That left us just four days to get hold of a Chinese visa.

Chapter 1

Rolling Out the Red Carpet for the African Continent

China-Africa Summit, Beijing, November 2006

> The twenty-first century is the century for China to lead the world. And when you are leading the world, we want to be close behind you. When you are going to the moon, we don't want to be left behind.
>
> —*Nigerian president Olusegun Obasanjo to Chinese president Hu Jintao, Lagos, Nigeria, April 2006*

Congratulations on the Beijing Summit.

On November 3, 2006, passengers arriving at Beijing airport cannot miss this greeting, which is plastered on signs all over in Mandarin, English, and French. But who is being congratulated, and for what? The summit has not even started yet. It's an idea particular to the Chinese to express pride in hosting an upcoming event by congratulating the guests, who, after all, are indispensable to the event's success. Other than five small African countries still considered enemies

11

of China because of links to Taiwan,[1] the entire continent has shown up for the summit. Even Senegal has come, even though it cut ties to Taipei only in October 2005. Chad, too, is a guest. It caved in to China's popularity in July 2006 and only because there was a gun to its head. There has never been a gathering of as many African dignitaries in one place. Forty-eight of fifty-three countries and forty-one heads of state, representing 800 million Africans, are expected here. If you include the population of China, a third of the world's population—2 billion people—will be represented at the Beijing Summit.

It's morning on Tiananmen Square. The flags of the countries attending the summit flap in the wind next to the red Chinese flag with the yellow stars. Banners hung in the streets display black hands shaking white hands: Africa meeting China. Other banners evoke images of Africa that have more appeal to the person on the street: elephants, zebras, and giraffes.

Autumn in Beijing and the sky is blue—unusually so. Normally, smog covers the sky over the capital, but today's clear skies aren't exactly a sign of good luck. For the duration of the summit, the authorities have banned one-fourth of Beijing's cars, half a million of them, from the streets, and many factories have been ordered to cease production in an effort to prevent smog formation. The emperors of China have always been "the masters of the sky." So now are the "Red emperors" like Hu Jintao.

The first Forum on China-Africa Cooperation was held in Beijing in 2000 and was greeted with relative indifference internationally. At the time, trade between China and Africa barely surpassed $10 billion. Then, Ethiopia became the first country in Africa to host the triennial summit in 2003, but again the Addis Ababa summit went almost unnoticed. The view in Paris, London, and Washington was that this kind of event, with its hollow talk about friendship between peoples, did not imperil postcolonial allegiances. By 2006, however, the West's alarms had started to go off as China had begun to spread its influence into nearly every part of Africa. The exponential growth of trade between China and Africa can be followed in the November 3 *China Daily*, which gives the numbers with a bit of Chinese pride. Trade between China and Africa rose from $12.39 billion in 2002 to $39.8 billion in 2005. It had risen again to $55 billion in 2006.

The media center of the summit has been set up in the News Hotel, a bland, sprawling building on Jianguomennei Street where forum organizers plan for nearly five hundred journalists to stay. What you notice immediately about these journalists is that there are no Europeans, Americans, Indians, Russians, or Japanese. It seems that the only journalists at the summit are African and Chinese, except for us and a handful of others, and we had to pester officials incessantly to get credentials. In fact, summit organizers managed to weed out others by waiting until the last minute to publish the exact dates, too late for anyone to plan to attend who did not already belong to an official delegation.

At any rate, the News Hotel is a long way—four kilometers—from the Great Hall of the People, where the summit will actually take place. So, we ask, how are we to access the officials?

"You won't have any reason to leave the hotel," Chenglin Shan, the head of the Press Office, assures us in excellent French. "Everything you need is here."

Plasma screens at the hotel are going to broadcast the events. There are water fountains, bags of green tea, and fortune cookies, too. Multilingual hostesses direct us toward welcoming gifts—a brand-new fountain pen, a leather-bound 2007 organizer, and a China-Africa 2006 T-shirt. As for food, the hotel offers a buffet every morning.

We head upstairs to the computer room, where a few of our African colleagues are on computers with high-speed Internet connections. "It's quite different here," laughs a man from Somalia when the official Web site of the summit blares the "breaking news" that a few African leaders are arriving. Chinese television crews have shown up to film the African journalists, whose distinctive clothing style, the safari jackets and the Mobutu-style suits known as *abacosts* (their style inspired by a trip Mobutu made to Beijing in the 1970s), makes them telegenic.

The presence of Africans in China is not a new thing. For many years, the Middle Kingdom has awarded scholarships to thousands of students from every part of Africa in the name of friendship between the two peoples. This scholarship program has expanded considerably since 2000. It used to be rare to see black students at universities in Beijing, Shanghai, Nankin, or even Chengdu, a city in the province of Sichuan, but not any longer.

"The Chinese never say anything to us," an African student confides to us. "I've been here for four years, and I don't have a single Chinese friend." Africans are active in the import-export business, as we were able to observe in the streets of Canton in 2003, but Africans and Chinese rarely mix despite Beijing's stated hopes that they will.

What's particularly novel about this summit is how big it is. It is an opportunity for China to make connections with the entire continent of Africa and for both Chinese and Africans to learn more about one another. Even though China and Africa are so distant—geographically and culturally—they actually have a lot in common. "China is the largest developing country in the world, and Africa is the continent with the largest number of developing countries," said President Jiang Zemin at the 2000 Forum. Six years later, his words have become a recurring theme at the forum.

While waiting for the summit to open officially, we watch the TV screens at the hotel. One documentary shows the 1963 African tour of Zhou Enlai, then minister of foreign affairs. Others show colonial atrocities juxtaposed with examples of gracious aid provided, no strings attached, by China—friend of Africa. African comrades, choose your sides!

A crew from Algerian television shows up with bloodshot eyes and looking disheveled. "We've been on the road for twenty-four hours. We had to go through Pakistan," they say. The crew leader then rushes to Chenglin Shan standing at the end of the hallway, ges-

* _The binding thread between the two._

ticulates, and returns with the news that TV crews will not be allowed to film inside the Great Hall of the People. All of us journalists are in the same boat.

The furious Algerians put away their microphones and cameras so that they can have a smoke. They tell us about the thousands of Chinese workers starting to gain a foothold in Algeria. "They're building everything. The ministry of foreign affairs, a major commercial center in Algiers, a thousand-kilometer highway," one of them says.

Are the Algerians happy about it? Not exactly. Especially since Chinese workers are supposedly paid more than the locals.

"At home, we call them the Ali-Baba." His colleague is a little more moderate. "Their crews work 24/7. You can't help but find them impressive," leaving us confused about whether Algerians consider the Chinese thieves or entrepreneurs.

The next day is November 4, the opening day of the summit. The sky is still blue, but the streets are blocked by a procession of official limousines. A traffic jam forces us to abandon our car and rush into the News Hotel to catch Chinese president Hu Jintao's inaugural speech of the summit at ten o'clock. Inside the hotel, an official from the Press Office apologizes upon seeing how much sweat we have expended and points out that a copy of the president's speech has already been made available. In the speech, Hu says, "Today, China-Africa friendship is deeply rooted in the hearts of our two peoples."[2]

After these conventional words, it's Ethiopian prime minister and forum copresident Meles Zenawi's turn to speechify. It's hard to believe that this diminutive bald man in glasses is responsible for the regime of terror that began in Ethiopia in 2005. Dictators like to speak of peace, and Zenawi is no exception. "It's in this spirit of friendship, of peace, of cooperation and of development," he says, "that Chinese and African officials are meeting to discuss ways to strengthen Chinese-African relations."

He mentions the colonial era only in passing, when, as he puts it, "China was always at the side of Africans, which created mutual trust

Zenawi's speech illustrates China's strategy in Africa but also the negative aspects of China's sovereignty policy.

between us. China also deserves credit for never interfering in the political affairs" of the continent.

At the time of Zenawi's speech the European Union is considering ending financial support for his regime because of atrocities it has committed. Ethiopia is totally reliant upon foreign aid, so the dictator later adds, "What we must do now is gain economic independence." In order for that to happen, "We will need China's help, since it has created a proven method of successful development. In return for China's aid, Africa is willing to supply all the energy and mineral resources that [China] needs." *BAD!*

These self-satisfied African allies are all too aware that they are being feted. They revel in Zenawi's speech, whose tone underscores themes that run through the summit. The hall is immense, and the mood solemn. Even some of these leaders, so powerful at home, allow themselves to feel impressed. The ceremony takes a softer tone when Zenawi recalls the glory days of the 1955 Bandung conference. That was when the nonaligned countries, led by Zhou Enlai, Egypt's Gamal Abdel Nasser, and India's Jawaharlal Nehru, raised their voices in unison, confidently announcing both the right of their nations to independence and their refusal to take sides with either West or East. Bandung marked the Third World's arrival on the international scene and was the basis for the nonaligned movement and for hopes of developing within Third World countries.

Zenawi returns to his seat, leaving the floor to the head of state of Congo-Brazzaville and the president of the African Union, Denis Sassou N'Guesso. Sassou greets the audience with a solemn bow like an orchestra conductor. Like Zenawi, he can't resist reveling in the glory days of Bandung as if those in the audience are the direct heirs of its spirit. In fact, some could have been present at Bandung, considering how long they have been in office. Sassou himself became head of state in 1970. Chased from office in 1992 by accusations of incompetent management of the government, of corruption, and even of murder, the ex-paratrooper retook the reins of power in 1997 with the help of France and Angola, along with a collection of mercenaries.

Fifty years after Congo-Brazzaville's independence, the Bandung spirit appears to have dissipated long ago. The country is one of the poorest and most corrupt in the world. However, Zenawi still proclaims that "real development between Third World countries is now occurring." After all, China has promised to cancel 10 billion yuan ($1.3 billion) worth of African debt.

"As usual, China has kept its word," Sassou emphasizes. In the future, "China is going to contribute to the revival of the Doha accords[3] of the WTO [World Trade Organization] and to meeting the goals of NEPAD [New Partnership for Africa's Development."[4] The maestro ends his speech by saying to thunderous applause, "Long live China-Africa cooperation."

By 10:45 it is time to move on to the long-awaited moment: the procession of African leaders coming up to the stage to shake hands with Hu Jintao. The screen focuses on Hu off to the left as his guests enter the field of vision one by one from the right. They greet him and then head off on the red carpet. The formality of the proceedings has the feel of a communist Versailles, but these few seconds with the red Sun King are very important to the African leaders. These images of their head of state with the second most powerful man in the world will be broadcast to the people back home, you see. The proceedings drag on, but the screen has no sound, as if mere images will suffice. After all, what more needs to be said? One leader, unsure of how to greet a Chinese person, nearly goes prostrate before Hu. Another leader lets his relaxed body language speak for itself. All kinds come up to the stage: the smiling, the chatting, the imperious, the stiff, the chummy, and one who is perhaps too casual. When one leader even embraces the impassive Hu, he is caught a bit off guard but manages to keep his composure.

Enter Robert Mugabe, the Zimbabwe strongman, with his little Hitlerian mustache. A pariah in the West, he is welcomed in Beijing. Since 2004, only Chinese financial, political, and even military support has kept his regime afloat. After all, in May 2005, on the twenty-fifth anniversary of Zimbabwe's independence, Mugabe said, "We must turn toward the East, where the sun rises." Then there's Sudan's Omar Hassan Ahmed al-Bashir. The international community has accused him of genocide, but Beijing greets him with open arms. BAD!

Every article in today's *China Daily* pushes the same theme—that China is active in every corner of Africa. A news item from China's official press agency, Xinhua, describes kung fu shows in the Shaolin style and dance performances in the Tang dynasty style in Cape Town. South Africa has the largest and oldest Chinese community in Africa, numbering 250,000 people.

Another article details the tragic fate of Madame Li Li, a forty-three-year-old nurse who left China to join her husband, Wang Chi, in Zambia, where he had started a farm thirty kilometers from Lusaka. He had 1,000 head of livestock, 2,000 pigs, and thirty-five hectares of land, but he died soon after she arrived. What did she do? She chose to stay in Zambia. "A perfect example of the cooperation between China and Zambia" is the conclusion the writer of the Xinhua dispatch draws. On the other hand, a revolt against the Chinese in the Zambian copper mines goes unmentioned.

A little bit later Mamadou Tandja, president of Niger and of the Economic Community of West African States (ECOWAS), gives a smooth speech to promote his region, a "huge 250 million-person market," which is "endowed with an extraordinary abundance of mineral resources," and which "hopes to form the same excellent partnership with China that China has had with others, a partnership that would enable it to envision great improvements in infrastructure like highways, railroads, and dams." Tandja speaks of a "long-term partnership" and of a "mutually advantageous relationship," but not of the trouble that has been brewing because of China's interest in the uranium mines of northern Niger.

It's only 11:00, but for ten minutes the camera has been filming a table decorated with fancy flowers in a vast, empty room: The interpreters have left to get something to eat. The "high-level dialogue between Chinese and African leaders and business leaders," as the program schedule calls it, doesn't resume until 3 P.M. Most of the journalists have been forced into idleness, since it's difficult to get around without an interpreter, without much of a schedule, and, for some African crews in particular, without money. All the high-tech, the gracious welcome, the staff at beck and call—all of this great fuss seems to be an attempt to compensate for the forum's lack of content. The press center is starting to look like a hall of smoke and mirrors.

Some journalists try, in defiance of the authorities, to make a foray into the Great Hall of the People, but the fortress proves to be impenetrable. The hotels where the delegations are staying will have to suffice. Delegations from Chad, Morocco, and Cape Verde are at the Hyatt, but the reception desk has been blocked off, and the desk staff's lips are sealed. The bellhops, baggage carriers, and doormen know nothing about the identity of the guests. Finally, at the Kempinski, we find that some Algerians have left their rooms and come downstairs. Luckily for us, one is standing in the lobby. The little man looks, in his nicely tailored suit, like a member of the National Liberation Front's old guard, but he is uninterested in conversation.

"We don't have the time, you know," he says. "The delegation is headed back to the Grand Hall any minute, and tonight there's another party." It's like this day and night. The schedule is completely stuffed with reception parties, visits to the building site of the 2008 Olympic Games, cultural performances, dinners, working breakfasts. Beijing pays the bills and sets the tempo.

Even so, we figure some visitors to the summit might rebel against the schedule and get some suitcases to stuff with purchases just as all foreign tourists do in Beijing. The diplomatic quarter of San Li Tun appears to be the best area to put such suspicions to the test. The Yashow shopping center is famous for its great selection of pirated goods and for its fierce haggling. Sure enough, our suppositions are verified when we see official limousines dropping off hordes of scurrying African officials in front of the shopping center. On the escalator, we surprise a Ugandan minister accompanied by women wearing boubous. His arms are full of packages, and he says with a bit of embarrassment, "Well, these are for friends, you know."

Later, we see an official from Congo-Brazzaville being guided around by a scarily efficient Chinese woman atop stiletto heels. "My translator," he explains. It turns out that the place and the time aren't really appropriate for talking in confidence, even if seeing these elite Africans rushing into boutiques when their poor countries are pleading for debt relief doesn't lack piquancy.

At any rate, these elites don't have much in common with the self-lessness of some Chinese veterans of Africa. We head off to the institute of a former diplomat named Mr. Xinghua. This professor of international relations welcomes us into his office, where he presents the image of a man of the people and of a distinguished ambassador. After apologizing for what is perfect French, he tells us his story. First, he was posted in the Guinean capital city, Conakry, where, he says, "I saw Zhou Enlai visit Sékou Touré in 1963." Then he held posts in Mauritania and in Mali. When the tea arrives, Xinghua closes the door and takes a more familiar tone. "I can be frank with you since I'm not a diplomat anymore. I don't want to engage in gobbledy—how do you say it?"

"Gobbledygook?"

"That's it. I don't want to talk in that dead language. Admittedly, China's attitude toward Africa was not always exemplary, but you have to admit that it has evolved quite a bit. There was a kind of golden age at first, a time when we gave aid without the expectation that there would be mutual benefit and when we had some very close relationships. That was Zhou Enlai's era. We respected the African people quite a bit, and diplomats were forbidden to act arrogant."

"Has that changed?" *KEY QUOTE*

"During the cold war, China became ideological rivals with the Soviet Union, which termed us revisionists. I think that's why we sometimes went too far and made it appear that we would rather work with the capitalists and allies of the West than with the allies of Moscow."

New market economy strategy began in 1990s to become a mutually beneficial relationship, and so began the China-Africa Summit

Rolling Out the Red Carpet for the African Continent 21

"Are you referring to China's alliance with the South Africa of the apartheid era and to China's support for Jonas Savimbi and UNITA [National Union for the Total Independence of Angola]?"

"Yes."

The professor hesitates a moment as if surprised by his boldness, but then he moves on to the next point.

"Then, at the beginning of the 1990s, there was the transition to a market economy. We told our African friends that our cooperation had to adapt to this new reality, and that our aid would no longer be as one-way as it had been before, that it would have to become mutually beneficial. The current period began with the first China-Africa summit in Beijing in 2000."

"What do you think of the 2006 version?"

"What's new is the international reaction. Europe is concerned about our relationship with Africa. European criticism may be unfounded, but at least they've noticed!"

"Is any of it legitimate?"

"It's true that Chinese cooperation in Africa is supposed to be more respectful of international norms and local concerns, but many Chinese take up residence in Africa only to make a lot of money. The government can't stop them, and our image suffers. Something of permanence should always be left behind for the locals. China also must stop giving the impression that its values conflict with the values of the West and that it is against human rights and democracy. We're making inroads with human rights in China, why not do so in Africa, too?"

"If so much work has been done in that arena, how do you explain the summit's taking place behind closed doors and its engaging mostly in cant and cliché?"

"There has been a lot of concern about security, perhaps too much, I'll give you that," he says. "As concerns political transparency, China and its African partners have not yet adopted, shall we say, contemporary ways. I cannot defend everything that my country does, but you

* Yes, China needs to stop antagonizing the West and respect international norms however, it efforts are being damaged by the minority of Chinese businessmen.

must have noticed that there has been a lot of progress. Give us a little time. Some vestiges of the old machine still remain." **KEY QUOTE**

We return to the News Hotel, where information technology and "the vestiges of the old machine" still exist side by side. It's 3:00 in the afternoon on this November 5, and as regards high-level "dialogue," we are subjected to wave after wave of smooth, polished, official debate. Algerian president Abdelaziz Bouteflika, a founding father of NEPAD and an ex-leader of the nonaligned movement, comes first, followed by Gabon's head of state, Omar Bongo. Bongo must be very familiar with Beijing by now, as he's on his tenth official visit to the city. He describes his Central African country as a "place of peace and prosperity." Perhaps he has simply chosen to forget about the 1998–2003 Second Congo War, during which 4.7 million people died, making it the bloodiest conflict since World War II. Bongo, like all the other leaders, goes on to exhaust empty phrases like "new horizons," "global dialogue," and "mutually beneficial trade." A new language has been born: Sino-Africanese. **POSITIVE SPEECH ACTS?**

Looking at the entirety of African leadership, some people are willing to make excuses for Muammar el-Qaddafi of Libya or Laurent Gbagbo of the Ivory Coast. The king of Morocco, Muhammad VI, doesn't require such pandering. After all, he received Hu Jintao in Rabat on April 24, 2006, to discuss ways of making the kingdom "China's springboard to Africa and Europe."

What does that mean? To find out we go to the Moroccan embassy and see Azzedine Haddaoui, a government adviser and vice president of the mission. Haddaoui is an enthusiastic, erudite man who is an expert on Africa, Europe, and China. Why is China interested in Morocco? Why has China signed seven cooperation agreements (on tourism, health, culture, infrastructure, and science) with Morocco that call for an infusion of $5.6 million into the country?

The diplomat smiles and says, "For the simple reason that we are the only country in Africa to have signed free-trade agreements with both the European Union and the United States,[5] and also with the United Arab Emirates and Turkey, Tunisia, and Egypt."

[Handwritten annotations: BUSINESS STRATEGY = Morocco has free-trade agreements with EU & USA, hence China has pursued them. China wins Because it is cheaper and respects locals by living as they do.]

In other words, products made in Morocco, even if they are made by the Chinese, can be sold tariff-free in Europe and the United States, as well as in many other parts of the world. How does China manage to get involved in so many large-scale projects? Haddaoui twirls his mustache confidently when he hears this question. He knows the magic words: the World Bank. The Washington-based bank has been pressuring Africa to allow open bidding on its infrastructure projects, and the Chinese almost always win the contract, thanks to China's low labor costs, economies of scale, and reductions in incidental expenses.

"They never bring vehicles with heated seats to the Sahel," Haddaoui says. "The managers of the construction site never stay at the Hilton like Westerners. They stay in the work camps, with the workers. That inevitably makes a big difference in price."

Night has fallen by the time we leave the embassy, which is guarded by two soldiers. We're approached by a wary man. "Salam Aleikoum," he says in Arabic but then switches to French. "Excuse me, I thought you were Arab," he explains. "What do you think of the summit?" he asks after we tell him our names, nationalities, and professions. This time it's us who are wary.

"There have been some good things," we say. "But . . . "

The man moves away from the doorway and the possibility that there might be ears turned our way. Avoiding streetlights, too, he whispers to us, "These Chinese, they speak of friendship and cooperation, but the real issue is colonization. You get what I mean, right?"

We get it. *The Threat!*

"Are you free tonight?" he asks after telling us that his name is Khaled and that he works in the embassy. "There's a restaurant near here called the Carthage. We can talk there."

Adel Rakrouki, the Tunisian owner of the Carthage, has lived in China for ten years. At the entrance to his restaurant, he has put up long-faded photos of the Mediterranean. The Carthage is where North African embassy employees come to relax and, sometimes, to complain. They have made the place a kind of mini–Arab Maghreb

Union. "Tonight we're riding Apollo 13," says a jovial Moroccan named Slimane. Translation: "Tonight, we're drinking." They drink to forget the dull, drab, and cold capital and to indulge in memories of the heat of Sidi Bou Said and Carthage. A half-Moroccan, half-Tunisian man named Muhammad sits opposite Slimane. He opens a beer and tells us that he is in China "on business." A couple of Algerians are hanging out, too. A few beers later, our new friends have gotten a little tipsy and have started to leave the clichés behind. Unequal trade, invasion, dumping, you name it. Even so, "the Mediterranean lifestyle is just different."

The couscous arrives. "It's my Chinese workers that made it," Rakrouki says with pride. "I taught them how." The friendly crew of Apollo 13 dips into the food, but their conversation inevitably turns to their problems with the Chinese. "Who is going to stop them?" asks an Algerian. "I don't know what my country is waiting for. We have to provide protections for our workforce." Slimane angrily flicks an olive from the plate. "Rubes are what they are, these Chinese. Just like everyone here. They don't have any taste."

The master chef ("You don't like my couscous?") comes over and sits down for a moment. "Ten minutes ago, a Chinese guy came in to sell some DVDs," he says. "Did you see him? What's he going to make tonight? One dollar? Doesn't matter. He'll work twelve hours if he has to, but he'll get his ten dollars a day. His wife will do it, too. I know because she works with me in the kitchen. They're saving money together, and one day they'll open their own small business. That's how the Chinese are! They're not lazy like the North Africans."

At the end of the night, the fellows begin to take their leave, and the Arab Maghreb Union of the Apollo 13 begins to break up. When the Algerians leave, the others start to run them down: "What lazy guys they are, real men of leisure." After the last Tunisian hits the road and the Moroccans are finally alone, they get really nasty.

"Look how messy that plate is," one says. "Ah, Tunisians. At least, we eat civilly in Morocco."

Rakrouki, who wasn't listening, says good-bye to us with these fitting words: "You see how it is? That's the best thing about the Chinese: They are united and have solidarity. They stick together."

As the summit comes to an end, Egypt is selected to host the next one in 2009. On the screens at the News Hotel, the heads of state reappear in order to hear the "Joint Declaration of the Beijing Summit" read by Hu Jintao in Mandarin, then in Arabic by Hosni Mubarak, and finally, in English by Meles Zenawi. It turns out to be a perfect example of the new language, Sino-Africanese, as demonstrated by the following extracted quotes:

> We declare that the development of our friendly relations and cooperation are in accordance with the Five Principles of Peaceful Coexistence as well as all the international principles that promote multilateralism and democracy in international relations. We urge that diversity of the world should be respected and upheld, that all countries in the world, big or small, rich or poor, strong or weak, should respect each other, treat each other as equals and live in peace and amity with each other, and that different civilizations and modes of development should draw on each other's experience, promote each other and coexist in harmony.

KEY Sino-Africanese concept: Developing Helping Developing

In the language of nonaligned countries, the Five Principles are mutual respect for territorial sovereignty and integrity, mutual nonaggression, noninterference in the affairs of others, equality and mutual benefit, and peaceful coexistence. The declaration refers to diversity because authoritarian regimes would rather talk about that than about grand, universal principles such as human rights. Continuing with the emphasis on multilateralism, the speakers also make appeals for "reforming the UN . . . which would give priority to increasing the representation of—and the full participation of—African countries in the Security Council of the UN."

More succinctly, the Africans and the Chinese are pointing out once again, and with considerable justification, that the Third World forms a majority in the General Assembly of the UN, and that the Third World is going to have to be given the representation it deserves if democracy in an international sense is to be honored. The implication is that China, as a member of the Security Council and a loyal friend, will help in reaching this goal, in contrast to the industrialized countries, which are only interested in finding objections to it:

> *We urge the developed countries to increase official development assistance and honor their commitments to opening market and debt relief, and call on the related international organizations to provide more financial and technical assistance to enhance Africa's capacity in poverty and disaster reduction and prevention and control of desertification, and help Africa realize the UN Millennium Development Goals.*

The industrialized world is a long way from fulfilling some of its pledges, like transferring 0.7 percent of GDP to developing countries. The declaration implies, however, that the carelessness is no more an issue since "the China-Africa friendship, having withstood the test of time and of global obstacles, is deeply rooted in the hearts of our two peoples and has become stronger and stronger." Therefore, the members of the forum are announcing the dawn of a new era.

> *We hereby solemnly proclaim the establishment of a new type of strategic partnership between China and Africa featuring political equality and mutual trust, win-win economic cooperation and mutually beneficial cultural exchanges.*

The end of the speech is greeted with silence.

"Now we are going to take a family portrait," the nasally voice of the interpreter in the headphones says. The screen is empty, though. There's silence again. Then the voice comes back. "The photo has been taken," it says.

That's that. The most important twenty seconds of the summit, other than the announcement that China plans to double aid to

Africa, have come and gone.[6] The photo that will be sent all over the world shows forty-eight high-level representatives of Africa standing at attention behind Hu Jintao in the Great Hall of the People. At the time of the photo, fourteen commercial contracts and agreements totaling $1.9 billion have already been signed and many others will follow. A Chinese-African development fund of $5 billion has also been created, a marketing coup for the autocrats and a source of pride for China—and a thumbing of the nose at the West.

At the very end of the summit, after the delegations have left town, the Chinese, Ethiopian, and Egyptian ministers of foreign affairs have to take one for the team and perform the most odious of chores for them: the press conference. Finally, one is tempted to say. Restrictions on journalists have been so tight, however, that most journalists do not even bother to show up.

Indeed, the hall is half-empty as the ministers pretend to answer questions that we pretend to ask. A journalist from *Chine Nouvelle*, apparently viewing freedom of the press in Egypt as worrisome, asks the Egyptian minister, "One can read in your papers of Chinese neo-colonialism in Africa. What do you have to say to that?"

The minister tells her what she wants to hear, but the real answer to the question will have to wait for 2007, a black year for freedom of the press in Egypt.

Someone from Radio China International asks next, "What will this partnership really accomplish?"

The Chinese foreign minister, Li Zhaoxing, answers the question with an irrelevant anecdote: "You know, when I called the Egyptian minister, he was in the pool. He told me that he often worked in the pool, too." An odd answer perhaps, but the officials share a good-natured laugh. At this stage, one has to wonder whether this is a comedy sketch, and it seems as if it is. If so, where is the hidden camera?

A journalist from the Comoros takes the mike and alludes to allies of Taiwan when he mentions that five African countries are still not participants in the forum. "How can we convince them to get on board with China?" he asks.

The expression on Li Zhaoxing's face turns grave as he explains that these countries, "which China has never harmed, by maintaining diplomatic relations with this province of China, are doing harm to China." The voice of the French interpreter in the headphones begins to quiver a little. Is she starting to find the whole thing amusing?

A reporter from Ethiopian television then asks, "What message does this forum aim to send to the international community?" The Ethiopian minister speaks of "mutual respect."

Li Zhaoxing adds that he would recommend to journalists who incessantly criticize China that they read the United Nations Charter. He reminds them of the six UN peacekeeping operations in which China has participated and China's considerable contributions of money for "keeping the peace" in Sudan. This comment is just too much for the interpreter. She's cracking. Her voice quivers again and starts to whimper, and finally she bursts into a liberating and telling laugh. The audience members in the hall who are listening in French glance around and laugh, too.

The Beijing Summit ends up resembling the punch line of a joke that no one gets. In a few days, a string of contracts and treaties, agreements and documents, is signed, and all of it happens without the West's being involved. No more of the compromises demanded by Françafrique—France's special relationship with Africa. No more of the smooth persuasion of London or Washington. No more African pessimism and fatalism. No more postcolonial dependence. The damned of the earth are rising up. All people are brothers. They're going to work together. A mirage? A lie? A fad? We'll see.

Chapter 2

How the Chinese Found Their Wild West and Called It Nigeria

"What do you call it again, that thing of yours
where everyone decides and nothing works?"
"Um . . . you mean democracy?"
"Yeah, that's it. We don't need it in China, and
we don't need it in Africa."
—*Conversation with businessman Roy Zhang,*
Lagos, April 2007

Two blue police cars make a Herculean effort to part the relentless metal and rubber tide of a Lagos traffic jam. Sirens blaring, they barge their way through the sweltering congestion, overtaking other vehicles on the hard shoulder as they crawl toward the Lekki Peninsula. Beyond the Falomo Bridge, traffic policemen peer through the glass with puzzled expressions, surprised to find that the driver of the lead vehicle is not a local police officer, but a small, bespectacled Chinese businessman.

Jacob Wood, born in Shanghai sixty years ago, is taking us to visit a 544-unit residential complex recently completed by his company,

Golden Swan Nigeria. After one last traffic jam, he takes off at high speed down the Lagos-Epe Expressway, finally free of the cars clogging the exit to this city of 16 million souls.

To our left runs a succession of supermarkets and builders' dealerships; to our right, a gray fortress flanked by four towers: headquarters of the global petroleum mammoth Exxon-Mobil.

"I was the first Chinese person from Communist China to work in Nigeria," says Wood. "My father fled Shanghai after Mao's victory in 1949, when I was a baby. In 1953 he opened a textile factory in Lagos, which back then was still a British colony. Growing up I was only allowed one letter a week from him, and even that was opened by the police. After Mao's death in 1976, the pressure eased up. I was finally able to leave the country, and I came here to get to know my father."

Jacob Wood did not stay long. He was sent by his father to study economics for three years in Toronto, where he worked hard, learned English, and was awarded a Canadian passport. Just a few hours before Jacob returned to Nigeria, his father arranged for him to meet Amy, a young woman from a prominent Hong Kong family who had just begun her studies in Canada. Both sets of parents agreed they would make a perfect couple. For Jacob it was love at first sight. Five years and many long-distance phone calls later, Amy put both Hong Kong and Toronto behind her to join Jacob in Lagos. By then Jacob's career was taking off, and he was working as the manager of the Shangri-La restaurant on the top floor of the Eko Hotel. This luxury establishment belonged to the "red capitalist" Armand Hammer, an American of Russian stock and CEO of Occidental Petroleum. Hammer was "an extraordinary man," according to Wood, whose friends included both Lenin and Ronald Reagan, and whose close business interests with the Soviet Union during the cold war caused an enduring controversy throughout his life.

Undaunted by the dark years of Nigerian military dictatorship and dwindling business travelers in the early 1990s, Jacob Wood opened a 1,500-seat restaurant, the Golden Gate, which specialized in banquets for Nigeria's rich and famous. Hot on its heels came the launching of Wood's first construction company, an event that coincided with China's emergence as a global economic power. Despite his deep-rooted mistrust of communist ideology, Wood discovered that his motherland was a reliable investor in Africa and an excellent source of skilled engineers for each of his industrial projects. Today he heads a corporation employing over 1,500 people, 300 of whom are Chinese. He provides the Nigerian government with so many services that, in addition to other privileges, he has been granted permission to register his entire fleet of SUVs as police vehicles.

"It's very practical for the *go slows*," he explains, using the pidgin English for traffic jam, "and it doesn't cost me anything. I just have to organize a banquet for the Association of Police Officers' Wives once a year. Every year they get hungrier, but it's still a good deal."

It is not just the traffic that justifies the price of the banquets. In one of Africa's most densely populated and dangerous nations, armed policemen make good travel companions. Nigeria, Africa's leading oil producer, has an exorbitant crime rate, compounded by the activities of guerrilla forces in the Niger Delta, where the oil wells are concentrated. MEND (Movement for the Emancipation of the Niger Delta) guerrillas kidnap expat workers on a weekly basis, in spite of the private armies that the major oil companies maintain to ensure the safety of their employees. Hostages are usually Westerners working for Shell or ENI, the giant state-controlled Italian oil, gas, and electrical company. But guerrillas were also quick to move when Chinese oil giant CNOOC arrived on the Nigerian scene. In January 2006 CNOOC made a $2.3-billion investment in an oil concession of French company Total. Four months later, during a visit by Chinese president Hu Jintao, CNOOC signed exploration contracts for four additional oil blocks, in exchange for a $4-billion investment in Nigerian infrastructure projects. Three days after the president's departure (May 2006) the guerrillas issued a proclamation: "Chinese citizens found in oil installations will be treated as thieves." They punctuated this declaration with a car bomb at the

China vs. Nigerian Guerrillas over Business deal for Nigerian Infrastructure and oil exploration.

Warri refinery in southern Nigeria. Groups of Chinese workers were held for ransom three times over the next two years.

As we approach the Nigerian Chevron-Texaco headquarters in the middle of the Lekki Peninsula, the two vehicles swerve left and head into a maze of small villas that seem more like Dubai or Bel Air than like Lagos. Jacob Wood stops his car in a courtyard strewn with electric cables and concrete rods. A Chinese engineer shows us into a shack furnished with three tables. His name is Reagan Shou,[1] and before he walked into Wood's Shanghai recruitment office, he had worked for a state-owned company in China. To date Shou has laid 110 miles of high-voltage lines in Surinam and spent three years in Kuwait. In Lagos, he is overseeing the final details on the 544 villas (completed in under two years) while he waits for official permission to begin work on 500 more.

"Everything is already sold," Shou says with a smile. "Chevron bought most of them for its Nigerian personnel."

Those who regard China's giant state-financed infrastructure projects as a simple down payment for Africa's raw materials should take note; Chinese businessmen and entrepreneurs like Jacob Wood are investing for the long term in private business empires on the African continent. But what tempts Chinese entrepreneurs to venture where indifferent or excessively cautious Westerners have feared to tread? Africa is a new frontier for the Chinese and a continent full of promise. They are not afraid to start small—a massage parlor, a restaurant, a little sewing shop, a pharmacy—anything that offers modest but quick returns on investment. A whole family in China will save for years to send one member to Africa, where the demand for services and goods is great and competition weak. African governments are by no means oblivious of China's growing thirst for investment opportunities. They are busy creating free-trade zones where Chinese investors and manufacturers can take advantage of tax breaks. Nigeria already has three; the largest, Calabar (bordering Cameroon), is overseen by the dynamic governor of Cross River State, himself a regular visitor to China.

Jacob Wood's intrepid investments are the perfect case study for Harry Broadman, a senior economist for the World Bank[2] whom we met in Washington, D.C., before embarking on our exploration of China's new ventures in Africa.

He told us, "If you look at the absolute levels of investment by the Chinese in sub-Saharan Africa, it's clearly in oil. But if you focus only on oil, you're missing the boat on what the Chinese are really doing in Africa. They are actually engaging in more fundamental investments: infrastructure, telecoms, textiles, tourism, food processing." It is these investments that will create longer-term returns: more jobs, economic stability, and technology transfer. *LONG- TERM BUSINESS*

Not far away, at another low-key office block in Washington, Mauro di Lorenzo, a research analyst at the very conservative think tank the American Enterprise Institute, was equally enthusiastic about the Chinese business venture in Africa.

"We Westerners are locked into a humanitarian vision. It's politically correct. Bono and his type want to lick the Africans' wounds, help them, cry with them because they have AIDS and are poor and innocent. But humanitarianism is also a means of control; it maintains the power relationship." Di Lorenzo goes on, "The only African stories we are allowed to tell are straight out of Joseph Conrad's *Heart of Darkness*: genocides, abominable diseases, the wholesale rape of little girls east of the Congo, ethnic cleansing here and there. In other words, the worst atrocities people can inflict on each other. The Chinese don't have these psychological limitations. They go to Africa to do business, profitable business. Hopefully that will be an eye-opener for us and we will follow their example. Our humanitarian aid has done its own share of damage."

Back in Nigeria, humanitarian interventions are the last thing on Jacob Wood's mind as we continue the tour of his industrial empire. Wood summons his police bodyguard, and we speed toward a workshop manufacturing machinery parts.

"Textiles used to be good business," he says. "A traditional African robe needs seven meters of material, a lot more than my T-shirt. But my father's factory went under because of cheap Chinese imports. In 2003 the Nigerian government took measures to protect its textile industry and it was right to do so. What we Chinese have to do is manufacture in Africa. Importing is a waste for everyone. Look at motorcycles. In 2005 the Chinese sold 300,000 to Nigeria for $100 million. Fine. The following year it sold 600,000 for almost the same price. Everyone is happy, especially the Chinese provinces that get a good reputation in the capital for their high export statistics. But just think about all the metal and electricity you need to make a motorcycle. China needs metal and electricity at home! I'm friends with Beijing's highest authorities, but when I tell them not to export this stuff they think I'm nuts." (Wood's concern about Chinese resources is even more touching when, two days later, we learn that he is the major importer of Chinese motorcycles to Nigeria.)

We pull up at Golden Eagle Ltd., a factory that turns out heavy construction machinery. Dozens of Nigerians are working in the main building, cutting, drilling, and welding parts to make concrete mixers, gravel graders, and vibrating plates. Only the engines that drive the machines are imported—from China. Occasionally we glimpse a Chinese foreman or technician behind a welding helmet, working among the Nigerians on the more delicate processes and maintaining the fast work pace. On the wall are posted regulations stipulating that if workers miss a day they forfeit their monthly 1,500-naira ($12.50) bonus; a second day results in docked pay, and a third day means instant dismissal.

Jacob Wood learned many things in Canada, but the art of political correctness clearly passed him by. "What else can you do?" he sighs. "The Africans are lazy, very lazy. It's not surprising in this place. When they want to eat, they just climb a tree and pick a mango."

Nearby is Wood's Golden Ever Ltd., which manufactures PVC windows and roof paneling.

"I use some of these windows on my own projects and the rest sell like hotcakes," he says in front of workers loading a truck. Walking us out, he turns around. "And did you know that an average house has seventeen doors? I am also going to open a door factory."

Jacob Wood comes from a long line of entrepreneurs, and over the years he has built an exceptional Nigerian network. In 2001, after donating a school large enough to house 4,000 students in Ikeja, a district near Lagos's airport, he was honored with the title "African chief" (proudly displayed on his business cards). In keeping with his title, and Nigerian tribal custom, Wood has become a bigamist. On discovering that his beloved first wife, Amy, was infertile, he took a younger second wife, also Chinese, with whom he has a seven-year-old. Wood does not draw attention to his polygamy but introduces both wives with no hint of apology. The arrangement is perfectly adapted to his business empire: The first wife runs the Millennium Inn in Lagos, the economic heart of the country, and the second wife manages the Golden Gate, his hotel in the political capital, Abuja.

But Wood is by no means the only prominent Chinese business-man in Nigeria. Many came from Hong Kong in the 1980s, such as Wenlong Li, who settled in northern Kano. Li's factories employ 2,000 workers and export sandals and plastic products to many countries, including the United States. In Lagos, Y. T. Chu owns a string of com-panies ranging from industrial bakeries to steel foundries. And a new generation of entrepreneurs is arriving that is as determined as it is young.

Twenty-six-year-old Roy Zhang, from Hunan province, is secre-tary of the Chinese Enterprise Association in Lagos, which boasts two hundred members.

"I moved here from South Africa seven years ago. Like everyone else I started off selling cheap Chinese goods. When the government raised tariffs, limited imports, and closed down the Chinese markets in Lagos, I opened a little shoe factory. Today it employs seventy people." Zhang raised some capital and in March 2007 opened a high-end restaurant called Mr. Chang on Lagos's main drag, Owolowo. The interior is sleek and modern, and both the decorator and the cook are accomplished recruits from Shanghai. Mr. Chang quickly became a chic venue for politicians and rich Nigerians.

One evening Zhang invites some fellow members of the Chinese Enterprise Association to Mr. Chang. The guests include the new Chinese consul, Guo Kun, as well as the correspondent for *West Africa United Business Weekly,* the first Chinese newspaper in Nigeria, with a circulation of 7,000 (Zhang is a founder). After a large banquet washed down with dozens of bottles of *bai jiu* (strong Chinese alcohol), the last guest staggers out and Zhang joins us for a beer.

"You Westerners, you're so patronizing. You come here and talk to the Africans about human rights, copyrights, all sorts of rights. You talk down to them. We get straight to the point. We talk business." Jane, Zhang's wife, locks the door, flicks off the lights in the dining room, and brings us three more beers. "France is a great nation," continues her husband. "I love shopping in Paris. But when I watch the Nigerians applying for a visa being humiliated at the French consulate here I think to myself, 'That's not smart. Some of these guys are very rich.'"

"Is the Chinese consulate better?"

"Oh yes! The consul sorts the good ones from the bad. If he has a query, he asks us. If the guy is important, if his business is good, he'll have his visa delivered on a silver platter. You can't imagine what we do for the consul and what he does for us. And you—I hope the French embassy pays you well for all the information you gather?"

"Um, no, not really. We're journalists. The embassy doesn't even answer our e-mails."

"That's stupid. I'm not surprised that Alcatel and Bolloré lose so many contracts in Nigeria. *Our* government helps us whenever it can: information, legal advice, interest-free loans. When we go back to China, it sells us land at discount prices to reward us for what we did in Africa."

In so many words, Roy Zhang sums up China's two-pronged partnership model, public and private, which aims to make China the number one player in Africa. Ambitious entrepreneurs break ground and invest, and at the same time, the Chinese government signs enormous infrastructure contracts with its eye on the exploration and extraction of precious natural resources. On the ground, it can count on a broad and organized Chinese diaspora for support, which in return is rewarded by Beijing.

In 2006 President Hu Jintao told China Southern Airlines to open air routes in any African location it chose, and a proud Jiang Nan,[3] formerly business manager at the airline's Dubai branch, was selected to find the right destination. Jiang eventually settled on Lagos after discovering there were 50,000 Chinese in Nigeria, and that the big Chinese projects in the country were going to bring in thousands more.

He was the only person we met who could give us an idea of the number of Chinese in Nigeria: None of the businessmen we spoke to were able or willing to do so—and the consulate was even cagier. One of these "big projects" is the construction of a railroad line between Lagos and Kano, which would employ 3,000 Chinese technicians in 2008 and 8,000 in 2009. Another is a 2,600-megawatt hydroelectric power plant on the Mambilla Plateau that will triple the current electricity supply.

On December 31, 2006, Lagos officially became the first African destination for a Chinese airline. The Beijing-Lagos flight runs three times a week via Dubai and fills to about 60 percent capacity. A second flight between Guangzhou and Lagos is opening soon.

"On this one we're going to offer first-class: Business class is not good enough for the Africans," laughs Jiang Nan, lighting a Panda cigarette. "Emirates is our biggest competitor in Africa, but we are going to eat them alive. As a Chinese company we have a huge competitive edge shipping the Chinese to Africa, and you just can't imagine how much the Chinese want to come."

Considering the country's track record in Africa, Chinese enthusiasm about emigrating is hardly surprising. But it is much harder to unearth the scale of China's success or its business formula. Even Pat

Utomi, 2007 Nigerian presidential candidate, director of the Lagos
Business School, and Nigeria's top economist, is mystified.

"I don't understand how the Chinese do it. *Our* entrepreneurs are
closing down their factories, while the Chinese open more and more."
He has asked his students to write a case study on Chinese competitiveness. We suggested that they visit the Newbisco factory, near Lagos
airport.

Founded before decolonization by an Englishman, sold to a
Nigerian group in the 1970s, and later palmed off on an Indian businessman, the factory is now owned by Y. T. Chu. When Chu, who de-
clined to divulge his first name other than its initials (Y. T.), took over
in 2000, it was a bankrupt mess of a company. Electrical engineer
Yechang Wang, who emigrated from China fifteen years ago, was
commissioned to get the factory back on its feet.

"We replaced half of the production lines with Chinese machines. They're four times cheaper than the European equivalent
and the only ones still compatible with the 1950s machines we have
here. We laid the factory's own gas pipeline when we replaced the
diesel ovens. We built a warehouse to stock enough flour, oil, and
sugar for round-the-clock production. We intensified quality control and motivated the factory's seven hundred workers by paying
them a decent wage and paying them on time. They now work in
two twelve-hour shifts."

The factory produces over seventy tons of biscuits a day, which
end up in the lunchboxes of schoolchildren across the country. Expansion is on the horizon.

"We barely meet 1 percent of the Nigerian market demand," beams
Y. T. Chu. At his house, built in the "English country style," Chu ex-
pounds on the differences between the "open, educated, sophisticated" Chinese of Hong Kong and those from the mainland, who still
need "a little smoothing." At the end of our tour of the factory, two of
his managers are invited to an upstairs office for coffee and biscuits. In
addition to biscuit production, Yechang Wang also handles technical
problems in the group's two foundries. He lives in very basic accom-

modations in the neighborhood and only returns to China to see his wife and son once a year. Benjamin Chen is responsible for flour and sugar purchases, and he also manages supplies for the electrical equipment plant, scrap steel, and all of the Chinese machines.

"We all do several jobs. That's the secret of our success. You did the same thing in Europe fifty years ago when you were still prepared to work, right?" Yechang Wang's wife has come to see him once, but he would rather she remain in China to raise their child. "There are no Chinese schools in Nigeria even though there are tens of thousands of us," he continues, "We prefer it that way. We're here on business, not to stay. We're not trying to enforce our culture like the colonialists."

At the end of the meeting the managers both fill in forms, jotting down the number of biscuits eaten and cups of coffee drunk. Hard work is not the only secret of Chinese success. Parsimony plays a considerable role. In Jacob Wood's Millennium Hotel a plastic-coated document sits on the nightstand, listing the cost of all thirty-five objects in the room in case of theft or breakage: electric kettle (3,000 nairas [about $24]), ashtray (300 nairas), TV (32,000 nairas), curtains (3,500 nairas), bath mat (1,200 nairas), lamp (1,500 nairas), and safety deposit box (12,000 nairas).

Chinese working practices may seem oddly penny-pinching, but from the new factories, growing payrolls, and vehicle fleets, Chinese business interests in Lagos certainly appear to be both considerable and expanding. Wood is building a television assembly plant in the Calabar Free Zone, near the Cameroon border, where he already runs an air conditioner assembly plant. Roy Zhang is next moving into Lagos's hospitality sector.

"Africa is just one immense opportunity that came at the right time for us," Zhang says. Jacob Wood goes even further: "I'm going to be honest with you. China is using Africa to get where the United States is now, and to surpass it. It is willing to do anything to achieve that, even build a Nigerian railroad that has no hope of making money [an $8.3-billion contract signed in November 2006] or launch a Nigerian satellite into orbit"—mission accomplished May 14, 2007.

※ The BUSINESS & POLITICAL goal /
Hegemonic threat.

Another way to estimate Chinese assets in Nigeria is to look at the wealth of China's Nigerian customers. Amy Wood invited us to Anthony Mogbonjubola Soetan's seventieth birthday party. The president of the Nigerian senate had rented the top floor of the Golden Gate in Lagos for the occasion. Wrists drooped with Swiss watches and necklines dripped with precious gems. Amy Wood was a little mouse in the midst of the elephantine women, all worth their weight in gold. The continental buffets overflowed with food, French champagne, and Saint-Emilion Grand Cru. Anthony Soetan thanked the owners of the Golden Gate in his speech. "This reception was a present from us," whispered Amy. "He is a friend."

The Chinese seem exceptionally good at keeping out of African politics while supporting the winning side. Y. T. Chu, the owner of the steel plant and the biscuit factory, considers himself a personal friend of the outgoing president, Olusegun Obasanjo. His living room proudly displays photos of the two of them under a tree.

"I was invited to his three-day birthday celebration in April," Chu tells us. "I was in London at the time, but the next day I brought a present to his farm, not far from my steel mill." Besides impromptu visits, the proximity of Chu's mill to the presidential home also has the advantage of a shared electricity supply. "Since no one would ever dare turn off the president's lights, my plant always has electricity," smiles Chu. His friend Jacob Wood advises the president on promoting enterprise in Nigeria. Wood also plans to work with the president's successor, Umaru Yar'Ardua.

Such proximity to power makes it easy to capitalize on the business opportunities inevitable at the start of every new administration.

"The new president and governors will embark on many new projects in order to rake in cash from a maximum of commissions. This is when everything is decided, and we are ready!" says Jacob Wood.

Y. T. Chu, on the other hand, is nostalgic for the string of military coups in the 1990s. "Each new dictator canceled his predecessor's projects and started new ones," he reminisces. "We salvaged high-quality steel from those unfinished construction sites. It was melted down and sold for the price of gold!"

Another police car, another journey through the city. Amy Wood is bored and her husband is in Abuja. It's dark and she wants to show us Lagos by night. "The first time I came to Nigeria was in 1985. I was traveling first class on a Swissair flight, and the man next to me snored so loudly I had to wake him up. He could have got angry, but he just laughed. As I got off the plane, the flight attendant asked me 'Do you know who that was?' I didn't have the slightest idea.

"'General Obasanjo,' she whispered. 'He often flies this airline!'"

In 1976 Obasanjo took over as military head of state, one year after the first military coup. In 1979 he voluntarily handed over power to a democratically elected government, overthrown four years later. A succession of dictators followed, the cruelest and most corrupt being General Sani Abacha in 1993. Obasanjo's open criticism of Abacha's oppressive rule resulted in Obasanjo's imprisonment. He was released in 1999, just in time to be elected president.

"After we settled in Lagos, his wife and I became very good friends," Amy Wood continues. "She came with me to China on several occasions, and I helped her manage a hotel in Lagos." Stella Obasanjo, apparently the president's favorite wife, died while undergoing plastic surgery in Málaga, Spain, in 2005.

"This is the red-light district," Amy says as we turn down Idowu Tailor Street on Victoria Island. At the sight of our police car the groups of prostitutes melt off the streets. We cruise past the empty pavement to be met at the Tower Casino restaurant by a fractious mob. In its center stands a thickset Chinese yelling abuse at a frail black man. It transpires that the Chinese man had opened his car door without looking and hit the Nigerian's *okada* (motorcycle taxi) with the Nigerian's wife and little girl sitting on the back. All three Nigerians went flying through the air. The Nigerian asked for money to have his daughter examined at the hospital, but the Chinese refused, accusing the man of taking advantage of a rich foreigner. Brushing off his wife, the Nigerian readied himself to fight.

"We don't need people like you here!" another local in the crowd yells. "You're worse than the colonialists. Go back to China!"

Amy Wood hurries through the door of the karaoke bar while we try to break up the argument. The furious Chinese man can hardly wait to lash out at the knocked-about and bruised Nigerian. After much effort we convince him to wait for us inside while we try to calm the witnesses, all of whom are energetically retelling the story, complete with mime.

When we finally make it inside, we find that the smoky casino consists of half a dozen roulette, baccarat, and blackjack tables. The owner, croupiers, and customers are all Chinese with the exception of one huge, profusely sweating Lebanese man. But the author of the ruckus outside the casino is nowhere to be seen. At the other end of the room a small door leads to the karaoke bar, where Amy Wood, in her pink-flowered outfit, having already knocked back several gin and tonics, is preparing to sing a Chinese love song to the video of two lovers sitting hand in hand by a shimmering river.

Pushing through a set of double doors, we find our man in the restaurant sitting beside his wife and a mountain of fried noodles. He takes a mouthful, listens to our remonstrations, and gives us a fifty-dollar bill.

"I'll win it back at the casino," he says, giving us a friendly pat on the back.

After crooning our way through the Chinese version of the Beatles' "Yesterday," we wobble back to the car. On the way home we pose a flushed Amy Wood a somewhat direct question.

"What do all these Chinese workers in Nigeria do for girls?"

"There are a few Chinese prostitutes, but not enough to go round. They wait to see their wives in China once a year."

"They don't go to African women?"

"Never! Not for sex. Nor marriage. I hardly know any mixed couples."

"Why not?"

"Simple. We don't like them!"

Amy Wood has no qualms about her comment, but when her driver, a smiley Nigerian called Monday, turns his head in surprise, we wince and start a new line of questioning.

"Would you marry a Chinese woman?" we ask him.

"Not likely. As we say here, 'Monkey no fine, but eem mama like am.'"

"Er, what do you mean?"

"I mean nobody go see eem mama whose soup no sweet. Best woman come from your village, who work hard and cook good!"

Chapter 3

In the Heart of the Congo Forest

> When a tree is moved, it dies. When a man moves,
> he can make a fortune.
>
> —*Chinese proverb*

Hilde and Justin live a short distance from one another. Their houses can be found in a remote corner of Congo-Brazzaville, in Conkouati National Park, a day's drive north of Pointe-Noire—the country's busiest port.[1] Both lead simple lives, still governed by nature's rhythms, rhythms that can be both luxuriant and pitiless. They breathe the same intoxicating fragrances of ancient flora and dank, earthy rot; they fall asleep to the vampiric cadences of the same malaria-laden mosquitoes; and they awake at dawn to the mighty cacophony of the same wild birds. Life here can be lonely, and for Hilde and Justin it is likely to remain that way. Star-crossed lovers they are not. In fact, they've never even met in person and would certainly loathe one another if their paths did cross as they went about their business in the jungle.

Hilde Vanleeuwe, a thirty-five-year-old Belgian woman, works for the Wildlife Conservation Society. She roams the forest in a pickup truck, monitoring the vegetation and wildlife, trying to understand and protect this immense trove of biodiversity. Justin Massalo, on the other hand, is Congolese and twenty-two. He lives in the Mpoumbou camp and moves on foot, hunting endangered species at night and marking trees by day. The ancient moabi trees on which he leaves his mark, a simple cross, will be cut down by his colleagues at the Mpoumbou camp, who, like him, work for Sicofor, the Chinese lumber company. He likes the Chinese because they're well disciplined and they pay on time. Hilde doesn't share this view.

All around her, she sees the natural landscape being churned up in one way or another to make it fit for human consumption. In one direction she can see the five-hundred-odd employees of BGP, the Chinese oil company, prospecting in the lagoon, clearing roads, and conducting seismic tests with dynamite for Zetah, a subsidiary of the French petroleum company Maurel & Prom. But how, we asked, were they allowed to drill for oil in a national park?

Hilde answers, "The government is aware that it is betraying its own commitments—we tell them time and time again. And not just its own commitments: The American government has invested a great deal of money in the park's protection, but the forestry minister in Brazzaville just tells us, 'I'll do as I damned well please,' or words to that effect."

And if she looks out to sea, she's confronted with destruction there, too. Chinese trawlermen are emptying the coastal waters with nets several kilometers long, plowing straight through those of the local fishermen. The fact that an area extending six miles off the coast is not only reserved for local boats but also is part of the national park means that this activity comes under Hilde's purview, too.

"One of the Chinese boats ran out of diesel the other day," she says, "so we took the opportunity to board her and conduct an inspection. We thought we had them, but they produced special licenses from the fishing minister."

And then, of course, there's the forest itself. She has to keep track of more than 5,000 square kilometers of national park with only twenty-two other rangers. In February 2007 they had intercepted a pickup en route to Pointe-Noire. Hilde and her group made the gruesome discovery of eighty-six animal hides in the truck, including those of gorillas and chimpanzees, which were thawing after having been stored in a freezer. The only deep freeze in the entire forest is in Sicofor's Mpoumbou camp.

• • •

As the sun sinks toward the horizon, we watch Justin as he slides three rifle rounds into his pocket, slings his gun onto his shoulder, and makes sure the headlight, which he wears to reflect in the eyes of his prey, is secure. The gun looks as primitive as the landscape through which he leads us. Tonight's hunt is a special one because Sicofor's director general, Zhang Ke Qian, has traveled all the way from Pointe-Noire to take part. Zhang's Congolese chauffeur is also with us.

Justin earned the honor of leading the hunt by emerging from the forest early that morning with a monkey he'd shot in the stomach while his colleagues were still sleeping; the nearest village big enough to boast a shop, Cotovindou, is a two-hour drive away, so in order to feed themselves Justin and his coworkers go hunting instead of shopping. Michael Lusaka, the Filipino in charge of Justin's outfit, told us, "Even if we deliver food to them, they still go and hunt for it. They think that only wild game gives them enough strength to cut down trees."

And they certainly need their strength. The forestry concession that grants logging rights includes cutting down a quota of 189 trees per day, a daunting task considering the sheer size of the trees, the poor roads through all-but-impenetrable terrain, and the company's far-from-reliable machinery. Nevertheless, day after day, tree after tree, Justin and his coworkers are participating in the deforestation of the Congo Basin, the largest rain forest in the world after the Amazon.

As he leads us slowly, carefully through the trees, Justin pauses occasionally to watch and listen. There is little enough game, it seems, for him to seek out. "We've hunted too much," he says in a low voice. "There's nothing left in the forest."

We cross a small river, the water coming up to our waists. We cross another. Or perhaps it is the same one? The hours roll on, guide and guided alike becoming increasingly impatient. Suddenly Justin holds up a hand, demanding silence. We all freeze. He imitates an antelope's cry, a pitiful, mournful whinnying, and is rewarded with a shivering in the undergrowth. At length, a rat emerges from behind a leaf. We breathe a collective sigh and continue on our way, walking ever deeper into the rain forest.

We ford another stream or two and disturb a handful of rodents before Justin admits that we're lost and will have to spend the night in the forest, surrounded by chattering insects and unidentifiable rustlings, animals large and small, and of course the relentlessly humid, stagnant air.

Zhang takes our predicament in his stride. None of us is overjoyed by the prospect of a night in the open, but this is the first experience of the African jungle for this refined, somewhat reserved man from Beijing. While Justin shuffles about collecting firewood, Zhang clears a patch on the forest floor, brushes some of the giant ants from his legs, and lies down to sleep. We follow his example and so find ourselves lying by a fire, unable to sleep for the eerie animal cries amplified by the darkness beyond our small, flickering oasis of light. We lie that way for an hour before Zhang, sensing that we are all wide awake, sits up, tosses a log on the fire, and tells us something of himself to pass the time, of how he came to be in Congo-Brazzaville and in charge of a lumber company.

In 1998, Zhang was in Brazzaville, where he was working for the Chinese news agency, Xinhua. "There weren't more than a dozen Chinese in the whole country back then," he recalls. "And most of them worked in the embassy. It was a pretty closed little clique; nobody went outside after five in the afternoon." At that time, the country was once again trying to find its feet, having emerged from a civil war, with the Marxist-Leninist dictator Denis Sassou N'Guesso triumphant once more after five years of quasi democracy.

"My life changed in April 2000 when I was asked to pick up a young woman from the airport who was flying in from China." He kicked a branch farther into the heart of the fire, provoking a flurry of sparks. "It was . . . how do you put it? Yes: Love at first sight."

The girl in question was one Jessica Ye. Twenty-three years old, she was coming to Africa from China on an ill-defined quest for adventure and fortune. Now, ten years later, she and Zhang are married, with a daughter. She, too, has businesses in Congo-Brazzaville, which employ eighty members of her extended and extensive family—but Zhang would come back to that.

On arriving in Congo-Brazzaville, Jessica worked for three months as an interpreter for the Chinese company that built the new foreign ministry in Congo-Brazzaville, before opening a small restaurant in July 2000. She soon sold it at a profit and got another job, this time in a nightclub, which she later bought. And while she was busy with all this, she was also importing Chinese goods, with which she stocked the seven shops she had acquired.

Zhang is interrupted by a far-off gunshot. Probably his driver, Felix Sitou, who went off in search of prey an hour ago. Justin remains sound asleep, twitching occasionally, no doubt dreaming of the big hunts to come.

"I used to break Xinhua's rules for Jessica," Zhang continues. "I'd leave my colleagues at the embassy watching the Chinese satellite channel, CCTV, and wait for Jessica at the entrance to her club or restaurant. Occasionally I'd grease the wheels for her with the Congolese officials if she had merchandise being held up by customs, but when they found out about all this, Xinhua recalled me to Beijing."

It was at this point that Jessica's brother, Philippe, appeared on the scene in Congo-Brazzaville. He had arrived to help his sister, who, with Zhang back in China, needed support. Like his sister and the rest of his family, Philippe hailed from Wenzhou, a city in the Zhejiang Province south of Shanghai. People from this particular place are often compared to Venetians: They have a taste for adventure, are wont to emigrate, and have business in their blood. A few days after the tragic events of June 1989 at Tiananmen Square in Beijing, Philippe illegally emigrated to France. He arrived in Paris and got a job in a factory making leather bags in the Belleville neighborhood, the Parisian Chinatown. He couldn't stand the smell of the glue, however, and got another job at a dressmaker's and then changed course once again, this time working nights in a restaurant. Toward the end of that year, he took himself off to Cannes, where he met a fellow countryman who had joined the French Foreign Legion. Philippe was impressed not only by the uniform but also by the man's praising the camaraderie of the Legionnaires. The next morning, the restless young Philippe set down his bag in the recruiting office of the Nogent-sur-Marne barracks and signed up for a five-year stint.

He was looking for adventure, and he wouldn't have long to wait. Four months, to be precise. Before he knew it, he was jumping out of a plane over the Arabian Desert. The Legion was helping to drive Saddam Hussein from Kuwait in Operation Desert Storm.

Philippe told Zhang that it was cold—really cold there. But they ate well. They ate so well, in fact, that the American GIs came over and ate with them. But they didn't see much of the Iraqis. In fact, the only ones they saw were dead.

After the war, he was posted to Djibouti for two years. His Chinese girlfriend joined him there and they set up a bar, but when a new law prohibiting the sale of alcohol was introduced, the bar went under. Then the regiment broke camp and headed back to Nîmes, where Philippe rented an apartment. He would soon be grateful for the toughening-up process for which the Foreign Legion is so famous, for Philippe found himself serving two years in jail after lending his apartment to an unscrupulous friend. According to Philippe, he had thought his friend just needed somewhere to stay. According to the police, however, Philippe was an accessory to the kidnapping in which his friend was engaged, holding his victim hostage in Philippe's apartment.

Usually, the only Chinese who go back to China are the ones who've made their fortune. Philippe, however, fresh from a French cell, was promptly deported and left France with nowhere to go but China. By this time Jessica was in a position to help him out and offer a new direction. She had just opened her first store in Brazzaville and needed someone on the Chinese end to organize the shipping of Chinese goods to Congo-Brazzaville. Philippe was more than happy to do this, and after a little while, he went to see Congo-Brazzaville for himself. The family business was expanding fast: There were shops in Brazzaville and Pointe-Noire, the club, and even a factory that produced aluminum window frames.

Meanwhile, Zhang was still cooling his heels in Xinhua's Beijing office. However, he spent his spare time expediting the visas of those family members who were going to work for the nascent Ye empire in Brazzaville.

We stop Zhang at this point in his story, not only to feed the fire that is quickly demolishing our log pile, but also to ask how a Chinese family business had gone from this relatively straightforward beginning to logging in the Congo River Basin. To explain this part, he tells us, he must digress a little and tell us about Xu Gongde.

Xu Gongde is Jessica's uncle, a man who has lived in Gabon since the late 1980s. He, too, runs a company, this one by the name of Gabon Timber Trade and Development Ltd. But, we ask, trying to solve this increasingly complex puzzle, what was he doing in Gabon back then, when there were surely even fewer Chinese in Africa than when Philippe arrived? Zhang raises a finger: good question. He is coming to this.

In 1987, Xu Gongde was a lowly lumber dealer back in Wenzhou. It was then *his* turn to get the call that would change *his* life. On the other end of the line was a man claiming to be his uncle, a man called Jean Ping. Jean Ping was Gabon's minister for foreign affairs, currently in China on a state visit with his president, Omar Bongo. Ping had managed to slip away from the official delegation to pursue a private agenda. He knew that his father had left a family behind in China when he moved to France in the 1930s and then, having little luck there, to the French colony of Gabon. Once there, he had married the daughter of an influential clan chief, in a Sino-African union, even rarer then than now, that had resulted in Jean Ping. Jean was sent abroad to be educated, to the best schools in France, and having excelled academically, he proceeded to excel in his diplomatic career, culminating in his being named president of the UN General Assembly in 2004. In his long and distinguished career he had mediated countless crises across Africa. Having tracked down his nephew in Wenzhou, Ping offered him an opportunity to come and help him in Gabon and, under his protection and with his support, develop the lumber industry there.

Ping didn't have to ask twice. Xu Gongde packed his things and never looked back. He made a great success of himself in Gabon. By the time his niece, Jessica, arrived in Brazzaville in 2000, he was a rich man. When in 2005 he heard that Man Fan Tai, a lumber products company in Congo-Brazzaville, was in dire financial straits, he got in touch with the Congolese forestry minister and negotiated the purchase of the company's assets. Thus Sicofor was born. Philippe, Jessica's brother, had assumed the role of interim managing director, but inexperienced as he was, the company needed someone a little more sophisticated and trained in the subtle art of negotiation. The Ye family turned to Zhang, who handed in his notice to Xinhua, got on a plane, and bent himself to the task of managing Sicofor's Pointe-Noire office.

"I jumped at the chance," he says. "Perhaps you've heard this Chinese proverb? 'When a tree is moved, it dies. When a man moves, he can make a fortune.'"

• • •

Zhang's story at last brings us back to the present, a present that finds us sitting in the jungle, the fire a small heap of glowing embers, and dawn bringing definition to the surrounding jungle. Sitou, Zhang's driver, returns with a small antelope called a blue duiker across his shoulders. In the distance, we hear the throaty buzz of chainsaws being yanked into life. We pack up our few belongings and head toward the sound. It takes us two hours to negotiate our way back to the access road, and when we finally reach it, we find a team of Sicofor lumberjacks preparing to cut down a twenty-two-meter-high moabi tree. We watch them as they work, as they load the felled, lifeless trunk onto a truck headed for Pointe-Noire, where it will be transferred to a ship that will take it the rest of the way to Zhangjiagang, near Shanghai. Zhangjiagang handles more tropical timber than any other port in the world. Valuable hardwood trees such as the moabi will be sawed to pieces for either British parquet flooring or furniture for IKEA, which gets 30 percent of its wood from China.

It takes about a hundred years for a moabi to reach maturity and, as we have seen, just moments to bring it crashing to the ground in a cloud of dust.[2] Zhang climbs atop the trunk and assumes a victory pose, surrounded by his men, before the tree is loaded onto the truck. On the way back to Pointe-Noire, he smiles to himself every time we pass one of these giant trucks laden with Congo-Brazzaville's hardwood trees.

In 2006 Congo-Brazzaville exported nearly a million cubic meters of wood. Unprocessed timber makes up two-thirds of this total despite the law that stipulates that a minimum of 85 percent of felled trees be processed on-site. According to, the Swiss company SGS, the world leader in certification and verification, China buys 60 percent of Congo-Brazzaville's wood, mainly the okume trees that are used in plywood. But China is not only Congo-Brazzaville's best customer; the majority of Gabon's, Cameroon's, and the rest of Central Africa's wood is shipped to China, too.

And since we're running the numbers: China consumes 32 percent of the world's rice, uses 47 percent of the cement, and smokes a third of the world's cigarettes.[3] In comparison, China's appetite for wood seems modest. In 2003 it imported only 10 percent of the global market (83.5 million cubic meters).[4] Even this amount, though, has caused a great deal of damage to the forests of Siberia and Southeast Asia. Forest Trend, a conservation group made up of private individuals and nonprofit organizations, has estimated that if logging continues at its current rate the forests of Indonesia and Cambodia will have disappeared entirely within a decade, Papua New Guinea's will be gone in thirteen years, and Russia's in twenty. Pressure on the rain forests of Africa and South America will then rise accordingly. The Congo River Basin, which covers both the Congo-Kinshasa (RDC) and Congo-Brazzaville as well as Gabon, Cameroon, and northern Angola, contains a third of the planet's vegetation. Its 200 million hectares of forest contain 438 reptile species, 336 amphibian species, 221 species of bird, and 270 different species of mammal. That we know of. Among the forest's 43 primate species are great pangolins, gorillas, and bonobos. It is also home to the ape formerly known as the pygmy chimpanzee, the ape genetically closest to humans. And then there are the elephants. The elephant population in the Congo-Brazzaville rain forest is the biggest in the world, but even this population is under threat, as 700,000 hectares are stripped every year.[5]

It's true that much of the damage is caused by itinerant slash-and-burn farming communities, but industrial logging is accelerating fast. The World Wildlife Fund estimates that at the current rate two-thirds of Congo-Brazzaville's rain forests will be gone by 2050.[6] According to a report by the American organization Woods Hole Research that was published in *Science,* one-third of the forest has been affected by logging already.[7] In addition to this danger to the ecosystem, the access routes cut by the logging companies are also used by poachers, allowing them ever greater access to the forest's fauna. The access routes are themselves as much of a problem as the logging: They account for 60 percent of Congo-Brazzaville's roads.[8]

The international community has often praised Omar Bongo's government in neighboring Gabon for creating thirteen separate national parks starting in the 1990s, covering 10 percent of the country, but it's worth noting that as of 2005, much of this land had lost its protected status due to the understandable attractions of mining projects and the associated revenues. The biggest such concession granted in a so-called national park in Gabon—for half a billion tons of iron ore from the Belinga site—was given to the CMEC (China National Machinery & Equipment Import-Export Corporation), a Chinese firm financed to the tune of $4 billion by the Exim Bank of China. The project will require the construction of two hydroelectric dams, one of which threatens Invindo National Park, and a 560-kilometer railroad for transporting the iron ore to a port that will also need to be built on the Atlantic coast. There are also plans in the pipeline for another Chinese company to extract iron from beneath the neighboring Minkebe National Park; additional plans for another Chinese giant, Wanbao, to exploit Moukalaba National Park; and, last but not least, for the oil company Sinopec to begin exploring the possibilities within Loango National Park.

But Zhang has other worries than to preserve the Congo-Brazzaville forests: "All the machinery that Man Fai Tai left behind is broken, and it seems that its workforce was made up exclusively of alcoholics." He says that Man Fai Tai was a major player in Congo-Brazzaville's forestry industry at the end of the 1990s, and that the company had been granted the biggest forestry concession in Congo-Brazzaville's history, which allowed it to work 800,000 hectares, 93,000 of which were in Congo-Brazzaville's Conkouati National Park. According to Zhang, the company was cashing in on "services rendered" to N'Guesso during the civil war, when it supplied transport for the president's Cobra militia and paid Ninja rebels to stay out of the armed opposition. But terrible management, combined with systematic violations of Congolese law, ruined the company, enabling Taman, a competitor run by Malaysian Chinese, to corner a 57 percent share of the wood-production market in Congo-Brazzaville.

Sicofor has expended a great deal of time and effort turning Man Fai Tai around. It's demonstrated that it means business and has earned the respect of fellow professionals in Pointe-Noire. The company's production has increased month by month, though it has not managed to reach the government quota of 234,000 cubic meters of wood in 2008 (which would translate into roughly 335,000 trees). A sawmill in Pointe-Noire that Man Fai Tai left pretty much in ruins has been revived, and by June 2007 was processing wood for export to the United States, France, and Italy. Another factory was waiting only for a shipment of glue from China before it could begin churning out plywood. Sicofor earmarked $40 million for investment in the industry by 2010, and it seems that's just for starters.

Xu Gongde, Jessica Ye's uncle in Gabon, has meanwhile launched another company in Congo-Brazzaville—Dejia Wood Industries—which has been granted a concession that allows it to work 636,000 hectares in the Kelle and Mbomo areas toward the middle of the country. Congo-Brazzaville's official newspaper declared that Dejia was the only bidder but hastened to add that they "would like to emphasize that the examination of this application was carried out according to a new system that conforms to the tenets of good government and of transparency in forestry management."[9]

· · ·

"China is one of the world's great powers and has enjoyed a long-standing friendship with many African countries. Therefore, it has good relationships with African governments that, in turn, enable it to obtain forestry concessions," says Zhang, winding down his window in an attempt to combat the ripe smell exuding from the antelope in the trunk. When Sicofor signed on the dotted line for its concession in October 2006, in order to lend gravitas to its application it had claimed that the Chinese government was among its stockholders. "Oh, that wasn't true," Zhang shrugs, looking out the window. He turns to us. "We only said that to—um—facilitate things."

What *is* true, however, is that Sicofor does boast a genuine big gun among its shareholders, one who is also in a position to facilitate things:

Henri Djombo, otherwise known as Congo-Brazzaville's minister for forestry and the environment. Djombo is a flamboyant character, combining his ministerial role with those of playwright and president of the Congolese Table Tennis Federation (the latter position taken on while Djombo was ambassador to Bulgaria in the 1980s). He is considered a potential successor to President Sassou, too, which might help explain why Sicofor was able to take over Man Fai Tai's assets without so much as bidding, a state of affairs that astounded the NGO (nongovernmental organization) that monitors Congo-Brazzaville's rain forests.

Due to his packed schedule, the minister is a very difficult man to find in Brazzaville. He likes to be seen in a wide variety of places— Paris, New York, Geneva, and so on—where he plays the defender of Congo-Brazzaville's forests, Pygmies, and great apes. In debate, he often lectures the international community on their responsibilities (to reach for their wallets, that is). Thanks to the resulting donations, he has been able to improve his department's effectiveness in its tireless efforts to combat illegal logging, poaching, and wildfires.

The West's support for these "initiatives" has led to the creation of a multitude of agencies and NGOs with peculiar acronyms (FLEGT, REM, WCS, CIFOR, GRASP, and so on), which expend most of their energies simply existing, coordinating their activities, and trying to minimize the damage inflicted by Congo-Brazzaville's own government.

Henri Djombo views these NGOs with the utmost suspicion. He has so far avoided getting caught up in any of their schemes. "The interests of certain countries," he says with the delicacy of a seasoned diplomat, "have made them turn to NGOs to attack other countries." He is referring to the competition his country's wood faces from Europe. And anyway, he says, eager to disparage the claims of the conservationists, "opening up the undergrowth to the logging of usable trees has allowed us to restore and rejuvenate the forest, creating better conditions for wildlife. Nowadays, you can find more wildlife in the parts of the forest that have been opened up to logging companies than in the National Parks. In fact, there's so much wild game in the logging areas that we're hoping to start holding big game hunts there."

It seems that the uneventfulness of Zhang's hunting expedition is uncharacteristic and that Justin is quite wrong about the animals.

Such claims would have the NGOs spluttering into their soup, just as they did following the minister's most recent act of folly: signing a contract with the American company Pioneer International Development that allows it to build hotels and casinos in the Conkouati National Park. Arnaud Labrousse, an activist with several books on what he calls the "pillage" of the African rain forests, did some research into Pioneer and discovered that the company claims to specialize in "ecotourism" (along with oil, gas, and mineral extraction). Pioneer shares its headquarters with another company, Avanta, on a small street in Salt Lake City. Avanta's activities include the recruitment of African nurses for American hospitals. The companies share not only their headquarters, but also their directors: two Mormon brothers from Kenya and a businessman from Kinshasa who has a nice little sideline selling diamonds on the Internet and lending money at high rates of interest.[10]

As soon as our group arrives at Pointe-Noire, Zhang rushes over to the Bel-Air, a beach restaurant that his wife, Jessica, has just bought and renamed the Yes Club. He wants to call his cousins together for a family picture. They interrupt a card game to join him, along with Jessica, who is preparing for a trip to China. As the sun sets, everyone strikes a pose on the beach, backs to the sea.

Zhang is in an expansive mood and gives us a brief lecture on the benefits of Chinese involvement in Congo-Brazzaville: "The Congolese often tell us it would have been better had China colonized the country, rather than France. The French have done nothing for this country—no roads, no factories, nothing. If the Chinese had come here earlier, the beach would be covered by skyscrapers."

• • •

Skyscrapers are something of which Wenzhou has several dozen. Six months after our initial meeting, we met up again with Philippe, the ex-Legionnaire, in his hometown in China. One of the skyscrapers is called the Trust-Mart Vegas KTV, and it has a famous karaoke bar on the fifth floor in which we get to hear Philippe sing, "Every time I close my eyes, you are on my mind/And it's like you never really loved me/Now that I am alone and hurt/I ask myself how you could have left me so heartlessly/Oh, I need your love and I'm begging you."

Philippe puts the microphone down. Singing the song has exhausted him. Madame Te, his business partner, extends two closed fists toward him. He is supposed to guess which one has a peanut in it. He guesses correctly, so it's Madame Te who has to down a glass of beer.

Philippe has a lot to celebrate. Since Madame Te has collapsed, a little overrefreshed, on the sofa, Philippe's fiancée, Ange, chooses the next song, a Faye Wong hit, and dances around while singing, "Your heart, your eyes, your ears and your lips are not my destiny/I have no one/I think that tragedy is returning and is going to strike us again."

There's also Sha Yue Ke, Madame Te's boyfriend, who tries for the third time to explain to us the recipe for Mushen, the alcohol that his factory produces. Apparently, there is a particular species of moth called *Cordyceps sinensis* that is found mainly in Tibet at an altitude of 4,000 meters. The larvae of this poor unfortunate are prey to an exotic breed of parasitic fungus, *Hepialus amoricanus ober,* which takes root in the caterpillar, devouring it from within over the course of the winter. When spring arrives, the fungus celebrates by growing up and out of the doomed caterpillar's head. The resultant mushroom is then ready to be dried, ground up, and sold as medicine. Some say it helped a Chinese athlete take forty-two seconds off his 10,000-meter time, and others maintain that its aphrodisiac qualities enhance performance away from the track, too. Sha Yue Ke mixes it with rice alcohol, puts it in shiny packaging, and claims that a bender on Mushen is like experiencing the fountain of youth. Only the previous year, the sale of this beverage was still reserved for the Chinese government, but Sha Yue Ke has just received a license to sell it to the "public at large," although since prices range from $700 to $7,000 a bottle, not every member of the public can afford it.[11]

Philippe is burning through his African earnings with glee. "I have not yet made a fortune," he explains. "Just a few million." Much earlier in the night, he had invited everyone to come to a party in the best restaurant in town that would be fortified with wine and the dreaded alcohol of the caterpillar fungus.

He has been in China only ten days, and his entire first week was devoted to escorting an important guest around, Henri Djombo's son. They visited the Zhangjiagang port, where the wood arrives from Pointe-Noire, and the wood-processing plant that is owned by his uncle in Gabon, but, most important, they have feasted day and night. As soon as Philippe returned his charge to Shanghai in fine fettle, he had to endure a tedious series of meetings with potential partners or employees pertaining to the development of his African affairs.

He started with some engineers who he wanted to help him assemble a system for importing car parts. He met with them in his brand-new apartment on the twenty-eighth floor of a tower overlooking the Oujiang River. He managed to hold the meeting without interrupting his breakfast of crabs, and he sucked down every one of their many appendages. The next day, he had a meeting with carpenters, with a view to staffing his new factory in Pointe-Noire, which will make furniture for the local market.

At dawn following a third consecutive night of drinking and singing, he left us, swaying slightly, on the pavement outside a bar. "I've got to rush off to Yunnan Province," he explained. "Can you look after yourselves? I've just heard about a cigarette factory that's up for sale. Perhaps I can dismantle it and ship it off to Pointe-Noire."

Chapter 4

A Short History of China and Africa from 1421 to 2008

> In the fifteenth century, colonial conquest and
> division of the continent put an end to friendly
> relations between China and Africa.
> —*Yuan Wu,* China in Africa, 1956–2006

The island of Lamu lies just off the coast of modern-day Kenya. To the east, the vast stretch of water that is now known as the Indian Ocean continues uninterrupted for thousands of miles until it washes up on the coast of the country known today as Malaysia. And until one morning in 1421, it's fair to assume that Lamu's fishermen were more interested in catching fish than in mind-bogglingly deserted waters that stretched as far as—and perhaps even beyond—the horizon. So when that morning the horizon was no longer empty but instead dotted with the masts of gigantic ships, it's understandable that some of the fishermen were stunned into silence, and that others, fearing the wrath of the gods, dropped their nets and started running back to their village.

61

Although, with their minds full of vengeful deities, it wouldn't have made a great deal of difference to the fishermen, it's worth pointing out to the modern reader that these ships had arrived more than sixty years before Bartholemeu Dias would sail around the Cape of Good Hope, and almost eighty years before Vasco da Gama sailed along Africa's east coast.

Onboard an enormous ship in the middle of this Asian armada stood Admiral Zheng. The admiral jumped to his feet as his vessel neared this exotic coastline. Whatever the gods had in mind for the fishermen, the waters were calm and the fifty-year-old commander was preparing to give the order to land. He hoped to discover yet more wonders of this new world for the Chinese emperor Yongle, third emperor of the Ming Dynasty. His five previous voyages to Asia and Africa had not disappointed his master,[1] and so this time he had been equipped with almost unlimited means. He had between twenty and thirty thousand men under his command, sailing in three hundred ships, some of them called the "Treasure ships" of so many legends. Quite how gigantic these ships were is not something everybody agrees on: One sixteenth-century adventurer's tale asserts that they were 130 meters long, 55 meters in the beam, and boasted nine masts. Contemporary Chinese historians concur, as does the British author Gavin Menzies in his controversial best-seller *1421: The Year China Discovered America*. Many rather more academic historians have reacted fiercely to these claims.[2] Even if the more widely accepted length of 60 meters is to be believed, that's still twice the length of Columbus's *Santa Maria,* and there's no dispute that Admiral Zheng's flotilla was the largest in the world.

It was also the most cosmopolitan. On February 2, 1421, Emperor Yongle is said to have hosted a summit to celebrate the Chinese New Year. Eighty chiefs and dignitaries from across Asia, Arabia, and Africa were invited to this, the most "international" summit ever organized up to that time, an event to showcase the influence of the Ming Dynasty and to present its credentials as an empire open to the whole of the known world. Part of Zheng He's mission was to collect some of the emperor's guests and ship them back to China. This, at least, is the account given by the revisionist historians of twenty-first-century China. As modern China strengthens its ties with Africa, it is understandably trying to recast Zheng He as an Asian Christopher Columbus.

However, as the admiral readied his men for the landing on Lamu, the bickering of unborn academics was probably not at the top of his mind, nor was the thought that he and all his many accomplishments would sink into oblivion after his death. For now, he dreamed solely of glory.

Zheng had spent twenty years exploring the China Sea, the inlets of Java and Sumatra, and the Maluku Islands. As his experience and responsibilities increased, his expeditions became more ambitious and dangerous. He reached Calcutta, India, and also Ceylon, where a pillar, inscribed in Tamil, Persian, and Chinese, commemorates his visit in 1409. He pushed farther west toward the Gulf of Aden, the Strait of Hormuz, the Red Sea, the coast of Somalia, and even Mecca. His groundbreaking expeditions allowed his emperor to extend the boundaries of the known world, to open trade routes, and to establish new missions.

Ever since the Yongle emperor had spotted him among the eunuchs at the imperial court, Zheng had inspired confidence. When he was a child, he had been captured and castrated during a raid against the last pockets of Mongol resistance in Yunnan Province and brought to the capital. His name at the time was Ma Sanbao. It is said that his father was a Muslim who had made the pilgrimage to Mecca and was a descendant of a king of Bukhara, but none of these credentials made much difference in the Chinese court. What mattered was Zheng's intelligence and his courage in combat, two characteristics that set him apart from the other eunuchs and that earned him from the emperor a name worthy of a leader: Zheng He, meaning "harmony" or "peace." Zheng was thirty-four years old when, in 1405, the Emperor Yongle entrusted him with his first expedition.

This emperor had a vision. He wanted to drive the Mongols out of China, strengthen ties with Korea and Japan, and, as is usually the case with emperors' visions, expand his empire. To the south, his armies occupied Vietnam, while Zheng He's naval expeditions ensured military supremacy in the China Sea. But the emperor wanted to go further still. In this era before Chinese isolationism, distant lands fascinated the Ming Dynasty, so much so that they built a flotilla that could pursue their expansionist agenda. Equipped with maps and charts, compasses, sophisticated flotation devices, paddle-wheel propulsion systems, precise astronomical tables, and other technologies far in advance of those of the European powers, these teak behemoths sallied forth from the Longjiang shipyard. Aboard these ships (crewed, as would become customary in so many nations' navies, largely by ex-convicts) was a whole cross section of society: cooks, scientists, interpreters, medical staff, monks—even concubines. According to the records of the time, this colossal undertaking was accomplished in just the sixteen years between 1403 and 1419. The construction of these 2,868 ships, of the Forbidden City, and of a major extension of the Great Wall entailed the destruction of half of all the forests in southern China and Southeast Asia, an ecological catastrophe that led to populist uprisings.

Zheng He was not, however, the first of the Chinese explorers to reach Africa, or such is the claim of a certain publication circulated at the Beijing Summit of November 2006. *China and Africa, 1956–2006*,[3] not the most academically rigorous of texts, was clearly published to advance China's political agenda in Africa. In it, the author, Yuan Wu, asserts that a Chinese emissary called Zhang Qian followed the Silk Road to the southern shore of the Mediterranean as far back as the first century BC, where he brought clothes to the notoriously fashion-conscious Cleopatra. Yuan also claims that a few centuries later the Tang Dynasty (618–907) was in direct diplomatic contact with the Arab conquerors in the Middle East. It's even claimed that some Chinese explorers crossed the Sahara.

The first mention of Africa in Chinese books, however, comes from a more reliable source, the seventh-century writings of Jing Xing Ji. There are also Tang Dynasty works of art depicting dark-skinned men whom captions describe as talented, courageous, intelligent, and "righters of wrongs." We know that the Tang Dynasty sold porcelain in North and East Africa, and Chinese coins of that vintage have been found in Kenya and Zanzibar. The next extant written account is by a ninth-century explorer, Duan Chengshi, who describes the city of Berbera on the coast of Somalia.

But it was the Song Dynasty (960–1276) that really developed nautical technology and made the trading contacts, bringing Chinese merchandise on a significant scale to places such as Ethiopia, Tanzania, and even Zimbabwe. Trade and maritime exploration survived the conquest of China by the Mongol hordes. Kubla Khan, founder of the Yuan Dynasty, even sent representatives to Madagascar. In fact, Africa's first appearance on a map, where it is depicted as an elongated triangle, is attributed to the Taoist monk and geographer Zhu Siben (1273–1333). African wildlife made as much of an impression on the Chinese as perhaps anything else. Figurines depicting big cats, ostriches, and rhinoceroses can be dated back to the time of Zheng He, though it was perhaps the giraffe, brought to China in 1414, that provoked the greatest interest, interpreted as it was as the mythical *qilin*— a cow/ox/lion/unicorn hybrid. Even to the modern observer, this is perhaps as fair an interpretation of that unlikely animal as any other.

Whatever the revisionism that can be attributed to the work of present-day Chinese historians, it cannot be denied that Zheng He's voyages made a strong impression on his contemporaries. The English may have Drake's Drum—the legendary instrument that can, when the country is in mortal peril, be prevailed upon to raise Sir Francis himself—but the people of southern China and Southeast Asia went so far as to make a deity of Zheng after his death in 1533. His seventh and final voyage took him to the Arabian Peninsula, but after that, Chinese exploration petered out. The business of China, from this point until relatively recently, was China. Zheng He's flotilla was broken up and destroyed; his tomb in Nanjing Province was allowed to fall into disrepair, overgrown with vegetation, its occupant sliding into ill-deserved obscurity for five centuries. His papers, including the designs for his ships, were burned, and—save for a few commemorative stones and a handful of work written by seafaring contemporaries—nothing remains.[4]

It may seem strange that the country that promoted and celebrated the man's achievements could so swiftly and deliberately let his memory die, but while Zheng was away, globe-trotting for the greater glory of his emperor, power at home was shifting. Confucianism, a tradition that put familial loyalty and, more important, the conservative elements of Chinese culture at the center of its system, was once more holding sway over government. The civil servants were encroaching on the powers of the eunuchs, who had had the ear of the emperor and his court. These Confucianists thought little of the outside world, a world they saw as populated by barbarians with nothing or little to offer a civilization as great as their own, and they didn't try to hide their contempt for ruinously expensive overseas expeditions.

Thus the writing was on the wall for the likes of Zheng He when Emperor Yongle died in 1424. The succeeding Ming Dynasty emperor, Xuande, launched one last expedition before he died prematurely eleven years later. His son, Zhengtong, acceded to the throne aged only eight, leaving the door open for the Confucianists to seize power. A small window of thirty years had seen China looking beyond its borders in a manner that would not be repeated for five hundred years.

Predictably enough, this isolationist version of events is not included in the Beijing Summit's official history as it struggles to explain the complete absence of any kind of relations between Africa and China in the past half millennium. It was those dastardly Europeans who were to blame, and the dastardliness of Europeans is—often fairly—proverbial. "In the 15th Century, colonial conquest and division of the continent put an end to friendly relations between China and Africa," Yuan Wu writes. China, too, was the victim of such colonialism, we're told. This shared adversity, this common fate, led to the strengthening bonds of friendship between China and Africa.

> *In the middle of the 19th Century, the aggression of the Western powers turned China into a semi-colonized country. From the 1880s, thousands of Chinese were forcibly sent to Africa to build railroads, work in mines, and farm the land. On railroads at Dakar and in Congo-Brazzaville and in the Ran gold mines of South Africa, Chinese workers poured out their sweat and blood, and these horrific experiences have created tighter bonds between Chinese people and Africans.*[5]

Since 1949, the People's Republic has supported African countries in their efforts to gain freedom from colonial powers. China's official reasons for this support were presented as nothing more than a moral imperative to help the oppressed, but China was also trying to garner backing for its effort to regain the UN seat that had been "usurped" by Taiwan, an effort that could be greatly assisted by the votes of newly independent African states. The conclusion drawn by Yuan is that "after fleeing to Taiwan in 1949, Chiang Kai-shek's gang continued to hold China's seat in the UN [and that] the support of African countries aided the governments of the People's Republic in the hard fight to secure its rightful place."[6]

This "rightful place" was secured in 1971, thanks to the assistance of the newly independent African countries, and in return China built "factories, farms, irrigation and energy projects, transportation and telecommunications facilities, and cultural, educational and sanitation projects along with other economic and social infrastructure. In total, roughly 900 projects were completed between 1956 and 2005."[7]

This account of mutual back-scratching and fraternal quid pro quo is not, however, as simple as its author makes out. He doesn't mention that the vast majority of these projects have come to fruition only since the late 1990s, or that relations between the two peoples have been blowing hot and cold since the 1950s. In fact, communist China had its ups and downs in Africa. In the 1950s, for example, China competed ideologically with the Soviet Union. At the time, it was the USSR that more often raised the red flag in Africa, and Sino-Soviet relations were rather shaky.

The 1955 Bandung Conference gave China the opportunity to present itself as a kind of locomotive for the Third World, a representation of itself that was given further credence among nonaligned countries when it broke from Moscow at the beginning of the 1960s. Zhou Enlai, China's most prominent foreign affairs official of the period, made well-received tours of Africa in 1963 and 1964, but despite the aforementioned fanfare, China's aid to the continent remained limited to a little money here, a little training there, and help with a few large construction projects (roads, bridges, sports stadiums, presidential palaces, and so forth).

However, spurred by what they perceived as "Soviet social imperialism," the Chinese were by the end of the 1960s increasing their spending in Africa. In 1976 China completed the Tan-Zam railway, which connected landlocked Zambia to the Tanzanian port Dar es Salaam on the Indian Ocean. This 2,000-kilometer project was supposed not only to open up the interior to trade, but to demonstrate China's technical prowess and selfless munificence: 60 of the 50,000 Chinese who built the eighteen tunnels and forty-seven bridges died.

History, though, looked as if it was about to repeat itself. Events back in China—namely, the death of Mao Zedong and the turbulent end to the Cultural Revolution—led, as in the fifteenth century, to official disenchantment with African alliances. In the wake of Mao's death, interest in Africa began once more to wane.

Relations resumed in the mid-1980s as a result of economic reforms undertaken by Deng Xiaoping. China's selfless generosity, combined with Africa's demand for China's goods and services, as well as the prospect of access to Africa's colossal energy resources and raw material, led to what China called "readjustment" and "healthy development of the economic and commercial relation with Africa."[8]

Roland Marchal points to two landmark dates that demonstrate how quickly Chinese attitudes changed over the "period of readjustment" and "healthy development," from the end of the 1980s to now, during which China sought to increase its presence and influence: 1989 and 1995.[9] Following the Tiananmen Square demonstrations that ended on June 4, 1989, China attempted to reemerge from the resultant ostracism by the international community by reenergizing such diplomatic relationships as it still had. Africa was an obvious place to start, for not only did Africa hold more than a quarter of the votes in the UN's General Assembly, but African elites wanted to strengthen their links with China as they faced the emergence of a stronger democratic movement on the continent. These African elites sided with China after the Tiananmen Square massacre, and the Chinese realized the benefits of courting the Africans once more.

The next "Great Leap Forward" in China-Africa relations came in 1995, the year in which President Jiang Zemin exhorted the Chinese business community to "Go abroad! Become world players!" And once again, Africa was an obvious place to start, a place in which the Chinese dragon might sharpen its teeth before taking on the big boys: Europe and the United States. By 2000, infrastructure projects in Africa were receiving full government backing from Beijing, as well as financial backing from the Exim Bank of China. Such fulsome support gave Chinese businesses the confidence to look for invitations to bid for contracts that would be hard to differentiate from developmental aid projects.

Yuan's official history, meanwhile, censures the West for its actions during this period. Since 1991, it says, the United States and Great Britain have, in their customary deceitful fashion, made democratic progress a condition of financial aid, a stance that's considered "interference in Africa as well as in China under the pretext of hu-

Chapter 5

Trouble Governing?
Outsource to China!

> The Chinese are a different race. . . . We need their hardworking culture. We need to take these things seriously.
>
> —*Omar Oukil, spokesman of the Ministry for Public Works, Algiers*

Peng Shu Lin sits on his bed. On his lap is a small black bag. Visible through the window behind him is the sprawling Huafeng factory that makes equipment for the People's Liberation Army, in which this thirty-six-year-old has spent half his working life. He is single, not least, as he tells us, because he cannot afford to marry. So he lives with his mother and his sick father in a cold apartment in Mianyang, two hours north of Sichuan Province's capital, Chengdu, a town wreathed in chilly fog.

Peng Shu Lin has never been on an airplane; he speaks no English; he has seen a black person only on television. But tonight, taking with him just this small bag, he is moving to Nigeria for three years.

71

"At the factory I make 600 yuan [$87] a month. In Africa, I'll make $500." The economics are compelling, and he smiles briefly. "The restaurant that my mother worked in just closed; my father retired last year and then fell ill. He can hardly walk anymore, and the insurance doesn't cover his costs. He never leaves the house. My brother moved to another province and now he sells detergent. He earns 3,600 yuan a month [$522] but he never sends any back," Peng says with a sigh. "He must lead a very extravagant life."

In the last fifteen years, 120 million rural Chinese laborers have abandoned the countryside for the bright lights of China's cities on the east coast. They arrive with little more than basic agricultural skills, hoping to find work in factories or on construction sites. For skilled workers in central China the story has been different: They have always enjoyed relatively secure employment (Mianyang is host to China's biggest manufacturer of color TVs), but rising inflation, compounded by inefficient management in a number of state-owned companies, has left life precarious for Peng Shu Lin and his peers. The state-run Huafeng factory has been hemorrhaging workers for years; they are scooped up by employment agencies that send them to Japan, Singapore, and Indonesia. Africa, though, is a new and different beast, and Peng is considered something of a pioneer, but he is drawn to Nigeria by more than just a pioneering spirit. If you want to work in Malaysia, say, then the agency application process alone will set you back $4,200. A Nigerian application costs only $1,800.

Peng Shu Lin is going to work for the Standard Plastics Industry, a member of the Hongkong Huachang Group, located in Kano in northern Nigeria. The terms of his eight-page contract appear straightforward. He will work for eighteen months, after which he will be eligible for a month's home leave. If he decides to forfeit the month off, he will be paid double. At the end of the eighteen months he can extend his contract for a further two years. His pay, in dollars, will be deposited in an account he has opened specially in Mianyang. This is not the sort of contract that anyone would sign without considerable thought, but once again the math is compelling: "I'll have saved $15,000—maybe even $20,000—by the time I get back in 2011." Perhaps, by that time, Peng will be able to move out of his parents' chilly apartment; perhaps he'll finally be rich enough to get married and set up some kind of shop. Another brief smile. "Perhaps an Internet café," he suggests. Little did he know that Mianyang and the surrounding area would be devastated by an earthquake that killed 69,000 in May 2008.

Peng Shu Lin is an unnaturally gaunt young man, thin from a lifetime of eating only enough to keep going. He looks around his room reflectively. No special meal has been planned for what may be his last evening with his parents for three years—or ever, given his father's poor health.

"He's my best recruit!" says Zheng Min, the petite, lively young woman who handled Peng's recruitment by Standard Plastics. She, too, worked in the Huafeng factory before opening an agency that recruits skilled workers for an employment agency in Chongqing. A large blue sign dominates her office:

Work Overseas and Live Your Dreams!

She proudly tells us she has eighty people on her books. Two of them are there when we visit. The details of their stories differ from Peng's, but the theme is the same: Mr. Tu is thirty-eight and waiting for a Nigerian visa. He's leaving so that he can pay for better schools for his seven-year-old son. Mr. Yu is unsure whether to take a job in Congo or Nigeria. He loves his son and his wife very much, he tells us. But he's willing to go away for fifteen years if it means a better life for them.

These men are symbols of a whole generation of Chinese. They are prepared to sweat ten-hour days in unknown, possibly hostile countries, far away from their families; they are prepared to sleep for years in company dormitories, eat in company cafeterias, and face the ubiquitous risk of malaria, all this without a sigh or a complaint.

Their motives are not hard to comprehend; the dollars speak louder than words. But their stories raise a question for Africa,[1] one that is less easily answered: How can countries like Nigeria, which face their own daunting unemployment rates and whose bright minds and skilled workers try to leave, justify importing Chinese labor?

The stock explanations—that the Chinese work hard while Africans are lazy, that the Chinese direct their own destinies while Africans leave their fate in the hands of God and aid agencies—are as logically flawed as they are racist. A brief glance at teams of African workers toiling under the equatorial sun, wielding axes to perform tasks long since assumed by machines in the developed world, is proof enough that the Chinese have no monopoly on hard work, in addition to the armies of African women who come home after a full day in the fields to the tough demands of housework, only to return to work the next day with their children on their backs. But as later chapters will show, in countries like Congo and Algeria, just as in every corner of the continent, a profitable African-run business—whether state-owned or private—is too rare. Successful businesses risk being looted by the political elites, whose predatory, corrupt practices have deliberately prevented the emergence of a middle class capable of threatening the status quo.

Zheng Min, the cheerful head of the recruitment agency, shows her new recruits a promotional video made by Hongkong Huachang Group. This hourlong tape is composed exclusively of scenes designed to reassure her audience: modern hotel lobbies, factories, and offices. In fact, if it weren't for the palm trees filmed through the windshield of a pristine 4x4, Nigeria could be mistaken for any number of China's industrialized zones. The film seems to have the desired effect, particularly the various factory sequences. The recruits mutter to one another when they recognize the machinery and laugh a little when they see an African performing tasks—very slowly, apparently—that they themselves perform at work. As the credits start to roll, however, they ply us with questions, interrupting each other as new, previously unformulated concerns occur to them.

"Is it really hot there?"

"Are there a lot of mosquitoes?"

"Is there a Chinese embassy?"

"Do the people there like the Chinese?"

"Surely you can get Panda cigarettes?"

"And what do they eat there?"

In reply to this last question, we assure them that reputable Chinese companies like theirs all have excellent cafeterias and Chinese cooks. But if they venture out into an African village to eat with the natives, well, then, they should beware: They may find a monkey on their plate. Sometimes, we tease them, if they're very, *very* lucky, they might even be offered a giraffe appetizer. They clearly have stronger stomachs than we do, for our tall tales seem to reassure them.

"Monkeys and giraffes?" says one. "Not a problem."

No doubt the producers of Hongkong Huachang's video are well aware that the prospect of lightly poached gorilla for lunch is the least of these men's worries. Although highly instructive when it comes to the company's forty factories, the producers fail to mention other aspects of this exotic home-away-from-home that these new recruits might want to know about—for example, the threat of kidnap by guerrillas, something that two Sichuan men, Li Shaofu and Gao Zeming, have learned firsthand. They were abducted by armed men from their camp in the south of Nigeria, where they were installing telephone cables. They were held captive for thirteen days and were released after a ransom was paid. The authorities would not disclose the amount handed over to the kidnappers, but it is likely to have been generous, for not long afterward, nine employees of the China National Petroleum Company were taken hostage, near where the first two men had been seized.

Li Shaofu and Gao Zeming were from a village called Jianqiang in a district, according to our map, called Renshou, less than three hours from Mianyang. We decide to take a drive and soon hit Chengdu's sprawling suburbs, which are lined with apartment blocks in various stages of construction. These forty-floor towers, designed to ease industrialized China's housing crisis, share the same aspirational and absurd names beloved of developers from Los Angeles to Singapore: "My South Seven Miles," "Living Park," "Agile Garden," "Cabin View," "Deluxe Hills," and the mythical "Dragon Hill Peninsula."

Renshou district has watched 100,000 of its inhabitants migrate to eastern cities and another 3,800 overseas, mainly to Singapore and Japan, but oddly, no one there seems to have heard of a village called Jianqiang, or of its two abducted sons. This is despite the Chinese press's making a great show of concern about the fate of these two men at the time of the kidnapping. Stranger still, nobody in the district has ever heard of any Chinese being kidnapped at all. We come to recognize, not for the first time, one of the many cultural differences that becomes painfully obvious as one travels between Africa and China: In Africa, China is a big deal. China's influence is evident everywhere and its presence is in itself a revolution, upending the old order. At home, however, Africa is just another place that isn't China.

In the end it takes us the entire day to find San E, the tiny hamlet that was once home to the two telecom technicians. We transfer to motorbikes to negotiate the rough roads that lead through terraced fields. As we arrive in San E, some of the inhabitants are watering their gardens with pails suspended from bamboo yokes. Old men, too frail for the yokes, are using primitive grinders to extract grains of corn from their husks. At last we come upon Gao Zeming's family home. Its covered portico, its new tiling, and the freshly painted calligraphy on its walls suggest a family a little better off than its neighbors. We knock, and wait. Eventually the door opens a crack. Gao's mother sees us and quickly slams it shut. "Go away," she shouts from inside. "I spoke to reporters before and everything they wrote was bullshit!"

We turn back the way we came and soon meet two men carrying a tree trunk between them. They are fractionally more talkative. We ask if they know where Gao Zeming is.

"He came home a few months ago," says one of the men eventually. "He rebuilt his parents' house with the money he made in Africa, but then he left again for Chongqing."

The second log carrier, it turns out, has also been to Africa. "The company kept back half of my last wage packet and said that if I talked to reporters I'd never see it."

We ask for directions to Li Shaofu's house and head off. We come to a muddy path leading to a farm that has seen better days. Li's mother is in the front yard, threshing beans with a bamboo flail. Her eyes are sunken, the creases around them fault lines in a face etched with years of fatigue. The gaps in her teeth seem to outnumber the teeth themselves. She's more communicative than her counterpart down the road. Her rapid, staccato speech is punctuated with regular grimaces as she takes out the world's many injustices on the plants at her feet.

"My three sons have all left. None of them send any money. The house is falling apart. There are holes in the roof. I don't have the strength to work the farm anymore. This year I managed to harvest only 150 kilos of wheat. That's worth two hundred yuan [$29]. I'm hoping to get 40 kilos of beans." She indicates the pile of vegetation in front of her. "That's one hundred yuan at the market."

"When Li left for Africa I told him to do what he wanted, so long as he sent money for a pig. Pigs are worth more than wheat or beans. The money never got here. Maybe he never sent it. I heard he had trouble with thieves over there. Either way—no pig. When the reporters came, they told me he was installing telephone lines in Nigeria. I told them that we didn't even have a telephone here. I told them we didn't even have a pig. When he came back, he told me it was very hot over there. I told him I needed a pig. Then he left again. He went to Shanghai. Or maybe Africa. It's all the same to me. Nobody cares about the house falling down around my ears. And I still don't have a pig."

The future seems less precarious when you look at it from the thirty-third floor of a skyscraper in Chongqing. The city is home to 31.4 million people, making it the biggest on the planet. The windows of the offices of the Chongqing Overseas Labor Company Ltd. provide a panoramic view of the city: the unfinished skyscrapers reaching ever upward; the highways, dotted with bright yellow taxis, roll out across an uneven plateau of glass and concrete; and through the center of the picture flows the Yangtze River. Life viewed from this altitude appears slow, even sluggish, and it seems impossible that today, like every day, 813 people will be born here, and the city itself, in a bid to make room for the new offices, apartment blocks, and factories, will expand by 137,000 square meters. Today, like every day, 1,370 new migrants will arrive in the city from rural China.

This last statistic clearly pleases Huang Yiming, the head of the company. "If they loved the countryside so much they wouldn't come here," he smiles. Some of these migrants come here to his offices for their last interview before contracts are signed and bags are packed for overseas jobs. Since opening for business in 1998, the Chongqing Overseas Labor Company has exported hundreds of such workers to every country in Asia and even to New Zealand and Great Britain. Since it has signed an exclusive contract of its own, however, to supply recruits for Hongkong Huachang, the focus has shifted to Africa.

"For 2008 I need a thousand new recruits, double the current workforce. Can you imagine the difference they will make?" Huang Yiming is a jovial man with a constant smile. "The Chinese work hard, you know." His smile broadens. "Perhaps you would like some of them in France? I can send you some next month!" He's still smiling when we leave to catch a plane.

• • •

Ten thousand kilometers from Chongqing, over the Himalayas, across the Indian Ocean, and past the Horn of Africa, we find ourselves at the home of Claude Alphonse N'Silou, the Congolese minister of construction and housing, in the capital Brazzaville. N'Silou seems content as he leans back in a leather chair, wearing an exquisitely cut blue suit and sipping meditatively from a glass of sparkling French mineral water. The water is to his satisfaction, and the servant who brought it glides off across the marble floor.

If there's one thing that N'Silou likes as much as imported mineral water, it's the Chinese flooding into his country. "They're magnificent," he tells us. "They built the Alphonse Massadena stadium for us, the Foreign Ministry and the television company's headquarters. Now they're building another dam, in Imboulou. They've rebuilt Brazzaville's entire water system." He counts these projects on the fingers of one hand and has to put his glass down to continue. "They built the airport, they're building the Brazzaville to Point-Noire highway. They're building apartment buildings for us, and even an amusement park on the river!" He can see he's going to run out of fingers and abandons the counting. The list is never-ending. "In Oyo, our president's native village, they've built a hospital, some more roads, and apartment buildings. It's all signed off! Done!" He raises his glass. "It's a win-win situation!" He then shakes his head, slowly.

"Too bad for you in the West, of course."

N'Silou forgets to mention that one of the projects the Chinese are also in the process of completing is the extravagant palace in which we're sitting. On our way into the mansion we passed sections still under construction, a series of columns leading up to an edifice so grand that the U.S. embassy next door, also under construction, seemed like little more than a bunker. This architectural one-upmanship might well have something to do with N'Silou's training as an architect in Italy, where he studied on an EU scholarship.

The minister's department has one of the biggest budgets in Congo's government, and he has the somewhat rare privilege of dealing with the Chinese directly. President Sassou N'Guesso had accorded him the task of improving Congo's housing, under the umbrella of a broader social development project grandiloquently titled New Aspirations, and it is a duty the minister takes seriously. He is to build 10,000 new "units," as he calls them, but in reality, this turns out to be a less daunting mission than it sounds. His job entails drawing up a broad outline for a project and giving it for implementation to the Chinese company WIETC (Weihai International Economic and Technical Cooperative), a company based out of Weihai in China's Shandong Province. WIETC has around fifteen such projects in hand in Congo-Brazzaville, which it staffs with nearly five hundred Chinese workers. In Africa, the company's assignment extends to hiring the labor force and importing the building materials. It works fast, too, and its quotes for these projects are unbeatably low. WIETC's official company Web site lists no fewer than six mottoes, including "Honor to those who uphold plain living and hard toil; shame on those who wallow in extravagance and leisure."

"We're rich now!" the minister tells us, once again raising his glass, referring to Congo-Brazzaville's 6 percent increase in GDP, thanks to rising oil prices. He shakes his head. "The French were with us through the tough times. Too bad they don't get to reap the benefit now."

France may not be sharing in the newfound, oil-based wealth, but WIETC clearly is. They're building not only N'Silou's own residence but also forty more villas down by the river in the Bacongo neighborhood. This project is particularly close to the minister's heart, and he describes the villas with relish. He sprinkles a bizarre assortment of exotic fruit through his description, and finally we realize that these fruity labels ("Mango" or "Papaya") correspond to the number of upstairs rooms in each house. Clearly the architect—in this case N'Silou himself—had the same lack of concern about semantics and the same love of whimsy as his counterparts in Chengdu. A modern Congolese family rich enough to afford a "Papaya" clearly leads a very comfortable life. The planners have envisaged a working couple, both driving their own cars. Each of their three children will have his or her own room, and the kitchens and bathrooms are top of the line.

The minister's enthusiasm for his residential fruit salad is infectious, and a few days later N'Silou personally escorts us on a guided tour. A yellow banner on the construction site goes some way toward explaining his interest in the project: "The passion to do more for you! Vote N'Silou!"

Improving the standard of living for the electorate is not the only duty entrusted to N'Silou. The president has also given him the task of getting elected to the assembly from the Bacongo District in the 2007 elections. This is comparatively difficult, because this same district is the home turf of one Bernard Kolelas, the former prime minister and leader of the rebel force known as the Ninjas, who fought against the current president during the civil war of 1997–2002. Bacongo itself saw fierce fighting at this time, which is why the construction project plays such a crucial role in the forthcoming election. The Chinese have been asked to finish it quickly.[2] The minister's path to a seat in the assembly appears smooth: Not only have the hundred-odd families that lived in the shacks where the villas are to be built been paid off handsomely, but a hundred more villas are planned. This means more compensation for those living on this land, and more votes for the architect. Those owning property near the development will also see the value of their properties rise, and the local shopkeepers are awaiting a boom time as affluent Congolese flood into the area.

For several days now, everyone in the neighborhood has been carrying large plastic jugs (made in China, naturally) stamped with the message "A Gift from N'Silou" in wheelbarrows (made in China) that also proudly read: "A Gift from N'Silou." They fill the jugs with water from new wells that are the fortunate by-product of the recent on-site drilling. Over one well hangs a large banner, proclaiming that the well and even the water itself are "A Personal Gift from N'Silou to Ease the Concerns of Families and to Prevent Children Drowning in the River. Vote N'Silou!"

In short—everyone is happy.[3] Everyone, that is, except the Congolese laborers working for the WIETC. Fortunately for N'Silou, these men aren't from Bacongo and can't vote here. At a cheap, privately owned canteen opposite the site, we found a dozen of them chewing cassava root and indulging in the favored pastime of workers the world over: bitching about their bosses. Their complaints, however, are of a different order of magnitude from those of their Western counterparts. Their conversation covers every aspect of their plight, and we rarely have to ask them to explain things in greater detail.

"How much are you paid?"

"Our basic wage is 1,800 CFA francs[4] [$4] a day."

"Are there many Chinese on the site?"

"About forty."

"And they work hard?"

"Are you joking? They never stop. They're not human."

"Not human?"

"They treat us like slaves. When we make a mistake, we get smacked with a shovel. We do something wrong, we get smacked with a shovel. I splashed a Chinese guy with a bit of cement once, and he hit me. He didn't bother with a shovel."

"Are there any accidents?"

"I cut my thumb once on the circular saw. They didn't pay me anything. Not even medical costs. Anyone who's more seriously injured is sacked."

"And what about when this project is finished? Is there more work?"

"There's no contract. Once a project is done, it's done."

"And are you charged for your meals?"

"Of course. A meal costs $1.12. And transportation costs that much, too. We only take home about $1.80 a day."

"What about vacation?"

"You don't work, you don't get paid."

Despite these conditions, Congo-Brazzaville does in fact have labor laws. There's a minimum wage of 50,000 CFA ($112) for twenty days' work a month, which amounts to 2,500 CFA ($5.60) per day. But only those with advanced skills and training receive that much in Bacongo.

Leaning against a villa wall, flashing a mouthful of teeth at a photographer, N'Silou strikes the pose of fearless defender of his country's labor force, someone who can keep the Chinese under control.

"The minimum wage is adhered to at all our sites. Our oversight is meticulous since the Chinese are . . . well, they have been known to fudge the numbers a bit. They don't seem to do it out of malice, exactly; it's just their way of thinking. The Chinese feel they have been sent on a mission. For them, doing business here is some form of conquest; their mission is to become the most powerful nation on earth, as they were a thousand years ago. They see Africa as a virgin space, abandoned by the West, and in need of a new conqueror." Suddenly, confronted by such issues, his attitude toward the Chinese seems suddenly more ambivalent, to say the least.

As we poke about the bedrooms of another villa, we mention the allegations of violence that the Congolese workers made against their Chinese bosses. We get a strong, well-rehearsed, reaction: "We are not like them. We have a different way of living and working. If the Chinese are in a hurry, then they simply work around the clock until the job's done. In Congo, we respect the schedule that's been set. Working someone—anyone—beyond their physical limits is an act of violence, and when that happens, which it does, I have to stop it. I can't—I won't—tolerate it. I've even had to have some Chinese deported for it."

We move along the line of villas and pause at one that it isn't as far along as the others because it is being built by young Congolese trainees. The locals are filling their big plastic jugs with water, and when they see us—or rather N'Silou—they start cheering. He raises his arms like a boxing champion and says, "See how happy they are?" We can, and we can also see how happy he is that they'll be among those putting a cross next to his name come election day.

We move on, and N'Silou resumes his geopolitical musings. "The Chinese are dangerous," he whispers. Dangerous? Dangerous how?

"I don't know how they do it. They study every manager, every minister. They always build the right relationships. Once, during a dinner given for a Chinese delegation touring Africa, I sat next to a big cheese in the Chinese Ministry of Trade. We got talking and it turned out that we both loved jazz and Greco-Roman architecture. It really was the most extraordinary coincidence. It turned out that we even had professional interests in common. Then, as the delegation moved onward, he called me from South Africa and from Angola, and then from China, just to keep in touch, just to check in and see how things were. I mentioned this to some of my colleagues and lo and behold! they had similar stories. Each one had his own Chinese guy keeping tabs on him! They're dangerous, the Chinese. You watch out—in ten years the world will be theirs."

Later on during our tour, N'Silou rediscovers his enthusiasm for the Chinese. Finding himself surrounded by WIETC supervisors, he suddenly seems to remember how much he owes the Chinese; everything from the wheelbarrows and wells to the villas and the plastic jugs, even his own house. He recognizes that if he is elected to the assembly, and if he can hang on to the title minister of construction, he owes it all to them. He turns to us for a moment: "They come from so far away, yet look how quickly they adapt. They live modestly, as we do, and we all get along very well with one another. And why?" He answers himself: "The Chinese *build* things and the Europeans don't."

Moving on, we have a look into a Papaya and then see what the Mangos have to offer in the way of closets and clever storage spaces under the stairs. We pass through to the kitchen and spend a great deal of time nodding and making the right noises as N'Silou waxes lyrical about the table design, before resuming where he left off.

"For Europeans, democracy is synonymous with progress. But the Chinese, like many Africans, think that more than a sprinkling of democracy is a dangerous thing. They worry that if China becomes too democratic too quickly and implodes, then the world will suffer the consequences. That's why the Chinese don't demand reforms from the African regimes they deal with: They understand that a little harshness is necessary. They sympathize."

Only on the way back to the minister's office do we get to the heart of the matter. "There are about 3 million people in our country, and about a billion in China. That's the reason our work ethics are different. Over there it's a matter of basic survival. And so it is here, but not to the same extent. It's our relaxed attitude toward work, particularly among our younger generation, that annoys them. I understand where they're coming from; we *can* be pretty laid back."

• • •

In an Algeria made sleepy by the summer sun, the only activity appears to be happy meanderings of flower-bedecked wedding convoys. Many Algerians who have emigrated to France have come back for the holidays, and holidays, as far as one can see, mean weddings. Lots of weddings.

Standing on the edge of the Mitidja plain, watching these festive processions, you need only to turn your head to see another kind of activity: employees of the Chinese consortium CITIC-CRCC out on the plain itself, working around the clock. On September 18, 2006, they started work on a 528-kilometer highway running east–west across the whole country, and if they complete it in the assigned forty months, they will have set a new world record.

Near the village of Arbatache, dozens of yellow trucks fresh off the boat from China are carrying earth from a rapidly disappearing mountain. The earth is unloaded onto the path of the highway and smoothed out by yet more trucks. Further along the prospective route, Chinese geologists, moving around without escort, take samples from the Ammal Gorge, through which they plan to dig two tunnels. They reply to our greetings with friendly bows. There's no reason that any of the men working on this enormous project should be particularly aware of the surrounding countryside and its history, but there is something to ponder about this particular spot, a story that illustrates how far and how fast Algeria is advancing. Only ten years before, this was the site of the bloodiest massacre of the Algerian Civil War. On the night of August 29, 1997, three hundred inhabitants of a nearby village, Rais, had their throats cut. The guilty parties have never been identified, but what is known for certain is that the Algerian army, stationed nearby, lifted not a finger to help.

Today's Algeria, under the leadership of President Abdelaziz Bouteflika, is doing its utmost to turn its back on terrorism and has instead embraced oil. It collects some $60 billion every year in revenues, which fund a panoply of ambitious—some might say grandiose—projects. Bouteflika plans to spend $140 billion on infrastructure by 2009, and Chinese companies are hoping for a lion's share of the contracts. It is no coincidence that the highway under construction will open on January 10, 2010, just in time for the general election, an election the president expects to win for the third time.

The sheer energy expended by the Chinese on the highway project astounds civil servants at the Ministry of Public Works, men like Omar Oukil, the ministry spokesman. "We've insisted that the workforce consist of at least 70 percent locals, but it's clear that the locals have some things to learn from the Chinese work ethic. The Chinese work seven days a week and do overtime. We Algerians could be more rigorous." He seems gloriously unaware of the irony of these words hanging in the still air of his office, which stands empty at 4 P.M. Indeed, Oukil hastily ushers us out. He should, he tells us, be at home himself. It's been a long day.

When completed, the highway will connect Tunisia with Morocco and will have cost 824 billion Algerian dinars ($13 billion). It is by far the largest construction project ever undertaken in the country and at its peak will provide employment for 74,881 workers, nearly 22,000 of whom will be Asian. Asia, however, holds no attraction for Omar Oukil, who, unlike a growing number of Algerian officials, has never been there.

"When I'm completely exhausted, I just go to Marseille," he shrugs. He does admit to a certain fascination with the Japanese, extending even to admiration. COJAAL, a Japanese consortium, has won the contract to build a third of the highway and is committed to keeping the same deadline as the Chinese. COJAAL, though, has a different approach to the task from the Chinese and has replaced part of its workforce with high-tech machinery.

"Every movement our vehicles make, every cubic meter of soil that is moved, every adjustment of a bulldozer blade, is directed by satellite," explains Atshushi Furuta, the chief COJAAL man, whom we met in his Algiers office. "That's how we make up for the inexperience of the local workforce and keep costs down. It's not exactly cost-effective to build a highway like this in forty months, so making savings wherever possible is high priority."

Omar Oukil approves of these methods. "On a Japanese site, their discipline commands respect. They seem to me to combine intelligence with a rare and genuine elegance. But then you go to a Chinese site and it's miserable. All they have to offer is toil and sweat."

Despite whatever Oukil thinks, this isn't the impression we get from the Chinese workers in the Khemis and Khechna sites we visit. Here, on Work Site No. 2, we observe young, well-dressed men and women working away on state-of-the-art computers, obeying to the letter the countless orders and decrees posted on the wall.

Nor are visitors exempt from the rules. As soon as we enter the site, and before we can even get out of the car, the manager approaches us, shouting, "Your mission is over!" Now we know how the Congolese must feel. It's true that we don't have authorization from CITIC-CRCC to visit the site, but it's also true that they never replied to the authorization requests we made, first in Beijing and then in Algiers. We have our precious Algerian press credentials, however, and also an ace up our sleeve in the form of Rachid Azouni, the director of the central section of the highway and a representative of the government's contracting authority. Imbued with the full dignity of his office, he yells back at the Chinese. The manager, who considers the work site Chinese territory, like an embassy, does not take kindly to this. The two officials settle down to a shouting match of epic proportions, and we take the opportunity to have a look around.

Perhaps the reason for all this shouting and screaming is that we have arrived at an inopportune time. Around thirty Chinese workers are just finishing their break and are in the process of feeding their leftovers to dogs and assorted cats that inhabit a patch of land amid the prefabricated homes. For the last few weeks the Algerian press has been full of accounts of strange goings-on at the Chinese sites. Apparently domestic animals are mysteriously disappearing, never to be seen again. One of Rachid Azouni's colleagues is wholly engrossed in what is becoming a really first-rate slanging match, but we tap him on the shoulder and ask him what he thinks about the stories. He can't quite bring himself to takes his eyes off the action, but he does whisper to us out of the corner of his mouth. "It's true. They eat them! I saw them strangle several dogs with a wire outside one of the kitchens." A particularly inventive gesture and an equally inventive piece of invective grab his attention once more, and we slip off to investigate the rest of the site.

Looking around us, we feel as if we've stumbled into a barracks. The entrance is protected by armed guards and the perimeter is lined with barbed wire. Loudspeakers are dotted around, too, and boom out stern exhortations about the benefits of hard work, interspersed with military music. We meet an Algerian technician who lives in the Algerian quarter of the compound. "The Chinese are squeezed like lemons here," he laughs. "That's why they're in such good shape."

We then come across a large, highly polished copper plaque, which provides a plan of the site, labeling each building in Chinese and French. According to this map, the "Head Progenerator" (that would be the head engineer) has an office opposite where the cooks prepare the Chinese workers' tofu, "The Soy Formation Room." Tiring of the linguistic intrigue, we spy a Chinese worker on the other side of the sports field; we approach him, and in time-honored journalists' tradition, we tell him that we've got official permission to inspect whatever we want to.

With immense pride he shows us around a dozen laboratories in which two hundred outlandish instruments used to test materials have just been installed. Most were made in China but have French names, though these names leave us none the wiser (though admittedly better informed) about their functions. The direct-reading calcium polyvalent sensor is clearly just the job for direct-reading polyvalent sensing; on the other hand, given the choice, it might be more useful to have an automatic compactor proctor-CBR if compactor proctoring's your game. Our guide is a little affronted when we tell him that his Blaine permeabilimeter is a little out of date with the latest permeabilimering trends, but our wide-eyed admiration of his electric core drill seems to mollify him. We earn his full respect when we examine his sand angulometer and profess ourselves unable to re-call having ever, in either of all our lives, seen a machine so effectively designed for the angulometering of sand. He feigns disbelief, and we reassure him that, wherever we may be in the world, when we want an angulometer, we'll consult him directly. A faint smile is the only out-ward sign he gives of being a man who believes wholeheartedly in the excellence of his work, of a life spent without hope of recognition or fanfare for his adept angulometering, but also of undeniable satisfac-tion at having met minds exalted enough to know the true value of well-angulometered sand.

He's a little embarrassed by the single Italian machine in the cor-ner. It's the only non-Chinese-made thing here. According to the label, it's a penetrometer, and although we're not sure what a pene-trometer is, it has a curious effect on our Florentine photographer, who is apparently wondering whether we have discovered a machine that could render Italian males redundant.

Our friend nods. "Twenty years ago I visited your labs in Europe. Now you're coming to us to see how things are done!" We thank him for his time, congratulate him once more on his angulometer, and make a break for it.

• • •

The CITIC part of CITIC-CRCC (China International Trust and In-vestment Company) is a state-owned finance company created in 1979 by Deng Xiaoping. It owns subsidiaries in forty-four countries and has declared reserves of 922 billion yuan ($13.5 billion). It has completed around a hundred major projects on five continents: bridges, dams, subways, ports, tunnels, and so on. The CRCC part (China Railway Construction Corporation) is the second biggest company in China, with 220,000 employees on its books.

"The companies whose services we retain are members of the global elite," asserts Muhammad Kheladi, the chief government official responsible for public works, as formal in his appearance as in his precise manner of speaking. His department sits atop Algiers and is a veritable hive of industry. One small section of the Algerian government, at least, has adopted a distinctly Asian work ethic. "We work eight days a week!" he jokes as he ushers us into his office, kindly finding the time to meet us between visits from Japanese and Chinese delegations.

Kheladi's job is to make sure that the aforementioned construction companies have no pretexts or excuses for delays or budget overruns. He has to make sure that the highway route has been cleared of residents, that the water and gas supplies are properly installed, that work sites are set up, that payments are made on time, that there's no trouble with customs officials, that Algerian workers get the appropriate training, and that work visas are issued for the huge influx of foreign workers. All of this he does under the threat of possible changes in the proposed path of the highway, such as a recent substantial detour to minimize the environmental impact on the El Kala National Park near the Tunisian border.

"The highway is going to bring the country together and accelerate development," he says. "Cities and villages will rise up along the highway, attracting investors and tourists."

At the highest level of government, the construction of the highway is viewed as a trial run for Chinese companies in Algeria.

"If they finish on time, then we'll open up every opportunity to them," an adviser to the president tells us. Some leaders, though, are beginning to show signs of disappointment with China.

When in 2001 housing shortages reached alarming proportions, the Algerian Agency of Housing and Improvement (AADL) was ordered to build 55,000 new housing "units." The AADL, in turn, entrusted the building of 30,000 of these to CSCEC, the biggest construction company in China. CSCEC was supposed to have finished the project in two years, but it is now three years late. When the public and President Bouteflika asked why, the AADL blamed the Chinese.

"The Chinese haven't done their best work on this [housing] project," according to Kheireddine Walid, the director of the AADL, but he's forced to admit, "We can't terminate their contracts because there's no Algerian company to replace them." His dissatisfaction with the Chinese should be taken with a pinch of salt, not least because Walid himself, it turns out, was brought before a court in 2001 and accused of misappropriating 9.5 million dinars ($156,000).[5]

Blame for delays cannot always be laid at the door of the Chinese. The Algerian government spent a great deal of time appropriating the land for the housing projects, some of which was later deemed too hilly to use. Five thousand visa applications were lost in Algeria's byzantine bureaucracy, and when they finally started to trickle through in 2003, a SARS (severe acute respiratory syndrome) epidemic broke out, and departures from China were put on ice for six months. Added to this problem were shortages of sand (angulometered or not) and cement and the failure of the Algerian companies responsible for building the access roads and the site development to fulfill their own contracts on time. These delays meant that, in places like Ouled Fayet, the Chinese workers, who receive no pay unless they're working, were essentially on unpaid leave on the wrong side of the world. They understandably began taking to the streets in protest.

Whatever the shortcomings of the construction sites, they are a striking example of globalization at work. Since the 1980s Western companies have increasingly outsourced their manufacturing to China. In turn, China's spectacular economic growth has led to an equally spectacular rise in demand for raw materials, such as oil, metal, and wood, sending the prices of such commodities skyrocketing. This boom in commodity prices has swamped African elites with cash because they find themselves sitting on significant quantities of these natural resources. In the four decades since the colonial independence of the African nations, successive African governments have failed to nurture their own technological and engineering capabilities and have allowed such infrastructure as was left behind by the colonial powers—arguably the only genuinely positive part of their legacy—to deteriorate. Their people are increasingly unhappy with the pitiful state of public services, and so African governments have relatively recently started spending the proceeds of the resource boom by paying China for the construction of highways, railroads, houses, utilities, hospitals, and schools, essentially outsourcing the very duties that traditionally fall to national governments.

Theoretically the next stage of this global process will ensure not only Africa's postcolonial survival but also its revival. As a continent, it is beginning to build up both the infrastructure and the requisite technological abilities to rise to prominence. Nevertheless, when you scratch below the surface, it's clear that the intricate sparring between the subcontractors and the subcontracted could still cause developmental gridlock. A visit to Ouled Fayet supplied a prime example of the two parties seemingly waiting for Godot.

SCENE: *The* FOYER *of a new, as-yet unused* APARTMENT BUILDING. *Two* ALGERIANS, JAFFAR TAHAL, *managing director of* AADL, *an official angered by construction delays, is engaged in conversation with* ABDALLAH DJAOUDA, *an engineer from the planning department of the Office of Monitoring and Supervision who is impressed by Chinese ways. Facing them is* MR. LI, *a busy, jovial fellow who is the general manager of Algerian construction sites for* CSCEC, *a Chinese company of some 122,000 employees. He has lived in Algeria for five years but does not speak a word of* ARABIC *or* FRENCH; *thus he has his* INTERPRETER *with him. The men have clearly been talking for some time, but the dialogue opens with* INTREPID JOURNALISTS *asking* LI *how the quality of the new-built houses here compares to that in China.*

LI: It's better in China.

TAHAL: Why's that?

DJAOUDA: It's a matter of discipline. The Chinese stick to the schedule. If the concrete's supposed to be poured at 8 P.M., the men who bring the gravel arrive on schedule. So do the men who deliver the iron. Nothing ever goes wrong. That's how it is in China. We're the only ones who can't seem to get anything done.

LI, *not waiting for the translator to finish*: You use the wrong materials. In China we use proper girders for crossbeams, and we use aluminum for window frames, not wood. That's why it's better.

TAHAL, *beside himself with anger*: So why don't you bring the right materials here? Perhaps they're too good for us, eh?

LI, *placatory*: No, no, no. It's just that in China people do the painting or tiling themselves, or they hire companies that specialize in such things. That's why it's better.

DJAOUDA: I admit that the Chinese are good at adapting. They're creative thinkers. Problem solvers. If A and B are the makers of X, but A and B are unavailable, the Algerians, like the Europeans, are stuck. The Chinese work around the problem. If in China a crane breaks down, they don't just close down the site until someone makes himself available to fix it.

TAHAL: The Chinese always make the right noises, but they were supposed to finish this project in twenty months. So far it's taken them fifty.

LI: Well, since it takes seven months to get a work visa out of the Algerians, we never have the workers we need.

TAHAL: That's the same the world over. A country can't just give out work visas like confetti!

DJAOUDA, *putting a hand on Li's shoulder*: And anyway, your workers are everywhere. Did you know that some of them are opening up *shops?*

LI: Not possible. Everyone coming here from China is checked out. Their passports are kept in a safe.

DJAOUDA: The Chinese are incredible. When they finish for the day at a construction site, they start repairing their machinery instead of just sitting around. Like in Ouled Fayet—they've never had to ship in a new machine because they've patched up broken ones that certain other people I could mention would have sent to the scrap yard.

LI, *increasingly uninterested in the translation*: The black sand we were using is, for some reason, banned here. We had to replace it all with regular sand. We lost eight months, just replacing sand with sand.

DJAOUDA, *also unwilling to wait for the translation*: Then there's the concrete molding. It's like concrete molding I've never seen before. It might be archaic concrete molding, but it works.

LI, *as if surprised by his own boldness, and seeming not to share this enthusiasm for scaffolding one bit*: Another problem, it must be said—no, no, let me finish—is the money. We always have to wait for months on end to be paid.

DJAOUDA: No, no, let me speak, I insist. We have a big problem here. We do not have skilled workers here in Algeria. The Chinese should take our young people to Beijing or Shanghai or wherever and train them. They could even train them here. Teach our young to work, and we'll look after ourselves.

LI, *looking at his feet*: It's not our problem. And why would we want to train Algerians? Just look at the differences in ability and diligence. Algerians simply aren't able to work as hard as the Chinese.

Silence.

DJAOUDA *eventually flicks his cigarette to the floor and stubs it out with the toe of his shoe*: Construction's the last thing we need help with from anyone, let alone the Chinese. Don't forget that it was us Algerians who rebuilt France after the war.

Chapter 6

Uranium Mania in the Sahara

Areva's monopoly has been smashed.
—*Aïchatou Mindaoudou,*
Niger's Minister of Foreign Affairs, Paris, August 2007

The little girl is singing in Chinese. She has the black, tightly curled hair of an African, an olive complexion, and Asian eyes. She is singing to us—for us—from one end of the Dragon d'Or, the oldest Chinese restaurant in Niger's capital, Niamey. The town by day is impossible to tell from any other dusty metropolis, bleached a uniform ocher by the sun and the desert dust that sweeps through it on its way south. But at night the heat dissipates a little, and it's cool enough to sit outside in comfort, on the long, broad terrace of the Dragon d'Or amid the red paper lanterns and the multicolored bulbs. A score of Chinese are sitting at our table, but nobody has eyes for anything but the singing child. Her mixed heritage is a sublime symbol of the union of two worlds: China and Africa.

But this union, in the hazy light of the Saharan sun, remains a mirage, and the guests who clink glasses in the numberless toasts know this all too well. In Niger the two worlds rub against each other. The previous day, February 8, 2007, Tuareg tribes attacked a military post at Iferouane, killing three soldiers and taking two more prisoner. The post is just up the road from the Agadez region, from which Chinese who had been prospecting for uranium were evacuated under tight security. In the days to follow, a previously unknown group calling themselves the Nigerien Movement for Justice (MNJ) will claim responsibility for the attack in a statement reminiscent of one of the Zapatista manifestos. The demands are these: decentralization of government, the appointment of MNJ members to all levels of power, the construction of roads and utilities by the government in the north, and scholarships for the Tuareg students. In short, they want at least some local benefit from the uranium extraction here. The demand for uranium is rising, the price has increased tenfold since 2003, and Niger is the third largest exporter in the world.

This particular incident goes nearly unnoticed. The government itself at the time describes them as "bandits," adding that the army will get all necessary means to make the area safe.[1] But six months later the tone is different. President Mamadou Tandja condemns the MNJ as a group of organized crime, of drug and arms traffickers, and promises swift, harsh retribution. Soon the situation will degenerate into open conflict; another ethnic group, the seminomadic Toubous, has joined the path to war. The Toubous come from the barren no-man's-land where Chad, Libya, Sudan, and Egypt meet, and they have their own small army in Niger known by its French acronym, FARS (Front des Forces Armées Révolutionnaires du Sahara). They have also, in the words of Niger's press, "threatened the abduction of Chinese workers exploring for oil in the Kawar region."[2] Kawar is an empty quarter, a relentlessly inhospitable area at the intersection of the Libyan and Chadian borders, where drilling is supposed to commence within the next five years.

In setting foot in Niger, the Chinese soon encountered more than they had bargained for; as the crisis worsened throughout 2007, one of the world's poorest countries split down unforeseen fault lines. It's a corner of the world in which armed groups bearing no particular flag operate, and where powerful nations spy on each other among the dunes. But being so rich in smuggling, corruption, and the promises of petroleum, and with the ongoing war for uranium as an overture, the desert has never seemed so crowded.

It is not entirely clear who is supporting the FARS rebels. The Niamey daily, *Le Républicain,* intimates a Libyan connection, though it is careful to stop short of actually accusing Tripoli. This connection is not out of the question. Libya's oil exploration of the Mangueni plateau in the extreme north is well under way, and Muammar el-Qadaffi has never disguised his sympathy for the desert tribes, nor has he kept his ambitions as a pan-African leader a secret. Nearly every national leader on the continent is in debt to the man one way or another, because Libya's own immense oil revenue has allowed it to make all sorts of investments across the continent. It's unlikely that Qaddafi—conspicuous by his absence at the Beijing Summit in 2006—is particularly enthusiastic about China's burgeoning influence, especially where this influence encroaches on his country's borders.

It's no wonder the colonel is suspicious. The Chinese have taken only five years to build solid ties with his neighbors: Sudan, Chad, Egypt, Tunisia, Algeria, and now Niger. China has even managed to become Niger's second largest trade partner after France.[3] But even taking Qadaffi's reputation into account, Libya isn't the only country interested in supporting attempts to thwart Chinese ambitions. France, too, has its reasons. The French company Areva, formerly Companie Général des Matières Nucléaires (COGEMA), enjoyed a four-decade monopoly on uranium exploration and extraction in Niger and can still use a few sharp elbows to keep the Chinese at bay.

This scramble for heavy metal is a comparatively recent phenomenon. For years, uranium was so cheap that even if one had a garden full of the stuff it would be more profitable to plant cabbages there.

But as the price of oil has shot up, so the humble uranium atom has been allowed back into an energy-hungry world's good graces. Nuclear energy is cheap, and even, some say, less polluting that the fossil fuel alternatives. Emerging markets like India, Russia, and China foresee their future energy demands being met by fission. By the end of 2007 there were twenty-eight reactors being built worldwide as China announced its intention to bring a new one online every year.

That reason Beijing has fallen behind on this self-imposed schedule is the depletion of its uranium reserves built up following the 1993 moratorium on uranium enrichment and from fuel salvaged from the decommissioning of nuclear weapons. Building the infrastructure necessary to exploit new uranium deposits will take some time, and some experts have predicted serious shortages of uranium. Worldwide demand for uranium reached 80,000 tons in 2006, but only 46,000 tons were extracted. The price of a kilo of yellow cake—unrefined uranium oxide—rose from $15 at the end of 2002 to $160 by the end of 2007,[4] outstripping even the rise in the price of a barrel of crude in the same period.

Eighty percent of France's electricity is nuclear-generated, and France cannot afford to let Niger slip off its radar. Similarly, Niger cannot afford to let France slide, as Areva is the country's largest private-sector employer. It employs 2,000 people in its Arlit and Akouta mines alone, as well as providing jobs nationwide whose beneficiaries number around 200,000 people. The relationship came under renewed strain in July 2006 when three Chinese companies signed contracts with Niger's government.[5] The president's son, Ousemane Tandja, was the commercial attaché to Hong Kong at the time and is given the credit—even if the French would not use that word—for attracting Areva's competitors. Right under France's nose, China acquired two zones ripe for exploitation: one in Teguiddan-Tessoum in northwestern Agadez[6] and the other in Madaouela, right next door to the French operation in Arlit.[7] It's unclear whether this transaction was simply the nurturing of healthy competition in the marketplace by Niger or a deliberate gesture of provocation toward France. The contracts were signed on July 14, the French National Day.

In the desert, one year later, the winds of change were blowing with a vengeance. A Chinese worker, seemingly chosen at random, had been snatched right off the sand by the MNJ. Zhang Guohua was the assistant director-general of Azelik, a subsidiary of the China Nuclear Engineering and Construction Corporation, which is itself an arm of the Chinese army, in charge of research and development. His kidnappers treated him well and after ten days dropped him off at the International Committee of the Red Cross along with a warning to Chinese mining companies. The statement criticized these companies for failing to employ local workers or to invest in local infrastructure. The most serious allegation, however, was that China had been providing weapons to Niger's army; the kidnappers had proof, they said, having confiscated Chinese-made arms during a raid on a military installation in Tazarzatt two weeks earlier, during which they also killed two soldiers and captured seventy-two more.

Once again the MNJ's actions produced results. All Chinese workers at the Teguiddan-Tessoum site were evacuated, and President Tandja promised revenge for the insult, accusing Areva of supporting the rebels. Popular protest broke out on the streets of Niamey, where chanted slogans directly accused the French company, slogans that Dominique Pin, Areva's director-general in Niger, called "outrageous and irresponsible."[8] In the good old days of Françafrique, the whole thing would have blown over and that would have been that. But with Chinese support, the Africans no longer had to take on the French single-handedly. Dominique Pin, once chief adviser to François Mitterand on African affairs, was unceremoniously deported back to Paris on July 25. This was more a symbolic gesture than anything else since Niger's authorities knew as well as anyone that in July Gallic minds tend to turn to vacations.

Still, Niamey's pointed insult to Paris had come close on the heels of a more discreet but more significant expulsion. Gilles de Namur, a retired colonel and an employee of Epée (an organization in charge of Areva's security), had been deported a few weeks earlier. De Namur was an old hand in Niger, having been sent there by Paris as military attaché twelve years earlier during the first *pacification touarègue* in the 1990s.[9] He returned to Niamey to deal with threats that rebels had been making against Areva. Not long after he returned to Niger he is alleged to have made contact with the MNJ, with a view to coming to some sort of agreement with them, and was subsequently expelled from Niger, though there is no proof that this contact was established.

More dramatic events early in July 2007 hardened Niger's suspicions of the French. Muhammad Ajidar, a commander in the unit of Niger's army tasked with protecting Areva's interests and employees, defected to the MNJ along with twenty-five of his men. After that, the MNJ seemed to lose interest in the French company. Its presence is even tolerated, provided that the uranium extractor attends to its environmental responsibilities. From now on, the rebels turned their attention to the Chinese.

• • •

Back in the Dragon d'Or, February 2007: the ideal backdrop for the opening of a spy novel. Its staff and clientele provide an accurate picture of China's infiltration of Niger, the place itself tucked away, the white-clad waiters clearing the tables of those Asians who have come to the capital in search of a little relaxation after the dangers and tension of the north. It's the kind of place that you always seem to wind up in if you're asking the kinds of questions we were asking. The little singer still mesmerizes her listeners, and as she finishes her number, a Chinese woman glides onto the terrace in a low-cut leopard-skin outfit.

"The owner," explains a waiter who overhears us asking about her. She comes to sit at our table.

"You've been looking for me," she says. Indeed we have.

"If the music bothers you, we could go and talk in another of my properties. The Shanghai, perhaps, or La Flotille. Or maybe somewhere even louder?" She smiles. "We could go to my nightclub, El Raï. It's the best in Niamey."

We'd been eating in her restaurant day and night for two days hoping for this opportunity, and going anywhere with air conditioning would have been fine. She takes us at our word, and we follow her into a back room.

"My name is Wu Wenyi," she tells us as she closes the door behind us, "but everyone around here calls me Wendy. I've lived in Africa since 1995. Aren't you going to ask why?"

We were, as it happens. Among other things.

Pull the thread of the Dragon d'Or, and the relationship between Niger and China unravels. The owner is also known by another name: Karda. Her husband, Aboubakeur Karda, is a Tuareg, and the young singer at the microphone is their daughter. She's finished singing for now and has come rushing in, glad to be in the safety of her mother's arms as she stares at the strangers.

Wendy is Cantonese but met her husband at the China Textile University in Shanghai. Their relationship would play an important role in Niger's future.

When Aboubakeur Karda completed his studies in 1993, he returned to Niamey and threw himself into the import-export business, primarily with China. His problems, though, soon began with the election of Mahamane Ousmane, the first democratically elected president of the country. Ousmane severed diplomatic ties with China in favor of Taiwan, a tactic used by several other African leaders since the late 1970s as they attempted to play one party against the other. The president's actions yielded $70 million for his country, $50 million of which came pretty much with no strings attached. This sum was enough to enrich what are known locally as the "itinerant Saharan bourgeoisie."

"After my husband's plans fell through, he went to Togo, and it was two years before I could follow him there. My family weren't keen on my going to Africa, but you can't escape your destiny, can you?"

Karda's sojourn in Togo turned out to be short-lived. In 1996, Colonel Ibrahim Baré Maïnassara led a coup, overthrowing Ousmane's Democrats and resuming relations with Beijing. And who was better placed to mediate between the new government and the People's Republic than a Tuareg called Karda?

"My husband worked on that a lot," Wendy recalls. She would say little else about that period, but it was obvious that Karda's experience in China and his knowledge of the language and culture eased his path back to Niamey. His work was well paid, too. Everyone in Niamey knows him; he's a successful and influential figure. On the other hand, things didn't work out nearly so well for Baré. He was gunned down by his own guards on the airport tarmac, "an unfortunate incident" in the words of one of the assassins, which did no harm to Chinese interests. On the contrary, the mutually beneficial relationship between the countries only strengthened under the supervision of the subsequent president, Mamadou Tandja.

A decade before the scramble for uranium, textiles were the thing to be involved in. This element of the country's history is also woven into the story of the Dragon d'Or.

"The first night you came looking for me, I was in here with the Chinese head of Enitex. My husband and I have not let our interests in the textile industry lay fallow, you know."

Enitex, formerly known as Société d'État des Textiles (Sonitextil), had been bought out by a Chinese company in 1997. The fate of the company is the stuff of Chinafrique parabola and is crucial to an understanding of how China has gained a foothold in Niger.

Originally Sonitextil had merged with the Companie Française d'Afrique Occidentale, or CFAO, a company that had employed eight hundred people to make traditional African clothing. In 1990 CFAO was bought out by the French Pinault Printemps Redoute, which had lofty ambitions about its profitability. Four frustrating years later the

French gave up on Sonitextil and turned their attention to maximizing growth opportunities in China, a common enough move among Western companies at the time, whose belief that business in Africa was doomed was not shared by the Chinese. So while the West chased business in China, China spotted the vacuum in Africa and jumped right in.

In 1996 pressure from the IMF and the World Bank forced Niger to privatize all its industries: cement factories, dairies, hotels, telecoms, utilities, and, that's right, textiles. Everything was sold off. It was a great opportunity for the Chinese. The following year President Tandja was invited to Beijing, and among his entourage was one Abdoubakeur Karda. His job was to find a buyer for Sonitextil, as the state, the only remaining stockholder, had mismanaged the company into the ground and bankruptcy was around the corner. Karda came up with the China Worldbest Group. "He negotiated the sale," says his wife with a smile edged with pride.

The new owners now had to see what they could salvage from their acquisition. A new name, Enitex, was only a first step. The day before we met Wendy, we talked with a man called Abdelnasser Seydou, an employee of Enitex and the secretary-general of the Union of Industrial Workers of Niger. When we asked him what happened to the company, he pressed his fingers together, marshaling his thoughts.

"The new Chinese owners promised to take on workers and renovate infrastructure," he said. "And, at first, that's what they did." Enitex quickly started struggling, however, in the face of cheaper imports, ironically enough, from China. Sales totalling 4.4 billion CFA ($9.4 million) in 2002 had been halved by 2005, the result being a similar drop in production.

The last straw was the end of the WTO's Multifiber Arrangement (MFA), which went into effect in January 2005 and concluded a system of quotas that had regulated the global textile market for thirty years. A massive influx of Asian clothing hit the African market, and three months later Enitex was forced to lay off 446 people, two-thirds of its workforce. Enitex was not alone. In Swaziland, 42 percent of the country's textile workers (12,000 people) lost their jobs. In South Africa, 15 percent (15,000 people). And in Lesotho, 26 percent (14,000).[10]

Competition in Niger is tough enough, but the corruption endemic in Niger's customs department makes the Chinese importers invincible. Smuggling goods into the country couldn't be easier, partly because of the cultural affinities between the people living along the border with Mali, Benin, and Nigeria, but mostly because a cartel of major retailers has simply bought off the customs officials.[11] In effect, business and government have become so intertwined that the political elites are running business, and businesspeople are running the country. To describe this as a conflict of interest is an understatement: In 2005, top government officials are even alleged to have speculated on grain prices during the famine. It's unlikely that such people would have had many scruples about sacrificing their country's textile industry for personal (and Chinese) gain. The people of Niger know this and long ago lost any illusions they may have had about the Saharan bourgeoisie.

In such a situation, when large multinationals and governments are busy eating one another's tails, gridlocked and redundant, individuals can often achieve a great deal more than such massive, unbending organizations. Hence, the decision by the Chinese to approach Wendy's husband to settle certain matters. "Aboubakeur was also of service during the Tagabati affair."

"I'm sorry, the Taga—what?"

The music outside is getting louder, and Wendy gets up to close the door, snapping at a waiter to keep it shut.

"Tagabati," she repeats, and tells us the story.

It seems that Tagabati, a Nigerien man living and working in the port of Lomé, managed to cheat the Chinese, becoming a local hero of sorts. He gained their confidence for a while doing regular business and then disappeared, along with several shipping containers full of merchandise that he then sold on the black market. The story is so well known that his name has been given to one of those transient places that encapsulate all the drama and comedy of Africa: the Tagabati Market.

It's an extraordinary place, a warren of narrow aisles made narrower still by the mattresses that obstruct the walkways and the tiers of motorcycles suspended from invisible frames. Everything, from the Chinese-made traditional African clothing to the Chinese-made multipacks of watch straps, has fallen off the back of a boat onto a lorry, from the back of which it's also been dislodged. It's a one-stop shop for those who just want to dash in, pick up three Chinese-made spoons, bumper packs of 6,000 triple-A batteries, and an enormous bra, and dash out again without traipsing all over town.

Mention of the word *Tagabati* in the Grand Marché next door provokes an excellent reaction, if you regard spitting and swearing as excellent. The undercutting has driven prices here into the ground. It's possible in the Tagabati, if you can avoid losing an eye to a motorcycle foot rest, to get an "imported real wax print" item of clothing—imported from goodness knows where—for a tenth of the price you would have to pay to an honest stallkeeper next door whose "imported real wax prints" come from the Ivory Coast. Or Germany. People, particularly the very poor, vote with their feet. Tagabati is a hero to the poorest of the poor and a legend throughout Niger.

Officials have naturally tried for years to close down the market, no doubt much to the amusement of its namesake. The amusement isn't apparent, however, in the many portraits that hang in the market. The man in the picture wears a silk uniform of a delicate pink that is at odds with the scraggly beard and melancholy face above it. Perhaps he's down in the dumps because, despite being lauded as an African Robin Hood, his name has entered the popular vocabulary to describe anything that's of outstandingly poor quality.

Tagabati HQ consists of a covered stall presided over, according to a large sign, by "ETS Almoustapha Abou Tagabati DG (General Business, Wholesale and Retail)." The man himself is nowhere to be seen, but then no one would be who has a squad of angry Chinese from Lomé after him. Karda had tried to negotiate a peace deal between the Chinese, the government, and Tagabati but, unusually for him, had failed.

The Dragon d'Or was livening up as the hour grew late, but it was time for us to go. A driver came in to collect Wendy and spirit her and her daughter away in a 4x4. Our exit was accompanied by the sound of karaoke. A woman we'd not seen before, a woman boasting an impressive pair of lungs it must be said, was telling the assembled diners that she was, if she had anything say about it, going to be "iron, like a lion in Zion."

Wendy broke off the hasty adieus to her patrons to tell us, "That's the wife of an IMF official."

IMF. A dreaded set of initials in Niger. For decades the International Monetary Fund handed down papal bulls to Africa telling it how it might get itself onto the right track toward an inescapable and ruinous spiral of debt called "development." When the Berlin Wall came down and the cold war ended, the IMF began to attach supplementary conditions to its loans. These conditions were not to the liking of many African leaders, who felt insulted that the West had withdrawn its tacit approval of their corrupt and despotic regimes. They felt badly treated, and naturally, their people bore the brunt of their leaders' anger.

Given enough time, international organizations can usually guarantee a certain level of suffering, and the IMF doesn't want to give the impression that it's bringing up the rear, or that it can't take a small economy and destroy it as comprehensively as any other organization. In the years since the IMF began supervising the economy in 1985, Niger has found itself competing with Sierra Leone for the distinction of coming last in the UNDP's Human Development Index. Clever new ways of structuring the economy itself have left the country permanently in debt and its social structure in ruins. Anxious not to be seen as leaving a job half finished, in 1996 the IMF implemented a wonderfully modern privatization plan that, alongside fantastic new cuts in education and health spending, has left the average Nigerien with a 17 percent chance of being able to read and a 66 percent chance of living below the poverty line. Luckily, Nigeriens who do find themselves living below the poverty line then can console themselves that they won't have to do so for long: The average life expectancy here is forty-four.

This road to hell is paved with the IMF's good intentions, and there's no question that the largest paving stone has been decentralization. Most people agree that the resultant lack of government control contributed significantly to the famine of 2005, when ten children a day starved to death. The liberalizing recipes cooked up by the "Washington Consensus"[12] led to failures that turned China's arrival in Niger, which was already looking likely, into a certainty. One of the World Bank's biggest boosts for the Chinese was its insistence that Niger allow international bidding for infrastructure projects in an attempt to stem corruption as well as to lower prices. The Chinese won every bid.

The World Bank's regional director is a certain Ousmane Diagana, a Mauritanian resplendent in an elegant gray blazer, a burgundy tie, and cuff links fastening the meticulously ironed cuffs that protrude precisely an inch and a half from his sleeves. When we saw him, he was addressing a delegation from Switzerland. Through him we learned that the Niamey office of the World Bank is positively crowded with twenty-five employees, and that he is satisfied with the progress being made in education, though he makes no comment on either the current teachers' strike (they've not been paid in six months) or the illiteracy of 50 percent of the Parliament. We're also relieved to learn of "the extraordinary freedom of the press in this country," particularly as we'd been momentarily concerned by news the day before that another journalist had been jailed and that Niger had been listed among the worst enemies in the world of this particular freedom. Diagana spoke in the language with which we're all familiar, that of the ideologue-cum-technocrat, so although we learned something of "maximizing the effectiveness of growth standards," he didn't dwell on the effects of decentralization, on good government, or on human rights. Nor did his speech concern itself with uranium or oil or the Tuareg rebellion. Or China's arrival and its implications. But no doubt it was a magnificent speech of its kind, one that would have brought the house down at the Beijing Summit. Or as a Swiss official, an expert in development, summed it up, "We didn't understand a word of that."

The trip back from the Dragon d'Or to the dreary Grand Hotel took us across Kennedy Bridge, built by the United States in the 1970s. It is the only crossing point on the Niger River that leads to the ports in Ghana and Benin. The Chinese are planning a second, six-hundred-meter bridge that they hope one day to drive trucks laden with uranium across. The contract for the bridge was signed on July 16, 2006, in Beijing, four days after the uranium contracts. The icing, so to speak, on the yellow cake. Even though the West is continuing to provide debt relief to Niger, whose debt fell from 90 percent of the GDP in 2001 to 50 percent in 2007,[13] the lessons so well learned from the IMF are not easily unlearned. Niger is looking for a new line of credit: from China.

The only adjective that properly describes China's attitude toward lending money is *seductive.* Borrow from the Chinese, and you are drawn into the bosom of its—highly profitable—family. Beijing is the Godfather, engaged in everything from textiles and infrastructure to uranium and oil. His bids are all interlinked and his motivation is constant. Such is his dependability that whereas Western companies such as Exxon, Elf, and Royal Dutch have thrown in the towel after twenty years of drilling holes in the Agadem site to see if any oil is sloshing about (they were pretty sure it was down there, 300 million barrels of it), he is still there, and if refineries and pipelines have to be built to get it out, then CNPC (China National Petroleum Company) will build them.

As a reflection of its interest in the country, Beijing built a vast embassy in Niamey's Plateau quarter, just opposite the equestrian club, so that the diplomats from the American or French embassies nearby have something nice to look at as they leave work for the day.

When we got back to the Grand Hotel, we watched the news and heard the glad tidings that the Chinese had announced a gift to Niger of half a million tons of corn. Before we called it a day, we heard the news also that a Japanese delegation was in town, visiting the Energy Ministry.

The next morning, as we were leaving the hotel, we found a group of U.S. soldiers on the terrace, wearing Oakleys, staying silent, acting distant, and drinking beer. In contrast, the driver who had just dropped them off in the parking lot wore the same government-issue Oakley sunglasses but was happy to talk. The troops were heading north to Arlit, where the United States had set up a base to train troops in the fight against terrorism. In southern Algeria, a group calling themselves the Salafist Group for Preaching and Combat (using the French acronym GSPC), but more commonly known as al-Qaeda in the Islamic Maghreb (AQIM), has been making claims that they're affiliated with Osama Bin Laden's al-Qaeda. The Americans plan to use Niger as a staging post from which, if necessary, they can attack the group from the rear. But of course, they're aware, too, that there's stuff in the ground up there.

Niamey has been swarming with discreet envoys ever since Niger's mining concessions came up for renewal in 2007 and this long-forgotten country found itself suddenly very popular. Areva, the first player at the table, still had a few cards up its sleeve, not least the geographical surveys it had carried out at the Madaouela site. When the Chinese won the concession, Areva refused to hand over the fruits of its labor, hoping that the Chinese would walk away and leave the site open once more. The gamble didn't pay off. When the Chinese backed out, the rights went to a curious company affiliated with the huge international mining company Rio Tinto: Ivanhoe. Ivanhoe is a company involved in the gold, copper, and oil trades, registered in Canada but also very active in China. Its founder and codirector is the 374th richest man in the world and goes by the name of Robert "Toxic Bob" Friedland, the sobriquet earned through a long career of leaving a trail of ecological disasters wherever he goes.

In Niger, "Toxic Bob" Friedland surfaced as the head of another company, Trendfield, based in Hong Kong. Trendfield served as an intermediary in negotiations between Chinese nuclear companies and the government in Niamey. It also advises CNPC in Niger and, in addition, has won key uranium concessions in partnership with yet another company, Govi. Govi, in turn, is owned by someone called Govind Friedland, though he, unlike his father and co-owner, doesn't have a catchy nickname. And as if the desert wasn't crowded enough, there are several smaller companies from Canada and India exploring Niger in the hopes of selling their discoveries to the bigger players.

If there's a distinctly American feel to the African desert as a result, it's worth bearing in mind that France hasn't entirely lost its touch. Niamey is aware that it was Areva's know-how and its colossal investments in the country that allowed the country to start exporting uranium in the first place, and also that none of Areva's competitors are in the position—in either the long or the short term—to maintain current production levels. Hence, the company's hard-won award of a mining concession at the Imouraren site in January 2008. The site contains the second richest uranium deposits in the world (4,500 tons a year) and will push Niger's total annual uranium output over the 8,000-ton mark. Of course, things have changed since the competition rode into town. Areva will have to pay twice as much to mine the yellow cake as it did previously and will have to surrender a significant amount of it to the government, that is, President Tandja and his inner circle.

Uranium mining in this area is a zero-sum game. Areva's gains mean losses for the Chinese. The latter must console themselves with the knowledge that their competitiveness, their talk of "mutual advantages," and their diplomatic cozying up to Niamey will encourage the government to squeeze all it can from the French. The Chinese have also made gains in their experience of doing business with Nigeriens, be they politicians, guerrillas, or other businesspeople.

• • •

When Tuareg rebels from the MNJ snatched the vice general director of the China Nuclear Engineering and Construction Corporation, the company came knocking at the door of the Dragon d'Or to consult with Aboubakeur Karda. Whatever other roles he may fulfill, Karda is primarily a well-respected businessman in Agadez, and so, with him as intermediary, the Chinese engineer was promptly released. Cue much mutual backslapping.

Unfortunately for Karda, the Niamey authorities were not among the backslappers. He was arrested, accused of participation in a plot against the state (he had, they said, offered too large a ransom to the MNJ), and convicted and received a prison sentence of several months. We have it on good authority that he was transferred from prison to hospital due to nebulous "health complications," and after nine months, apparently due to pressure from the Chinese, he was freed.

The fates of people such as Karda, though, are just sideshows in the tough, relentless, and highly complex arena of Saharan uranium exploration. The politicoeconomic stakes are high in a struggle that is only just beginning there, far away from the relative limelight of issues such as the dying textile industry or the World Bank's futile interference. Even though it seemed as if uranium prices had peaked in 2007,[14] the nuclear ambitions of the emerging world are guaranteed to keep the mania going.

In Niger, the risk is that this uranium mania will help fuel the Tuareg rebellion, which foreign powers tend to support to a greater or lesser degree, and similarly bolster the determination of the government in Niamey to keep the rebels—and the mineral deposits—under its control. According to Human Rights Watch, the Nigerien army has already carried out punitive missions to that effect, missions that have started to resemble war crimes more than legitimate military action.

Chapter 7

An Invasion of Junk

If you see a goat at the mouth of the lion's den, fear the goat.

—*Malian proverb*

A young unemployed Cameroonian felt that he had stumbled onto a magic formula: He stood by the side of the road in the suburbs of Douala, collecting loose change from motorists in exchange for filling the road's many potholes. He carried a placard, as much a political statement as it was a guarantee of his work: "Stronger than Chinese."

It hurt to see him this way, with his ragged trousers, the holes in his shirt, shovel in hand, standing there. He personified the scorn implicit in his boast: Stronger than Chinese. It's a bold claim, because in Cameroon "Stronger than Chinese" is a contradiction in terms, an impossibility, like being harder than a diamond. The adjective *Chinese* is synonymous with excellence, perseverance, and achievement. The Chinese have transformed the country. The Chinese built all the country's stadiums, most notably the Multisports Palace in the capital, Yaoundé. The Chinese have offered the local police thirty beautiful new motorbikes. They are restoring the water-supply network. And of course the Chinese are looking after the people's health, too: They've built hospitals and clinics in even the most remote and inaccessible regions of the country. They have introduced in Cameroon and elsewhere in Africa a miraculous plant, *Artemisia annua,* which has been found to be so effective against malaria.[1] As for transport, twenty-eight ultramodern buses from the Zonda Industrial Group now get travelers from the port of Douala to Yaoundé in record time. And while the country's people go about their business, they can go about it to the sound of the late Liu du Kamer, the Chinese star of Cameroonian Makossa music who died in 2006, blaring from their Chinese-made radios. There's hardly a single aspect of the country's life that hasn't been upgraded, replaced, or otherwise improved by Chinese intervention.

The thing that has *really* won the admiration and gratitude of the populace, however, is the restoration of two sections of Douala's ring road by the China Road and Bridge Corporation (CRBC). Though the project, like the company's name, is prosaic enough, it is by any standards a magnificent achievement. Not only was the job completed a whole month before the deadline—something unheard of there or indeed anywhere else—but CRBC had built sidewalks, crosswalks, and traffic circles, all as smooth and untrammeled as a baby's proverbial behind. The grateful nation responded in traditional Cameroonian style and pinched all the traffic lights; one would have to think, "Here before me stands the last word in illuminated traffic-signaling technology," actually to want to tear it out of the ground and lug it all the way home. The tarmac, too, oozes pure quality, but it's been stuck to the ground so effectively that it's still there, unvandalized. In fact, the Cameroonians can't get enough of driving on it, and the traffic that plagued downtown Douala for decades has finally been relieved.

In fact, if there's one criticism leveled at the Chinese, it's that they're "*too* strrrong," the *r* rolled until one gets the idea it may go on rolling forever. And there's some justice in this criticism. Chinese consumer products are sold at rock-bottom prices all over Africa. As well as the spoons, triple-A batteries, voluminous bras, and mattresses of the previous chapter, there's everything else: clothes, shoes, shampoo, pumps, generators, telephones, jugs, nougat, watches, glasses, kettles, dishes, toys. You get the idea. The list goes on and on, like God's "to-do" list on the third day. And all of these items sell at a fourth or a fifth of the price the people have been used to paying. The stock sells out fast, and more and more Africans wonder how they ever got through life before without a small purple plastic frog that croaks when you punch it on the nose (that is, if they bought the batteries—not included). Cheap goods can be an even more habit-forming drug in poor countries than they are in rich ones.

Chinese president Hu Jintao began his 2007 Africa tour in Yaoundé. The visit was a triumph in the way that arches are triumphal; millions of Chinese soldiers armed only with cheap goods had already conquered the place. David Zweig, professor at the Hong Kong University of Science and Technology, knows all about it: "In the past, if a state wanted to expand, it had to take territory. You don't need to grab colonies any more. You just need to have competitive goods to trade."[2]

No empire, mighty in arms or economics, ever succeeded without a few bumps and setbacks along the way, and in Cameroon—the so-called Country of Lions—the Chinese found no exception. Which might explain why, not satisfied with their unchallenged superiority over the spoon and bra markets, they felt obliged to corner even the humble doughnut.

Only American police officers come close to Cameroonians in terms of respect for this jelly-filled comestible. It's a veritable institution here and has been dubbed "Ça va se savoir" (which, loosely translated, means "It's going to come out," hence the saying's adoption as the title of a Belgian TV show, very similar to *The Jerry Springer Show*, also broadcast in Cameroon; the Cameroonians' appetite for gossip, shame, and scandal is, we might point out, matched only by their appetite for doughnuts). But as MBAs and fans of *The Wire* will know, cutting costs and selling shoddy merchandise form a tempting strategy when one is trying to corner a market. The Chinese "doughnut"—and it deserves every ounce of disrespect that the quotation marks can convey, by the way—sells for 10 CFA francs less than the real thing and is made with highly questionable flour. Nevertheless, these doughnuts are taking over despite the patriotic fervor of some who will never surrender, who will never give in, and who will accept only the authentic *Ça Va Se Savoir* during daytime television. Thus the Doughnut Wars began.

Yet the doughnut, despite its sugar-sprinkled popularity, is only a symptom of a much larger problem. Skilled Chinese workers and professionals like doctors and engineers are needed in Cameroon, but of street vendors and prostitutes the country has a sufficiency. The latter only serve to reinforce the image of the newcomers as tricksters and con artists who pirate DVDs and undercut locals in business because they'll do anything, just *anything,* to make a sale. There are roughly three hundred prostitutes in Douala, who congregate in the more down-at-the-heels areas like the Quartier Village or Carrefour Elf Aéroport. Chinese prostitutes will turn tricks for as little as 2,000 CFA ($4.25), whereas the locals, the famous Wolowoss, won't get into bed for less than 5,000.

Part of the reason that the Chinese practitioners of this, the oldest profession, can charge so little is that they also have day jobs, frequently in the many dingy shops in the least desirable neighborhoods, such as Douala's Douche Municipale.[3] The district gets its name from the "public baths," but don't go expecting refreshment or cleanliness. We arrived at three in the afternoon, the heat pressing down on the former baths, which were themselves formerly a colonial mansion. The place was a ruin, like everything around it. The streets reeked of urine, burned plastic, and decomposing trash, and the stench was so bad that it was impossible to believe that people might ever have come there for pleasure.

The once-grand five-story buildings had been derelict for as long as anyone cared to remember, and it was only the most desperate, the most impoverished of the Chinese immigrants who were willing to call them home. They put up with the appalling conditions to be near the Congo Market, one of Douala's main attractions.

The neighbors have nothing but scorn for the Chinese, who rent wretched houses at wretched prices and pack themselves in ten or fifteen to a room. They keep their overhead low and then open up shops to compete with local tradespeople and artisans such as basket weavers, tanners, jewelers, and tailors.

We decided to go to one of these Chinese-run shops. Cameroonians, the broad-shouldered kind more commonly employed as "security" at a club, stood behind piles of merchandise. The piles were covered in dust and grit that had blown in, like us, off the street. The security detail kept a close eye on us as we looked around, and another close eye on their boss's goods.

"We're looking for Mr. Wu," a representative of the local Chinese community, we told one of them.

"Not here," said one, while his colleagues meandered round the shelves pretending not to take an interest in us. We could see their eyes pressed up to the gaps in the shelves.

"When will he be back?"

"Three hours," the man said. Three hours' time meant nightfall. We were neither brave nor stupid enough to wait until then. The mood in the Douche Municipale was ugly and the tension palpable: A young Chinese man had recently been stabbed there by a local gang, and violence was on the increase. Chinese shopkeepers had come out onto the streets in protest but had been promptly and harshly dispersed.

"Don't come to our country and do what you wouldn't do in your own" was the unapologetic attitude of the commissioner of public safety. So the Chinese appealed to their own president, Hu Jintao, who happened to be visiting the country shortly after the crisis. They asked to meet with him and make their complaints about the violence, blackmail, and brutality.

This approach was more effective. Two weeks later the protesting Chinese awoke to find that a phone booth had been erected on the street. Upon closer inspection they found that they couldn't make calls from the little hut, not least because it was inhabited by two burly policewomen who, presumably tired of the endless strangers trying to use the telephone, had written "Police Station" on the outside. This done, they sat back down on their chairs and looked out onto the street from behind reinforced glass.

"By order of the mayor," they explain to us. "The Chinese—they're fed up with being attacked. Now that we're here, they've got nothing to worry about."

"And this is it? For the whole quarter? And nobody's attacked you?"

"Well, the Chinese look after themselves, mostly," says the burlier of the two. "And anyway, I can defend myself. I've even been knifed a few times."

Before we can ask how these last two claims go together, she lifts up her shirt to show us the scars. Her colleague adds, "There are others out on patrol, too," but we didn't see any for the rest of the afternoon.

However capable these two were, we couldn't help but wonder if they weren't going to have their work cut out for them in the near future. Seen from China, Cameroon is still a dream destination, a kind of summary of the continent at the intersection of West and Central Africa, bilingual (French and English), offering a great range of opportunities. The land is rich in raw materials: oil, gas, bauxite, tin, gold, uranium, and, particularly, wood. It's nearly as big as France and has merely a quarter of the population, but that is set to change.

Due to various pacts between Yaoundé and Beijing, the Chinese are the only foreigners granted eighteen-month residence visas without a work contract.[4] At the end of February 2007, the Cameroonian embassy in Beijing announced that it had already received 700,000 applications for these visas.[5] It's impossible to tell how many Chinese will settle in the Douche Municipale, under the watchful eyes of the two sedentary policewomen.

· · ·

It seems that every country in Africa is facing the same dilemma: how to satisfy the people's demand for cheap Chinese goods without being overrun by the Chinese themselves. Take Senegal, for example. The country is inundated with the aforementioned merchandise. The Boulevard du Centenaire in Dakar is symptomatic. This highly symbolic thoroughfare was once called Avenue du Général de Gaulle and still hosts Senegalese Independence Day parades, but on every other day of the year the place is unrecognizable to the Dakarians themselves. However, they've evolved a solution of sorts to their problem.

The conquest of the avenue happens in a uniquely Chinese and inconspicuous fashion. First, one shop changes occupancy, then the one next door, then one across the street, and so on and on. The method is always the same: Convince owners to rent out old garages (at very generous rates, of course), and then set up shop in the garage. A bit rough around the edges, but then Rome wasn't built in a day. In Dakar the Chinese found no shortage of people looking to rent out or even sell their properties because the cost of living shot up following the four years of high inflation between 1994 and 1998—during which the CFA franc, a currency that took its fixed exchange rate from the French franc, and now from the Euro—saw its value slashed in half. The inflation problem was compounded by the conflict in the Ivory Coast, which led the majority of large businesses and other international organizations to crowd into Senegal. In August 2004 there were three hundred Chinese-owned businesses in Dakar, and the number had more than tripled by 2008.

But the influx of the budget goods in which these businesses deal has been predictably popular. On the Boulevard du Centenaire, a certain Mr. Diop can get a machete (nothing sinister: It's for Tabaski, the Muslim Festival of Sacrifice) for next to nothing. He can admire the keen edge or the burnished steel and run his fingers over the inscription on the handle: "Made in China." The women he knows walk up and down the road in brilliantly sparkling native dress, so brilliant, in fact, that for a moment you don't see the piles of garbage and ubiquitous plastic bags over which they're stepping. Even the people themselves barely see them. As they push up against the stalls, all they notice is that their money's going further these days.

The shopkeepers themselves are as reserved as their customers are ebullient. If they speak French at all, it's impossible to tell. Senegalese teenagers came to our aid, however. They've figured out the problem words and did our bartering for us. When you ask the Chinese about their lives, however, the only thing you get—if you get anything more than silence—is "Meyou." We know what that means. It means "No." Mr. Diop, luckily for us, was happy to advise us. "Don't ask about that. Ask about the *prices*. Believe me, if you're talking money, you'll find they speak any language you want!"

Some Senegalese take a dim view of the Chinese, mostly because they are convinced that the only reason a Chinese would come here is to set up a brothel or a gambling den, or both. Or they believe the rumors that all the Chinese goods are smuggled into the country, and that disputes are settled exclusively with knives. In reality, of course, such rumors aren't really the issue. The Senegalese love a drama, though, so even if they knew that the rumors were false, the idea of strange-looking men from far away stabbing one another over boot-legged carrier bags is just too appealing to dismiss. First and foremost, however, it's the established merchants who have the biggest gripe and the loudest voice.

"Unfair competition," claimed the Senegal Trade Association (UNACOIS). It denounced the Chinese shopkeepers for "not respecting the customs or the financial regulations," and for "importing containers of so-called 'spare parts,' only to reassemble the parts into finished products and so pay reduced taxes."[6] UNACOIS, which is nothing if not a lobby for the big French, Lebanese, and Senegalese merchants, went so far as to claim that the Chinese imports were poisonous, that the leather in the belts "caused allergies," and that the flower pots killed the plants put in them. There's a protectionist wind blowing in Dakar, whipped up by the scapegoat issue of globalization.

On July 1, 2004, the members of UNACOIS threatened to ransack the Chinese stores and close them down vigilante-style. The members' secretary-general told them, "We've imported everything there is to import from China, everything except for genuine Chinese shopkeepers." He went on to explain that the Chinese so-called shopkeepers in Dakar were "nothing but a mafia gang. They are wanted everywhere for underhanded business practices and shady dealings that range from prostitution to drug trafficking. Today it's Dakar, tomorrow it'll be the suburbs, and then the entire country."[7]

Whatever the accuracy of his claims, UNACOIS soon grew fed up with their negotiations with the authorities and three weeks later delivered an ultimatum to President Abdoulaye Wade, giving him a month to "drive all the Chinese from Senegal." It seemed as if, one way or another, this was crunch time.

But for two reasons, nothing much happened. Granted, there were a few attacks, but nothing like the full *Kristallnacht* promised by the union. First of all, the arrival of the Chinese had inspired a broad shift toward a more tolerant Senegalese outlook; for whatever reason, social or purely commercial, there were many who welcomed the Chinese presence. The Association of Senegalese Customers (ASCOSEN) even organized a march against what it called "the intolerance, racism and xenophobia of UNACOIS."

The second reason is that Senegal has often played a better political hand than many of its neighbors when it comes to the Chinese. When the dispute between the two groups flared up, the government in Dakar wasn't on speaking terms with the Chinese because of Senegal's temporary alignment with Taiwan (1996–2005). Though this meant that the Senegalese couldn't expect the Chinese to help them stem the flow of immigrants, it also meant that Senegal had a valuable bargaining chip when it came to Dakar reestablishing diplomatic ties with Beijing, as it did in October 2005.[8] In partial exchange (one part being the restored diplomatic relations) for the granting of several large construction projects to Chinese companies, Senegal was able to negotiate an almost complete cessation of visas issued by its Beijing embassy and also an increase in visas for China issued in Dakar for Senegalese.[9] The Senegalese merchants were thus able to haul in profits of 80 billion CFA ($160 million) in 2006. According to Xinhua, China's official press agency, "incomplete statistics [lead us to believe] that the number of Senegalese in business in China has overtaken the approximated 1,000 Chinese currently in business in Senegal." In just two years, 5,500 entry visas and residency permits were issued by the Chinese embassy in Dakar. Xinhua concluded its statement by quoting a Chinese shopkeeper in the Dakar neighborhood of Sandaga[10] as saying, "Senegalese merchants now have containers of goods sent to them from China. They pay less duty on their imports than we do, so it has become very difficult for us to keep our heads above water." It is no doubt scant consolation to the man that it was the rock-bottom prices that he and his fellows had been able to offer that led eventually to his native and adoptive countries' doing business with one another.

• • •

These Senegalese merchants, and indeed the majority of the African community in China, have settled in Yiwu, a city of 650,000 people in the Zhejiang Province, southwest of Shanghai. It seems strange that only very few people have heard of this city, but if you've got a Rolex with a stationary second hand or an exploding Du Pont lighter, the chances are it comes from Yiwu.

Toward the end of the 1980s, Communist officials from Yiwu had a very bright idea. Yiwu was then an undistinguished and indistinguishable village, a miserably poor place with an agriculture-based economy, among many other miserably poor places with agriculture-based economies. These officials knew that their own village had an informal market, where farmers came to buy provisions, and they also knew that an increasing number of foreigners were turning up at the trade fairs that the big cities were beginning to host. The bright idea was to turn the informal market into a permanent trade fair, a wholesale market where the region's producers and growers could sell their wares. Twenty years later, Yiwu is the biggest wholesale market in the world.

It's big. Really big. *Numbers* big: 200,000 businesspeople go there and spend 287 million yuan ($41 million) on 4,300 tons of cargo. That's every day. These purchasers find that that the prices of 320,000 listed products are less than half the prices being negotiated in Beijing. The site is 2.5 million square meters, and to spend just one minute in each of the 34,000 shops would take seventy days. Yiwu has 8,000 foreign residents, the majority of whom are African and Arab Muslims, for whom a number of mosques have been built. And on the subject of religion, you can, of course, buy any religious artifact you might need. In Chen Xiao Ping's third-floor shop you'll find Virgin Marys with flashing lights; mirrors engraved with scenes of Mecca; mosque-shaped alarm clocks that beep out the five daily calls to prayer; other clocks with hands sweeping over the friendly face of Ali, the first Shiite imam; faux bronze renderings of Christ on his cross; and miniature Buddhas, their plump faces serene amid all these ecumenical commodities.

. . .

No doubt the enlightened little Buddhas would have beamed with equal serenity on the comparable clutter of Cairo's Khan al-Khalili market. The Egyptian guides would have you know that a stroll through this place is like walking into the fourteenth century, but if this is the case, China had a bigger medieval empire than even the Chinese claim. Walking along Muski Street at the southern edge of the market, we felt as if we'd time-traveled back only as far as the early twenty-first century. Cursing our DeLorean and its flux capacitor, we found ourselves struggling through drifts of T-shirts, knocking into luggage racks, getting shouted at and our toes crushed, and ducking the jeans that were being flung from one hawker to another in the manner of some violent and obscure sport akin to fourteenth-century football. Everything on sale bore the legend "Made in China," even if the vendors themselves, unlike in many African countries, were locals.

It was with relief, therefore, and not a little surprise at our good fortune, that we discovered we'd made it past the Muski "Strip" and into the market proper. Here, among the local artisans, like leather-workers and tile decorators, we felt as if we were getting somewhere closer to the guides' visions. We were still shouted at, of course, but our mood had improved to the extent where such pushy, almost inco-herent yelling takes on a rare veneer of charm. Consider, if you will, the small plastic pyramid we bought. It's a wretched object—it really is. It's a misconceived hybrid of a snow globe and something used to stop airplane wheels from moving. Inside, covered in the snow for which Egypt is so famous, sits a disgruntled little figure. At the time of purchase, however, we felt that this little ornament deserved to be behind bulletproof glass in the Hermitage. Never had yellow plastic seemed so perfect a material in which to render the sun-warmed stone of the pyramids. We agreed that if only Peter Carl Fabergé had had the material available to him, he'd have gone on to achieve great things instead of meddling with eggs and such. And the disgruntled little man within wasn't a disgruntled little man, but a god (Horas, the ancient Egyptian god of the sun, the seller assured us, and we knew his words to be the truth). As we turned the pyramid, there was revealed to us a hawk, the animal manifestation of this deity, staring disparag-ingly through the flurry of snowflakes. And on the base these words appeared, evidence of the ancients' eye to posterity: "Made in Egypt."

"Yes, yes. Made in Egypt," the shop owner said, adding, "You'll find them for sale even at the foot of the great pyramids themselves," by way of proof. This we had to see.

At the foot of the pyramids, in Giza, a new civilization has arisen from the antique sands. This modern-day phoenix is an area—more accurately a *city*—of souvenir shops catering to every budget. With the help of a friend, Khaled, we set off to solve a mystery that would have baffled a sphinx. We found for sale another priceless relic, in this case a porcelain bust of Nefertiti (the combined stepmother and mother-in-law of Tutankhamen). Knowing that we held in our mortal hands one of a very few extant remains from the period in question, we asked after its provenance, lest there be other archaeological gems waiting to be uncovered at bargain prices.

The vendors were unanimous, and scrupulously honest. It turned out that what we held was, for all its beauty and craftsmanship, merely a replica. All of them swore up and down that it was hand-painted and, from that point of view, that every piece they sold was unique, lovingly crafted by noble artisans. Not far from here. Just around the corner.

"And what about our snow globe? Is it possible to visit these artisans? To look upon them as they go about their ancient craft?"

"It's time for lunch," the vendors explained.

It was, as they said, near enough lunchtime. The sun was overhead, and though the pyramids could cast no shadow on us pilgrims at that time of day, our minds were becoming clouded with doubt. Would we never find the people who made such masterpieces?

"We should go to Alexandria," suggested Khaled. Perhaps our friend knew of some secret, some clue to help us on our quest. "That's where all the cheap Chinese goods come into the country. I know the place well. It's my hometown."

The highway to Alexandria was lined with an astounding number of pigeon coops and then a brief glimpse of a banana plantation about a hundred kilometers out, after which we saw nothing but a succession of military bases, police training camps, prisons, and labor camps, interspersed with five-star golf courses, a business center, and upmarket gated communities to which the residents could escape from the simply ghastly hoi polloi of Cairo.

Khaled wound down the window to get rid of the smell of turpentine that pervaded the car. One of us had greatly displeased Horas, and so great and swift was his divine vengeance that he had torn asunder the plastic that enshrined him. Whatever spell had caused us to think that buying this piece was a wise move was wearing off.

The most striking thing about the highway, however, wasn't the lengths to which the well-off had gone to keep themselves apart, but the number of Chinese cars on it: Chery, Geely, the Zhonghua—all unknown in the West. Because there are only 2.5 million cars on the Egyptian roads and 80 million Egyptians aspiring to drive them, this is a huge potential market for the manufacturers. Chery Automobile and the endearingly named Brilliance China Auto (a partner of BMW) are among those building assembly plants here.

Accompanied by Horas's sacred stink, we finally made it to Alexandria, which appeared over the horizon like an Arabian Riviera with its fort and Mediterranean beach. Though clearly proud of its history and antiquity, it did possess one strikingly forward-looking monument: the new library, opened by UNESCO in 2002 to replace the one that, as legend has it, went up in smoke, along with its 700,000 volumes, when Julius Caesar lay siege of the city.

Although Egypt may have been fought over and even fought through for thousands of years, it has never submitted willingly to foreign invasion, except for now. The shipping containers of cheap imports are stacked high all along the harbor. Some of this merchandise is sold on the spot: prayer mats (with built-in Mecca-finding compasses), halal cellular phones (including polyphonic calls to prayer), djellabas, lanterns for Ramadan, and even copies of the Holy Koran printed in Yiwu. So unanimously popular is prayer here that even such enormous containers cannot satisfy the demand for these objects.

To continue for a moment on the religious theme, social injustice in Egypt is widespread and serious, serious enough to engender the kind of frustration among the people that can fan the flames of the occasional blaze of violent Islamism. President Hosni Mubarak occasionally takes it upon himself to suppress these flames with a zealousness that is too extreme even to gain the approval of the United States, which, as a result, has reduced its military aid to Egypt. Formerly this aid was about $2 billion a year. But for 2008, for example, the American Congress attached certain conditions concerning the improvement of the police force and the judicial system, and reduced the aid package to $1.3 billion. Conversely, with no such squeamishness, Chinese military aid has risen, matching the rate at which the Egyptians soak up the Chinese-made religious trinkets.

"The Chinese door-to-door salesmen have spread inland," Khaled tells us, "and have infiltrated every last corner of the country. They knock at my front door the whole time, unpacking their wares and trying to sell me stuff despite not speaking a word of Arabic."

This is precisely the kind of information for which we should have been looking, but it seemed we were still not free of Horas's spell. Though his private snowstorm had dropped to a level just below his nose, his eyes told us that he was still a force to be reckoned with, and we were once again possessed of an urgent need to find the true origins of this divine relic. The sky god's turpentine had soaked our clothes, the smell producing a force field that kept the path of our quest clear. Khaled directed us to a friend who sold souvenirs by Alexandria's harbor.

A little later, we met this man, Mahmoud: two large, bright eyes peering out at us from a sky-blue djellaba with a Lacoste alligator on it. He had in his arms several packages for our delectation. First, he produced a Nefertiti head in its original box, exactly the same as the one we had unearthed by the pyramids, only smaller. He also had an ashtray inscribed with strange runes or hieroglyphs, as well as a set of three miniature pyramids that shone and sparkled like Swarovski crystal. The latter were a considerable improvement on anything we'd seen Swarovski produce lately because the artisan who had hewn it from the glass had ingeniously inserted holograms in the center of each pyramid. Amazing. We started to get our wallets out, hoping we might be able to take possession of these unique objets d'art, but we were rendered motionless by the merchant's last three prize items. He had a snow globe identical in every respect to ours, though the god within had not yet expelled the turpentine from his transparent sphere. More astounding still, the merchant revealed from within the folds of his clothes a small figurine, an amalgamated buy-one-get-one-free rendering of the Sphinx (with nose intact, testament to its antiquity) and one of King Tut. These figures were cast in some rare and exotic material as bright as gold though a fraction of the weight—as light as plastic. We agreed that they must be almost priceless and, defeated, returned our wallets to our pockets.

Mahmoud then began to disabuse us of our illusions. "These are all from Yiwu. Look, 'Made in China' is written on the box in Arabic." Fakes? We were dumbfounded. "I haven't gotten around to erasing the origin yet, but I will. Everyone here does."

He asked us to look closely at the mysterious calligraphy on the ashtray: "Chaozhou Jiahua Ceramics Co., Ltd." The company is based in Chaozhou, as the name implies, a region known as "Ceramics City" by aficionados. We were familiar with the maker by experience: When the tea is finished and the cup empty, it's worth reading the legend on the bottom: "Not intended for the service of food or beverages." Most encouraging.

We were back almost at square one, with nothing genuinely valuable save the original Horas, who was expressing his contempt by secreting turps into the bottom of one of our camera bags. Nevertheless, Mahmoud was keen to make a sale. He fished around for something and at last pulled an ace literally out of his sleeve—a gold-painted ballpoint—but found that the pen no longer worked. "Khalas!" he exclaimed. "All this stuff is shit. I sell shit. We *all* sell shit."

His disgust seemed to us to cover not only the deplorable quality of what he was trying to sell, but even the contribution he continually made to the disappearance of local artisans.

The flash of regret passed quickly, and we told him we'd take a sphinx and a Nefertiti off his hands for 35 Egyptian pounds ($6.38), but that we'd want a good deal on the trio of glass pyramids. He said he'd be robbing his kids if he went lower than 30 pounds ($5.48), but that if we wanted a pen, too, he could do that for 7 pounds ($1.28), so long as we bought an ashtray for another 7 pounds. We agreed, cunningly insisting on a pen that worked. Total: $12.

And Mahmoud's profit?

"Usually it would be a dollar or so, but I sold everything to you at cost price," he said.

Ninety-one thousand Chinese tourists came to Egypt in 2007, and hundreds of Egyptian tour guides are learning Chinese to cater to the potential millions expected to visit annually so that the tourists can take home a special reminder of their visit—a roundabout route for them to buy local.

Chapter 8

For Sale

Weapons for Dictators (Made in China)

Obtain safe passage in order to conquer the
Kingdom of Guo.
—From 36 Stratagems, *a Chinese collection*
on how to beat the competition

Clouds of dust marked the soldiers' passing. The column of rebels several hundred strong had crossed the border from Sudan and into Chad, heading for the capital, N'Djamena. The date: March 30, 2006. These men, members of the United Front for Democratic Change (known by the French acronym FUC), had one goal: to overthrow the president, Idriss Déby. The soldiers had added to their ranks along their route a hundred or so beige pickup trucks and military vehicles carrying enough water and fuel to give them an operational reach of several thousand kilometers. The soldiers in the backs of the trucks puffed out their chests with naked pride, both in themselves and in the green battle dress, headscarves, and red berets that marked them as Mahamat Nour's men. Their weapons, like their clothes, were brand-new. Snipers kept watch from the roofs of the trucks, scanning their sectors, making sure the surrounding desert held no surprises. In addition to their rifles, they carried QLZ87 35mm grenade launchers manufactured by Norinco, a Chinese company well known throughout Africa.

It was clear by now that the recently signed peace accord had been nothing but a ruse. Even as the agreement was being signed by Chad and Sudan in Tripoli two months earlier, Chadian rebels were congregating in el-Geneina, a village in Sudan's Darfur region, to train with the FUC to ready themselves for this attack. Even at that time, there was evidence of Chinese involvement. The Chinese consulate in Lagos had made subtle overtures to the rebels, urging them to ally themselves with the FUC, and claims had been made that the column had stopped to fill up with gas at a Chinese oil facility.[1] At the beginning of April, as these rebels headed west toward the capital, another group moved across the border into Chad, this time from the Central African Republic. This group, too, was equipped with Chinese-made arms; it would have been unusual had the arms come from anywhere else, for the government of the republic had been facing such financial difficulties that it had had to turn to Beijing for money just to pay its own civil servants.[2]

This attack had been a long time in the making and was the result of pressure from various quarters. Chad had been discovering, extracting, and exporting its own oil since 2003, and China, already a player in neighboring Sudan, harbored hopes of replacing Déby with a pro-Sudanese—and by implication pro-Chinese—puppet such as Mahamat Nour. China's ambitions were heightened because Chad was one of Taiwan's few remaining "oil allies" in Africa. Chinese confidence in the success of the plan to replace Déby was founded on the Chadian president's poor standing internationally. In January 2006 the World Bank had suspended loans to the country after the Déby government passed a law that effectively abolished the allocation of the newfound oil revenues to the fight against poverty; the law violated an agreement that the same government had signed with Exxon Mobil, an agreement that had been presented at the time, 1999, as a showcase for "development through oil." As if this were not enough for the embattled President Déby, it all came on top of his main concern: He had six simultaneous rebellions on his hands, and his army was hemorrhaging men through defection and desertion. It looked as though the slightest shake would bring the whole regime tumbling down.

One of the biggest questions, from an international point of view, was what France's reaction to this coup attempt would be. Twelve hundred members of the French armed forces were still stationed there as part of Operation Epervier, originally sent to protect Chadian interests from Libya in the 1980s. France, for its part, had been responsible for putting President Déby in power to replace Hissene Habre sixteen years earlier, but its protégé's wretched human rights record, combined with the contempt he inspired more generally in Paris, had given the rebels reason to believe that these twelve hundred would watch from the sidelines. The rebels found out the hard way that they had been mistaken. Jacques Chirac ordered the French military to provide aerial support for Déby, a crucial move that gave the latter time to muster his reserves and beat back the rebel forces. It was a close-run thing, for on April 13, the FUC had covered eight hundred kilometers and reached the outskirts of N'Djamena. It was rumored that the first rebel into the city got lost and had to ask the locals for directions to the palace; they sent him not to the presidential palace but to the Palace of January 15, home of the National Assembly, on the edge of the city.

But for this farcical incident and French support, the writing would have been on the wall for Déby. He was clever enough to realize, however, that he had come to within an ace of being deposed by an outstandingly inept band of rebels, and also that he couldn't count on French support forever. He placed his future, therefore, in the hands of the Chinese. China had kept itself far enough removed from the various rebellions for there to be no bad blood between the countries, and anyway, as Michael Corleone might have explained, the Chinese involvement wasn't personal; it was strictly business.

Beijing recognized a good thing when it saw one and welcomed Déby's entreaties. Déby had simultaneously gained a powerful ally and rid himself of dependence on the French. Of course, Chinese support wasn't unconditional: The president promptly slammed the diplomatic door on Taiwan. "There is only one China," he bellowed. In Beijing, a canny government had learned that a little support could go a long way. It was as if the politics of the cold war had returned to Africa.

China's strategy in Chad was not a new one. The same game of playing off rebels and governments against one another had been used with marked success by the likes of France, the United States, and the USSR. The circumstances in this instance were remarkable, however, in that, according to a sensational report by Amnesty International of June 2006[3]—two months after the failed rebellion— China had just become the world's biggest small-arms exporter. The report went on to denounce China for "having supplied a vast selection of military, security and police equipment to countries accused of massive violations of human rights." It's impossible not to feel that the likes of Britain, the United States, and France must have been just a little annoyed that China was doing it so much more effectively than they were.

Accusations of "amoral" Chinese arms trading were being made long before the rebels crossed into Chad, and the fact that their equipment boasted "Made in China" was no surprise. The Chinese arms industry had been through a revolution in the 1980s. Hitherto the policy out of Beijing had emphasized domestic production, but reforms introduced by Deng Xiaoping authorized previously state-run institutions to engage in for-profit commercial enterprises. To the military-industrial complex, this was a license to export arms.

The Chinese People's Liberation Army was divided into five branches: navy, army, air force, a space division, and a separate entity in charge of nuclear weapons. These branches went on to spawn ten profit-oriented companies,[4] the names of which can be seen all over Africa, among them Norinco (China North Industries Corporation), XinXing Corporation (run by the army's logistics corps), and the Poly Group (run by the army's general staff).

The Chinese have sold arms to both Sudan and Zimbabwe (both of which stand accused of widely publicized human rights violations) and regularly flout international sanctions and embargoes against these two countries. Atrocities all over Africa have been perpetrated with Chinese weapons—in Congo-Brazzaville, Tanzania, the Great Lakes Region of East Africa, Chad, and Liberia.

The Chinese dealt with Amnesty International's claims in the only way it knew how: It produced a member of the Chinese Arms Control and Disarmament Agency, one Teng Jianqun, who mourned "the most dreadful" consequences of the illegal arms traffic and added that China, of course, had always abided by international agreements in plying its trade in this arena. In addition, he said, "China imposes very strict control on its exports . . . of military technology," which therefore made Amnesty's claims 'baseless."[5]

In China's defense, Teng pointed to the figures published by the Stockholm International Peace Research Institute (SIPRI), a global index tracking the arms business. According to the statistics collated between 2000 and 2004, arms exports from the United States had risen to $25.9 billion, and China's had not exceeded $1.4 billion. At the United Nations, China often went on record to express its support for initiatives aimed at combating illegal arms trafficking. For example, in 2002, Beijing announced that it had updated its system for supervising arms exports, and in January 2006, the Chinese delegation to the UN called for a conference to implement a plan of action specifically targeted at the small-arms market.

All in all, China simply expects to be taken at its word. The main stumbling block, though, comes from its unwillingness to open its books for inspection. Beijing has failed to supply sales figures for conventional arms to the United Registry of Conventional Arms for over a decade. Customs statistics, collected by Comtrade, the UN's Commodity Trade Statistics Database, suggest that China is the eighth most active arms exporter in the world, and there is a widely held belief that these figures don't reveal the whole story.[6] Further research, this time courtesy by the U.S. Congress, listed China as the third most active supplier of arms to Africa between 2001 and 2004.[7] In real terms, this evolution can be expressed by the fact that since 2000, the majority of muggings and robberies committed in South Africa have involved a Norinco 9mm pistol. This particular gun is widely available on the South African market but doesn't appear in any of the UN's custom statistics. Sometimes China doesn't even go to the bother of *selling* guns: It just swaps them for other things it needs, like Sudanese oil or Congolese mining concessions, thereby keeping the arms sales under the counter and out of all those inconvenient trade statistics. Other times it just hands arms over as a somewhat macabre sign of goodwill.

It's worth pointing out that an understanding of these statistics is incomplete if one takes into account only the dollar value of exports. For example, though the United States might sell a fighter such as the F/A-18 Hornet to Kuwait, this sale has a much smaller effect on the local population than spending that same money on assault rifles (300,000 in this case).

According to Small Arms Survey, another organization that tracks arms dealing, China is much nearer the number one spot in international ranking when it comes to the sale of small arms.[8] Even the term *small arms* can be misleading when one considers that the large-scale supplying of small arms turns them in effect into weapons of mass destruction, as has been the case in the Great Lakes Region; 17 percent of the 1,100 weapons seized in a MONUC[9] operation in Bunia—in the eastern part of the Democratic Republic of the Congo—were Type 56 Assault Rifles, or 56ers, Norinco-made copies of the AK-47 Kalashnikov. Sales of guns such as these have made Norinco a global leader in the manufacture of heavy machine guns and submachine guns. When it comes to the ever-popular cult classic Kalashnikov, Russia makes only about 12 percent of the million sold world-wide every year;[10] it spends quite of lot of time trying to protect the brand from the pirates who sell their forgeries to the likes of the Democratic Republic of the Congo (DRC), Uganda, Rwanda, and Burundi.[11] Often, the imitation firearms come from China, but they also come through third parties in Albania or Zimbabwe.

Also, a fair number of the hundreds of thousands of machetes—the trademark of those who committed the Rwandan genocide—don't show up in arms-dealing statistics, even though they were, according to a UN report,[12] imported into Rwanda from China for just this purpose between 1992 and 1994.

On top of all this, it's hard to see exactly what the "international norms" are that China claims to abide by. The OSCE (Organization for Security and Cooperation in Europe) agreed to the regulation of sales of conventional weapons in 1993, and Canada, the United States, and even Russia have followed this example, trying to stem the sale of arms "that could be used to violate or suppress human rights and fundamental liberties." If Teng Jianquin, the Chinese government expert on arms dealing, is referring to these agreements, then China can hardly be said to be complying with them. On the other hand, in a document drawn up in 2002, the Chinese outlined their own guidelines to follow. China will sell arms only if

1. The importer's ability to defend itself, as long as it has a legitimate government, is strengthened.
2. Peace and global or regional security are not threatened.
3. The arms will not be used to interfere in the internal affairs of other countries.

But one might ask what exactly the term *legitimate government* means in the context of Africa.

One of the most obvious examples of indiscriminate arms sales to African dictators concerns Zimbabwe, formerly Rhodesia. Since 1999, despite recent talk of power sharing, Zimbabwe has been suffering under the terrifying reign of Robert Mugabe. Ostracized by the international community and the Commonwealth of Nations, Mugabe has had to resort to arms in order to retain his position as president. Sanctions imposed on the regime initially made it difficult for him to find new weapons or, indeed, the equipment necessary to maintain his existing stock, though it didn't take him long to find a supplier willing to do business. In June 2004, China sold the Mugabe government $240-million worth of weapons, including twelve fighter planes and one hundred assorted military vehicles.[13] Included in this price were less blatantly warlike technologies, like water cannon and telephone-bugging devices that would come in handy during election time to keep his "enemies of the state"—the electorate and the opposition party—in line. In April 2008, Mugabe made a great deal of noise about holding open and fair elections, when something happened that succeeded in uniting the whole of Africa against China.

On April 18, dockworkers in the South African port of Durban refused to unload cargo from the Chinese-registered *An Yue Jiang*, citing as their motive solidarity with Zimbabweans. The ship's load had come from Tianjin in China and was en route to the ministry of defense in Harare. A maritime agent, under condition of anonymity, gave us a copy of the manifest or "bill of loading." The list was shocking in its simplicity and brazenness. But the impact of the document wasn't so much what it included (3,080 boxes of ammunition of various calibers, 1,500 rockets, and 2,700 mortars; the document even listed the price of a single round of the 7.62mm ammunition for an AK-47: sixteen cents), but what it left to the imagination: the human cost.

The following day, the *An Yue Jiang* sailed out of Durban, leaving in its wake a political crisis in South Africa and a show of solidarity across the region. Zambia's president, Levy Mwanawasa, declared that China should find more constructive things to do in Africa than deliver armaments, and he called on neighboring countries to work together to block such transports.

The last radio message received from the *An Yue Jiang* as it sailed off read, "Next stop: Maputo." As intended, this ruse directed attention to Mozambique, when in fact the ship had sailed in the opposite direction, toward Cape Town, where it was spotted on April 22. The ship next showed up in Angola's capital, Luanda, where officials confirmed that it docked and took on cement and other construction materials on May 5. Officially, where the ship sailed from there is a mystery, though the Zambian secret service claims that it did eventually arrive in Mozambique.

Later, a Zimbabwean official was imprudent enough to be heard boasting about the delivery. The rumor then making the rounds was that the arms had finally arrived in Harare from Luanda on an Ilyushin aircraft. The Chinese embassy in Namibia vehemently denies this version of events, claiming that the ship took its cargo of weapons back to Shanghai.

"The story about the Ilyushin plane was a smokescreen," an agent of the Zambian secret service told us, under condition of anonymity. "The solution the Chinese found was, as usual, simpler and cheaper," he added and told us that "the ship stopped in Beira, Mozambique, at the end of May . . . where the arms were loaded onto trucks bound for Harare."

But, we asked, what about China's assurances, admittedly made under international pressure, that the *An Yue Jiang* would not deliver the arms?

The agent was adamant. "There was never, not even for a second, any question of whether that ship would complete its delivery. No Chinese ship has *ever* gone home without completing its assignment."

Liberia, too, has been on the receiving end of such Chinese deliveries, thanks to the Dutch arms dealer Guus Van Kouwenhoven. He served as an intermediary between President Charles Taylor and China from 2001 to 2003, procuring large quantities of weapons in violation of a UN embargo. Taylor urgently needed these weapons for the murder of 300,000 people.[14] In exchange for the necessary hardware, Liberia gave China, among other things, wood, which came as no surprise to those who were aware of Van Kouwenhoven's presidency of a lumber products company—the Oriental Timber Company (OTC)—in Liberia's capital, Monrovia.[15]

But of all the many African countries crying out for the means to kill and maim their people, it is Sudan that received the largest amount of military aid. This "aid" included the fighter planes used in the 1983–2001 civil war, during which aerial bombardments and famine wiped out between 1 and 2 million civilians. China also supplied the Z-6 helicopter troop transport and the Mi-8,[16] which, despite being ostensibly a civilian cargo plane, can be converted into an equally effective military aircraft.

According to the most recent available data, Sudan imported nearly $100 million worth of Chinese armaments in 2005 alone.[17] The military journal *Airforce Monthly* claims that in December 2006, not only did the Chinese company AviChina deliver six K-8 fighters, but they even supplied training—including flight simulation equipment—on how to get the most out of the planes. The journal also claims that six more K-8s are currently on order.

In August 2005 a group of UN observers in Port Sudan reported seeing a convoy of military trucks manufactured by another Chinese company, DongFeng. A year later, a UN Security Council report, drafted by experts sent to Sudan to supervise the implementation of sanctions, stated that Chad-based FUC rebels were in possession of an arsenal of small arms that complemented the existing QLZ87 35mm grenade launchers. This sale was clearly a contravention of the arms embargo imposed on Sudan by Resolution 1556 of the UN Security Council in 2004, but the evidence for the report is clear: The Janjaweed militias that carried out the Darfur massacres had the backing not only of the government, but also of the FUC.

China, lest we get too complacent, is hardly alone in illicit arms exportation. Photographs in an Amnesty International report of May 2007 taken at the Nyala airport in southern Darfur show not only

Chinese A5 Fantan bombers but also Russian Mi-24 attack helicopters as well as an Antonov 26 (a light transport plane) disguised in the UN's distinctive white livery. And the West is hardly in a position to lecture either Russia or China on the rights and wrongs of the arms trade. Great Britain, under the leadership of Tony Blair, quadrupled its sales of arms to authoritarian regimes in just five years, between 1999 and 2004,[18] receiving a billion pounds ($1.7 billion) from African states alone during this period. France became the foremost supplier of arms to Africa, a position it held between 2001 and 2005, surpassing even the United States, Russia, and China.[19] Russia, however, is said to have stolen the top spot from France in 2006, though so many reports are published each year it's difficult to know which one to believe.

One thing we can be certain of, though, is that the United States is the true leader when it comes to the global arms trade. For the fiscal year 2007–2008, U.S. arms sales rose to $33.7 billion, up from $23 billion the year before and only $12 billion in 2005.[20] By our own count, forty-two of the top one hundred arms manufacturers—a list compiled by the Stockholm International Peace Research Institute— are American, including eight of the top twelve.

According to the same source, Africa's military expenditure rose by 51 percent between 1997 and 2006, and according to Refugees International, the Bush administration attempted to disguise its garnering of juicy contracts that flooded the continent with weapons.[21] The report, released in July 2008, stated that the U.S. Africa Command (Africom) had authorized the U.S. Defense Department to take funds allocated to it and use them to improve the Pentagon's image in Africa.[22] In the late 1990s, a mere 3 percent of America's humanitarian aid budget was distributed by the Pentagon, but that proportion had risen to 22 percent between 1998 and 2008, and the Pentagon, being the Pentagon, wasn't using it for purposes that might commonly be called "humanitarian." In Liberia, for example, the Pentagon spent $50 million training 2,000 soldiers. "What good does this do?" one might ask. The answer, whether you're the Pentagon or China, is "a great deal." According to William D. Harting, arms control specialist for the New America Foundation, "That is surely a quick and easy way to cement alliances."[23]

The amount of military aid, both purely financial and also for training purposes, given by the United States to a lucky few African countries (ones considered "strategic") in the Saharan belt more than trebled from 1997 to 2008. From 2002 to 2008 the Pentagon dispersed $500 million to Mali, Chad, Niger, and Mauritania to help these countries build up their border security. Between 2002 and 2008, the U.S. International Military and Training Program (IMET) spent $10 million training African personnel. Precise sales figures for Africa, however, are as difficult to obtain from private American companies as from their competitors overseas.

It is no coincidence that international criticism of China over its arms trade has become more outspoken since the Chinese gained a foothold in this expanding market. In 1998, the world managed to spend only $745 billion on armaments manufacturing, but by 2006 this figure had doubled, reaching levels not seen since the cold war. Of these sales, the United States was responsible for 46 percent, and France, the United Kingdom, and Japan accounted for 4–5 percent each. These proportions remained fairly static for a while, but the new and more disturbing figure—if you're a Western arms manufacturer or an African—is that China's exports are catching those of Japan and the Europeans.

China's attitude toward arms trading is a complex one. It's not content merely to sell arms or to use them as bargaining chips: It wants to share its knowledge and know-how, too. China has military agreements with forty-three African countries, and between 2001 and 2006, leaders of the Chinese army went to Africa thirty times.

Take Egypt, for example, itself the recipient of many of these high-level visits. Military cooperation between China and Egypt has grown apace. In 2005, Beijing gave its Egyptian friends permission to produce its K-8E training planes, which can, if required, be adapted for combat roles.

In the five years from 2001 to 2006, China presided over 110 such bilateral strategic consultations, and this involvement has been increasing. Chinese military instructors are being sent all over the continent, magnanimously offering advice to the likes of Ethiopia and Egypt.

China's growing interest in UN peacekeeping missions to African countries reflects its investment there of both financial and political capital. Four of the six countries with which China maintains high-level relations—Algeria, Nigeria, Sudan, and Egypt—are also countries from which it buys oil. It is fair to say, as it is often fair to say of peacekeepers, that there has been a self-interest motivating China's involvement in the six peacekeeping operations in which it has taken part: against terrorism, gun and drug trafficking, and organized crime in the Ivory Coast, Liberia, the Democratic Republic of the Congo, Eritrea, and Western Sahara. Only modest numbers of Chinese troops were dispatched—a few dozen observers and soldiers at most—but it's a start, for as China insinuates itself more and more thoroughly into Africa, it must also deal with all the problems faced by the previous colonial masters.

In addition, China has, officially and unofficially, had to confront hostile rebels in Ethiopia, Niger, and Nigeria, and it looks very much as if Sudan will soon be added to this list. Indeed, in the last days of October 2008, five Chinese oil workers were killed by rebels there.

Chinese officials are more used to red carpets and photo opportunities with heads of state than to negotiating with rebels out in the bush, but they've learned on the job. A number of signs suggest that China is even willing to reconsider its policy on troop deployment. Its policy so far has been simple: It doesn't "do" troop deployment. For the moment, however, Beijing finds it more convenient to use mercenaries—or "private defense contractors," as they're now known—to protect its interests at its many infrastructure projects, as it has done already in Sudan, with 5,000 men guarding the country's oil pipelines.

Whether it likes it or not, China's policies on military intervention are beginning to resemble the policies of the former European colonial powers. China appears increasingly willing to support repressive African regimes and rebellions alike, and to profit from the resulting chaos by selling weapons and improving its access to natural resources. All Beijing's posturing, its talk of "ethics" and the rest, seems merely cosmetic, a way of presenting itself as a responsible, benevolent ally of the suppressed that refuses to get involved in conflicts so as to arbitrate disinterestedly and secure the pax Sinica. It's nothing but a public relations exercise, and if you doubt it, just go and ask one of the Chadian rebels who were so effectively hung out to dry when they tried to depose Déby with, they thought, Chinese support.

• • •

Two years later, in February 2008, the same haphazard collection of FUC rebel factions tried again, this time with three times as many men. Once more, they dashed into Chad from Sudan and made a beeline for N'Djamena and were now not to be misled by the locals; they knew precisely where they were going and went straight to the presidential palace.

Once again, with China's interests aligned with Déby's, and with France's continued support, the president clung to power.

Chapter 9

Gaining Ground in Sudan

> Thank you for your visit and your support of the
> Merowe Dam Project.
>> —*Sign in Chinese and English at the entrance to the
>> work site that forced 50,000 farmers off their land*
>
> We're sorry for the inconvenience.
>> —*Addition to the Arabic version*

"Chinese farmers in Sudan? You're joking! There's no such thing."

Draped in white from head to toe and slumped in a soft leather armchair, Youssef Ahmed Osman, editor of *El Hayat (Life),* was uncharacteristically energetic in his denial. We'd shown him a story from the Chinese news wire about the fabulous success of Zhang Fenghua, thirty-three, who arrived in Sudan in 2001 and has become the most successful foreign vegetable farmer in the country. "If there were any Chinese in our countryside, I'd know, believe you me!"

So we went to the Chinese embassy in Khartoum, to knock on the tiny little door in its great white wall and see if we could find out more about this Zhang Fenghua. The door didn't open, but the intercom crackled to life and a metallic voice was happy to help.

"So talk to our news agency, Xinhua. Follow the wall."

We followed the advice, and the wall, and after a couple of hundred yards we came to another tiny door in the great white wall. It gave the impression of being firmly locked. We pressed the doorbell and heard nothing but a dog howling, so we pressed it again. We weren't sure it was working. It had that look about it that malfunctioning doorbells sometimes have. Not everyone recognizes it, but we had become experts at getting no reply. We gave the bell a few more presses and the door an exasperated thump. Perhaps the bell had been wired up to the dog, for it kept howling, and suddenly a man poked his head out. He looked annoyed. Perhaps it was *his* dog.

"We're all very busy," he snapped. "I'm a diplomat *and* a journalist, so why don't you go and bother someone else? Go ask your question at one of our other offices in Port Sudan, Geili, or Juba." There ensued a stony silence, but we must have had the expressions of people willing to torture dogs for as long as it took because eventually he said, "Hold on," disappeared. Then he came back with a phone number scribbled on a scrap of card: "Ask for Miss Lin."

Miss Lin, it turns out, is a nineteen-year-old from Shandong Province, a place famous for Tsingtao beer. She's fluent in English and tells us that she'll meet us at the University of Khartoum, where she's studying Arabic. And so we find her, the campus's aging brickwork so redolent of the British Empire. Her pert teenaged looks make her easy to identify among the veils.

"My father runs a company in Halfaya, fifteen minutes from Khartoum," she says. "I'd be happy to take you, but he's away at the moment."

Perhaps she can help us with something else, then. A young Sudanese friend of ours, Muhammad, arrives to give us some good news. "One of my uncles rents his land to some Chinese. It's an hour away, and I've brought my car. Shall we go?"

We will need a translator. We look at Miss Lin.

"*Insh'allah,*" she smiles. Muhammad laughs, and we hit the road.

. . .

A few green shoots are visible among the dry, withered stalks. Land punctuated only by the occasional date palm stretches to the horizon in every direction. It's three in the afternoon, and a thermometer, hanging in the shade by the small farmhouse, informs us that it's 120 degrees Fahrenheit. Du Fujun and Chao Baoguo see us looking at the thermometer and open the gate without hesitation. We head to the bare concrete block that is the dormitory.

Du and Choa, both forty-three, work for Wei Feng, a farming business based in Henan Province that has twenty such employees on this farm.

"But we're expecting a lot more," Chao assures us. There's a pause, during which we take in our surroundings: Two beds and a rickety ceiling fan of the sort that Vietnam veterans would find familiar. A TV in the corner that has been wired up to receive CCTV—Chinese government television—via satellite. We sit down on two plastic chairs next to a Mickey Mouse dresser, leaving Miss Lin to sit on the comparative softness of the bed. The thermometer outside is having an easy time of it, for the fan simply makes sure that every part of the room is equally, unbearably hot. What have these people been doing for eight years, stuck in this furnace, working this land, which seems to interest most people only in terms of what's under it? What is Mickey Mouse doing here?

The first question, at least, must be written all over our faces. Chao tries to explain.

"It's hard here. There's not enough water."

"What about beer?" we ask. "Do you get any of that?"

We're not dropping hints. Our interest is purely ethnographic in nature. It doesn't matter to us whether they have a six-pack of ice-cold

Kronenberg, beads of condensation dripping slowly into the crushed ice in which they're embedded. Alcohol is illegal in Sudan, where the laws are based on Sharia.

"We sometimes get a little beer," confess the farmers, one stroking his beard and glancing yet again at Miss Lin. Whatever they have been doing in this godforsaken dump for eight years, these two men have not been doing it in the company of a fresh-faced nineteen-year-old girl; that much is clear. Both Du and Chao are married, with two children each, but they get to see their families only "when the company allows us to go home." That's once every other year.

We ask them what the forty-odd local laborers on the farm are like.

Chao drags his gaze back to us. "Well, they pray five times a day. That, um, surprised us at first . . . "

His comrade interjects, "Why not just say they're lazy?" Chao doesn't contradict him.

Neither man speaks a word of Arabic, and the laborers wouldn't be laborers if they spoke Mandarin. Gesticulation is their only means of communicating. We change the subject.

"What do you grow?"

Chao's attention has wandered again. He has to look very closely at Miss Lin if he's to understand her translation properly. "Eh?"

Du answers for him. "Chinese vegetables. Hard to grow in Sudan."

"Do the Sudanese like Chinese vegetables?"

Du's attention has wandered, too.

"Do the Sudanese like Chinese vegetables?"

Miss Lin translates. Silence.

"Eh?" Chao comes to his senses. "Oh, um . . . No! No, no, no! We don't sell them to the *Sudanese!* We sell our produce to the Chinese who live here."

"We have a lot of fellow countrymen in Sudan," Miss Lin volunteers. The count varies anywhere between 10,000 and 60,000. Enough, either way, for a Chinese basketball league in Khartoum. The Chinese also have their own travel agency and a supermarket with imported food, the Zijing center.

Because the Chinese in Sudan shy away from local food, growing Chinese vegetables can be highly profitable. "In Henan, we earned 2,000 yuan ($300) a month. Here, we can make ten times that!" say the two farmers, slapping their thighs. "Chinese workers building the cement factory in Berber, up north, drive three hundred miles to buy vegetables in Khartoum," Muhammad tells us by way of explanation.

China has found it in its interests to grease the wheels in Khartoum, and to that end it has invested $15 billion in just ten years in almost every sector of the economy. It has built most of the Sudan's oil infrastructure, including a 1,000-mile pipeline that pumps the black gold from the southwest of the country all the way to Port Sudan on the Red Sea, and another, only marginally shorter, running from the Melut Basin in the southeast to join the first near Khartoum. The wheel greasing also runs to three-quarters of a billion dollars to upgrade the international airport, another hundred million for the textile industry, and further funds to develop the fishing industry. Moreover, China wins a great many of the infrastructure projects, such as the Chinese Engineering Works' $79-million contract to modernize and expand Port Sudan. Chinese companies are also building pumping stations along the Nile, as well as several new bridges: two north of Khartoum and two to the south of the city on the Blue Nile and White Nile. CMIC, a Hunanese company, has won a $373-million contract to build an aqueduct that will divert water from the Nile at Atbara toward Port Sudan. Apart from the oil contracts, though, the biggest Chinese project is the Merowe Dam on the Nile, built and largely financed by Beijing at a cost of $1.9 billion. But before we go any further, it's well worth noting the circumstances surrounding China's arrival in Sudan.

In 1978, the American multinational Chevron discovered oil—a lot of oil—in the south of the country. On receiving the news of this major new find, the dictator, Gaafar al-Nimeiry, attempted to change the provincial borders of the country with a view to guaranteeing the north access to southern oil supplies. His move led to rebellion in the south in 1983 and the formation of the Sudan People's Liberation Army. This Christian black-African force fought for ten years with the Arab-Muslim Nimeiry regime, which had allied itself with Hassan al-Turabi's Islamists. A year after war broke out, Chevron was forced to suspend its operations. Throughout the war, the U.S. government ratcheted up the pressure on Khartoum, accusing the leadership of all manner of crimes. Finally, in 1996 the United States accused Khartoum of harboring a man with whom the United States had been wanting a word: one Osama Bin Laden, who had been living in Sudan since 1993. In 1997 U.S. president Bill Clinton put in place an embargo against Sudan, provoking the expulsion of Chevron, General Motors, and many other U.S. businesses. General Omar Hassan al-Bashir, who had staged a coup in 1989, was now in a position to accept the help that was being quietly offered by the Chinese. His military/Islamist regime needed help, having proved no more successful in bringing prosperity to the country than in winning the war against the south. China had little to lose by helping and a great deal to gain; since the Tiananmen Square massacre, the government in Beijing had been taking heat from the West, and if there was oil to be had, and the Sudanese needed China's help to get it, then far be it from China to withhold assistance. But, Sudan told China, we've got to win the civil war for starters. Not a problem, said China; perhaps these guns might help.

Back on the farm, so to speak, the temperature has sunk to a relatively breezy 100 degrees. Du and Chao are anxious to show Miss Lin the fields, and so we tag along, too. Just as we're leaving the dorm, Muhammad's uncle, Amin Abdulwahab, runs over, seemingly furious and brandishing a plastic bag. He arrives in front of the two Chinese and continues his yelling, emphasizing the odd point here and there with a flourish of his plastic bag.

"He's already told them," says Muhammad, "not to leave plastic litter around as it damages the land." If the two farmers could understand what Uncle Amin was saying, they'd have to agree with him, since, we were to discover, he's the one with a doctorate in chemistry. Miss Lin offers to translate.

Uncle Amin bends down and comes back up with a handful of earth, holds it in front of the Chinese faces, and lets it pour through his fingers. Du and Chao look at their feet, like schoolboys, waiting for the storm to pass.

"Call this 'earth'? This is *sand*. D'you understand? *Sand!* You keep saying that the soil's no good, but this isn't even soil. It's *sand*. Can you understand what I'm telling you? You have to mix this *sand* with *silt*, or nothing will grow! Understand?" Uncle Amin is exasperated. The two farmers scuttle off.

Amin turns and introduces himself. "I rent out fifteen fedans (acres) to them for $10,000 a year. It's a bargain! But what do they do? What thanks do I get? They just complain about the soil." If the land is cheap, it's because there's an awful lot of it. Sudan is a place with 40 million inhabitants spread over an area four times the size of Texas.

On the way back to Khartoum, Miss Lin and Muhammad chat about the expedition, while refreshing themselves with water bottled in Khartoum by the Chinese. Sitting in the back, Miss Lin is proud of her people's contribution to this country, a country under development that could, she says, be so rich. But proud as she is of her country, she has a confession.

"I feel *free* here. My father lets me go out, I can see my friends whenever I want, go to the movies, or even drive out into the countryside with complete strangers. It's a safe country for a woman."

Muhammad looks up from the driver's seat and addresses her in the rearview mirror. "My father worked in Beijing for a long time when I was young," he says, treating her to a winning smile. "I was there for a year and a half before I went to study in London, and it was in China that I felt free. I loved it there." Was Muhammad discussing the concept of freedom? Or was this a line?

"Hey, Miss Lin," he says suddenly, "do you have an Arabic name?"

"Why?"

"Well, you know, the Chinese often take Christian names to make contact with foreigners easier, so why not an Arabic one? How do you like 'Leila'? Leila's a pretty name."

Miss Lin does not appear receptive to our friend's smooth moves. It's not because she's inundated with friends, though; her life here seems quite lonely. She has three friends in Sudan, all Chinese students. "One of them's a guy called Ma San Fu." She turns to stare out of the window, lost in thought. "He converted to Islam," she tells us with a sigh. It's Friday, the weekend, and remembering this, Miss Lin cheers up. It turns out she's arranged to meet him at the African University, north of the city, where he's studying Arabic and the Koran. "Why don't you come with me?"

Play gooseberry? Us?

This pleases her. "No," she laughs.

We meet Ma San Fu, a handsome twenty-three-year-old, in a halal fast-food place. Although he's Muslim, he isn't dressed as we'd expected. He's wearing jeans, sneakers, and a white T-shirt. He's fascinated by the Koran, which he studied for six semesters in Beijing before coming to Africa for the first time six months ago.

"I can read the Koran, you know," he tells us. This does not sound as boastful as it looks on the page. There's a wistfulness about the man, and the impression we get is that this is his only boast. When he came here, he left behind his peasant father, three brothers, and an unhappy love affair. He now devotes his broken heart to Allah. We ask him if he likes it here.

"It's hot and it's very poor, but the people are friendly."

"He's a little lonely," Miss Lin chips in. "Sometimes he comes over to dinner with my parents."

"Allah allowed us to meet," he confirms.

"What do you like about the Koran?" seems to be a key question to ask, so we ask it.

"The Koran is like medicine for Muslims who are sick, money for the poor, company for the lonely. Allah is there, and they can talk to him."

Born in Shanghai, Mr. Wood has lived in Nigeria since the 1970s, building an empire including hotels, restaurants, construction companies, and factories. Now a Presidential adviser too, he has a police escort to ease his way through Lagos's continual traffic jams. Here, with a member of the Nigerian police that function as his private guard, Wood was on the site of a 544-villa development he was building for Chevron employees near their local headquarters on the Lekki Peninsula. *(Lagos, Nigeria, April 2007)*

Nigerian workers are under Chinese supervision at Federated Steel in Ota, Ogun State. The Chinese technicians must keep up a ferocious work pace and train their charges. Despite the language barrier, they often succeed. *(Lagos, Nigeria, April 2007)*

Dinner with the Association of Chinese Entrepreneurs of Lagos at Mr. Chang, one of the city's many Chinese restaurants. Most of the association's members are very young businessmen, new to Africa, who meet to network and celebrate their growing success. *(Lagos, Nigeria, April 2007)*

A Chinese technician and a Congolese worker at the Bacongo site where Chinese company WIETC is building forty villas for wealthy Congolese. The site previously held hundreds of shacks lived in by locals. *(Brazzaville, Congo-Brazzaville, June 2007)*

At the Bacongo site, two Chinese WIETC employees and their Congolese translator take photos for potential investors back home. *(Bacongo, Congo-Brazzaville, June 2007)*

Mrs. Wood presses the flesh in her five-story, 1,500-seat restaurant, the Golden Gate. Senator and polymath Anthony Mogbonjubola Soetan (second from left) was celebrating his seventieth birthday with three hundred of his nearest and dearest. *(Lagos, Nigeria, April 2007)*

A night watchman at the Jiang Su headquarters located in Lobito, Angola, enjoys the company of a young local woman. Both the Chinese and the Angolans discourage such relationships, and Chinese workers found to be involved with local women are summarily fired and sent home. *(Angola, October 2007)*

Lunch in a canteen near the WIETC building site. These workers are paid about $4.00 a day, half of it needed to cover food and travel. Because of the poor pay and working conditions—they have no contracts and claim they are beaten for the smallest errors—anti-Chinese sentiment is rife. *(Bacongo, Congo-Brazzaville, June 2007)*

Ke Qian Zhang outside his home, formerly the official residence of the German consul. Zhang worked for the Chinese state news agency Xinhua before meeting Jessica Ye in April 2000 and then leaving journalism to take charge of Sicofor, the family timber firm. Sicofor owns over three-quarters of a million hectares of logging concessions in the Congo basin. (*Pointe-Noire, Congo-Brazzaville, June 2007*)

In a matter of minutes, a Sicofor employee fells a supposedly protected, 22-meter-tall moabi tree that took a century to mature. The timber will be loaded onto a truck to Pointe-Noire, shipped to China, and eventually make its way to Europe or the U.S. as furniture or flooring. *(Conkouati National Park, Congo-Brazzaville, June 2007)*

Chua Booan Lee (right) at the timber processing plant he manages for Sicofor. Congolese law states that 80 percent of the country's timber must be processed at plants like this before export, but shipping unprocessed logs directly to China is so profitable that such regulations are widely ignored. *(Pointe-Noire, Congo-Brazzaville, June 2007)*

At one of China International Fund's many projects in the country, a Chinese laborer and his Angolan coworker brave land mines to rebuild a critical Angolan road that was all but destroyed during the civil war. *(Coastal highway between Luanda and Lobito, Angola, October 2007)*

Chinese and Angolan employees of TEC, a Chinese construction firm, weld rails for the Luanda-Malanje railroad. This stretch runs between the bustling Luanda harbor on one side and the infamous Boavista slum on the other. *(Luanda, Angola, October 2007)*

Zambia's Victoria Falls and the Great Wall of China are uneasy companions in a montage commissioned by copper giant China Nonferrous Metal Mining for the front of its headquarters. *(Chambishi, Zambia, June 2008)*

Wang Xin (right) is one of the men responsible for Chambishi's special economic (free trade) zone in the heart of Copperbelt Province. The two men beside him are part of a delegation inspecting the plan's implementation. Wang Xin's job is made difficult by frequent strikes among the underpaid Zambian workers; their protests have been met with violence by Chinese security personnel. *(Chambishi, Zambia, June 2008)*

At a Chinese base camp, prefabricated homes provide temporary lodgings for some of the many Chinese working on the country's East-West Highway. Here, a CITIC-CRCC employee tries to bar our way despite our Algerian governmental passes; the site, he maintains, is Chinese territory. *(Khemis El Khechna compound, Mitidja Plain, Algeria, July 2007)*

"Would you like to get married and settle here for good?"

He thinks about this briefly. "Yes," he says, "but to a Chinese Muslim." Miss Lin's smile fades, and it is her turn to look wistful.

Ma San Fu has to leave us, he tells us: It is prayer time. As he leaves, he greets the owner warmly, a Sudanese man who answers him in Mandarin. When Ma San Fu has gone, the owner sees the surprise on our faces. "I spent five years in Guangdong Province on business," he chuckles. The city abounds with similar stories; it seems as if there's nobody here who isn't in some way connected to China.

• • •

On the morning of Monday, June 11, 2007, we waited for Bernard Kouchner to begin the press conference. We sat in the heat, and eventually the Frenchman turned up, his teeth gritted and his jaw grinding. He looked as if he'd had a tough week. In the days before he became foreign minister, he used to say that everyone would really get to see what he was made of if he was in charge of Darfur. Then, as soon as the new right-wing French president, Nicolas Sarkozy, made him, a socialist, the unexpected head of the Foreign Office, he headed to Darfur. His sense of urgency is well-founded: 200,000 dead and 2 million refugees.

In order to get aid to the refugees, Kouchner suggested what he calls a "humanitarian corridor" protected by a mixed UN–African Union force. The previous day, he'd gotten a tentative go-ahead from the Chadian president, Idriss Déby. Déby's permission was qualified, and the qualifications were set to be discussed at the international conference on Darfur in Paris on June 25. It was yet another well-considered, well-meant initiative doomed to failure, a failure brought about by the fact that Saudi Arabia, Egypt, and Libya were also, simultaneously, preparing their own peace initiatives. So busy are the four parties in their quest for peace that they're unlikely to find the time to sit around a table and talk to one another. That morning Kouchner's plan seemed, like everything else, to be being buried in the sand. His

Sudanese opposite number, Lam Akol, suggested that perhaps the Paris conference was "ill timed," and that there were already "too many Darfur initiatives." He told Kouchner, "We don't want any distractions."

During four long years of war, the regime of President Omar Hassan al-Bashir has blown hot and cold over this issue of peace, has made promises and then broken them, has given the occasional ray of hope and then brutally extinguished each one.

It is true that Chinese interests have benefited from the war in Darfur, but contrary to popular belief, China had nothing to do with starting the conflict; it has been content, rather, merely to take advantage of it, to do business and to veto any proposed international intervention in Darfur. Ahead of the Beijing 2008 Olympics, however, its position has evolved.

The war in Darfur began in the spring of 2003. In April of that year, the rebel group that came to be known as the Sudan Liberation Movement announced that it had taken Al Fashir, the capital of Darfur. The Justice and Equality Movement, dedicated to bring together Islamists disappointed by al-Bashir's presidency, soon joined the insurrection. While this was happening in the south, to the north the Darfur Liberation Front took control of the city of Gulu. Very quickly, the rebellion seemed to involve every one of the African (as opposed to Arab) tribes, even if this is a false distinction, given that both sides contain Muslim, black, and Arab-speaking people.

The reasons for all this are not new to history: There's oil in Darfur, or so they say. The province is the size of France, and in the south of it are Chinese-owned drilling concessions. But the oil reserves have not yet been exploited and are only in part the cause of the conflict; disputes stretching back to the civil war and Darfur's precarious relationship with both the government and the Sudan People's Liberation Army contribute to the conflict.

The Darfur tribes, which supplied Khartoum with the majority of its fighters in the war against the south, realized that they had been fooled by the government. In 2001, Khartoum and John Garang, the southern leader, signed a draft agreement in Nairobi to end the conflict and divide the oil "pie," once again neglecting Darfur, which is literally translated the "House of Fur," which lacked everything from schools and hospitals to electricity and clean water. The ancient and ongoing struggle for access to wells and grazing among nomadic and sedentary groups is often perceived as the main reason for the violence, but this, too, is simply popular opinion and myth. According to Gérard Prunier, an expert on the region based in Ethiopia, "This cliché, like all clichés, contains an element of truth," but it doesn't, he says, stand up to scrutiny.[1] How does one explain, for example, that the large-scale abuses currently occurring are incomparably greater than any in the past and cannot possibly be the work of traditional nomadic herdsmen?

In fact, right from the very beginning, Khartoum has been sending its air force to bomb the province, while on the ground it has utilized the services of local militias—the infamous Janjaweed. The Janjaweed, equipped with Chinese-made weapons, among others, had carte blanche to pillage, and very quickly the situation descended into a humanitarian tragedy, a tragedy long ignored by the international community. In early 2004 at least one highly placed UN official made a reference to "ethnic cleansing," but it wasn't until April 7, 2004, and the commemoration of the Rwandan genocide that UN Secretary-General Kofi Annan called for international intervention. It was a call that would go unanswered. Two months later, in July, the U.S. Congress, alongside U.S. secretary of state Colin Powell, uttered the word *genocide,* which led to UN threats of further sanctions of Sudan. The rhetoric and threats continued for another year, and only in March 2005 was the situation in Darfur, with its death toll approaching 180,000, referred to the International Criminal Court (a course of action initially vetoed by the Chinese when it came before the Security Council). As for the United States, it retreated from its definition of *genocide* and the moral imperative of intervention that went with it; the experts doubted that Khartoum was deliberately targeting a specific ethnic group by official policy, even if its subcontracting of large-scale slaughter produced the same results. No doubt the fact that Sudan had been an ally in the "war on terror" since 2002 wasn't far from the minds of these legal experts as they drew their conclusions.

American popular awareness of the situation didn't really begin until May 2006, when George Clooney, following an episode of the TV show *ER* featuring Darfur, appealed to the UN Security Council. On May 10, 108 members of Congress called on China for the first time to apply appropriate pressure to its ally, Sudan. The letter to which these members affixed their signatures even went so far as to hint at a threat of boycotting the 2008 Olympic Games in Beijing. The tactic seemed to work, for the next day Beijing announced that it had appointed a special representative for Africa, Liu Guijin, a high-ranking diplomat who had previously headed the Africa section of the Chinese Foreign Office from 1998 to 2001. It seemed as if the threat to China's reputation, as a member of the Security Council and an Olympic host, was enough to make it take the Sudan situation seriously.

All this Clooney-inspired hard work went for nothing, however. In August 2006 the Security Council passed Resolution 1706, sending 17,300 blue helmets in a mixed UN–African Union force to Darfur to relieve the 7,000 overwhelmed African Union (AU) peacekeepers already there. Khartoum, to judge by its reaction, was neither intimidated nor impressed; relations became even more acrimonious, and on October 23 Jan Pronk, special representative of the secretary-general and head of mission for the UN Mission in Sudan, was expelled from Sudan. Over that month and the next, the crisis spread to Chad and the Central African Republic, where refugee camps were attacked and pillaged and the occupants raped and massacred.

By early January 2007 the number of such refugees had reached 2 million, representing nearly a third of the entire population of Darfur. The same month, the UN Security Council's assessment mission produced its report, accusing Khartoum of having "orchestrated and participated in" war crimes and crimes against humanity. For a short while it looked as though China's support of the regime might have consequences—consequences in the area that would hurt it the most: the Olympics. In March the actress Mia Farrow took up the cause and called for a boycott of the Beijing Olympics. She published a piece in the *Wall Street Journal* likening the events in Africa to the Holocaust and expressing her regret that artists such as Steven Spielberg—a consultant for the Olympic Games' opening and closing ceremonies—were helping to embellish the Chinese regime's image. "Does Mr. Spielberg really want to go down in history as the Leni Riefenstahl of the Beijing Games?" she asked.[2] In France, two of the three presidential candidates, Ségolène Royal and François Bayrou, also called for a boycott. A few days later the White House added its weight to the argument, publishing thirty-one publicly listed Sudanese companies with which Americans were henceforth forbidden to trade. But all three efforts were wasted, for the Olympic ceremonies went off without a hitch (despite Spielberg's eventual abandonment of his mandate). Nothing, from China's actions in Tibet to its support of the Burmese regime, could cast a shadow over the Olympics.

International opinion did have some limited effect. Beijing announced that it was prepared to participate in a Darfur peace mission, leading to Khartoum's accepting, at least on paper, the deployment of 20,000 soldiers and 6,000 police in the form of a UN-AU hybrid force (UNAMID). Further, the nomination of a Chinese special representative for Africa also indicated that China was going to restore not only peace in Sudan but also its international image. As we made our curious way along the Nile, we found out exactly how.

· · ·

The lobby of the Taka Hotel in Khartoum was unusually lively. It's not exactly buzzing at the best of times, and one o'clock in the morning is considered by regulars among the worst of times. The capital has little to offer in the way of entertainment, and we were usually fast asleep by then, but that night the place was positively crowded—if it's true that "three's a crowd."

"Hey you, over there! Which paper do you write for?"

We stared at the speaker blankly. As expressions go, the blank one has been among our most often used, usually when we're not sure what any other reaction would provoke. Luckily the man seemed friendly; he smiled widely and introduced himself as a fellow journalist, from Pakistan. He jerked a thumb at the others. "The two mustachioed guys are with Iranian TV." The mustaches nodded. "Khartoum's packed with foreign journalists, you know! So! Are you going on the cruise tomorrow?"

We'd not been there long enough to have seen all these other journalists and had to admit that we were a little surprised. Obtaining Sudanese visas for journalists is no mean feat, and we had been pretty proud of ourselves for having managed to get "visitor visas," but we soon got an explanation. The Sudanese government had invited thirty journalists from all over the world to come visit for a week. The previous day they had all been to Darfur: a flight to Al-Fashir, a ceremonious greeting at the airport by local bigwigs, a good deal of handshaking and speech making, followed by lunch and a display of traditional Sudanese dancing; back on the plane and off south to Nyala for more handshaking and speech making, a slickly organized tour of a model refugee camp, and then back on the plane to the capital.

The next morning, the itinerary centered on a cruise on the Blue Nile on a heavily guarded Chinese boat equipped with two decks and all the mod cons, including a Filipino crew. The journalists themselves were from all over: Malaysia, the United Arab Emirates, South Africa, Kenya, Algeria, Pakistan, Iran, Italy—even a pair from ABC in the United States, kitted out in identical safari gear. We settled in among them and the Interior Ministry's MC, the latter dressed immaculately in white and sipping hibiscus tea. We were treated first to a concert to welcome us and then went out on deck for some air.

Leaning on the rails in the bow, we took in the scenery as it washed by. From this vantage point, it was almost possible to watch the city's metamorphosis as it happened in real time. Sticking up through the canopy of the oldest buildings were ultramodern ones, such as the al-Fatih Hotel, a nineteen-story, $80-million, egg-shaped present from Muammar el-Qaddafi. "It looks more like a grenade," observed the Algerian standing next to us.

Next to this "grenade" and in front of al-Bashir's presidential palace, shutters closed against the sun, an off-white building stretched off downriver. The plot on which it stood was lined with trees, above which four giant letters stared down: *CNPC*. This, then, was the headquarters of the most important Chinese oil company in the country.

Having soaked up enough of this richly varied architecture, we headed back inside just as a gourmet lunch was being served, which we ate to the accompaniment of local songs, more specifically, traditional Darfuri songs. The atmosphere, had it not been for the armed guards scattered about, could almost have qualified as jovial. After lunch we had the epiphany shared by anyone who's ever been on a cruise: If you're not eating, drinking, or sleeping, there's precious little to do. We headed off to the stern to see if things looked different from there and were pleasantly surprised. We passed two mighty pillars of the new Chinese-built bridge at al-Mugran, where the White and Blue Niles converge. It is here that the government plans to build a futuristic city, redolent with insane large-scale projects that will rival those currently under way in the Persian Gulf. The Arkeweet area, with its palatial Salam Rotana Hotel and its unnaturally green lawns all around, will look like a miniature version of Dubai, though for the moment it was surrounded only by sand.

Not far from the Rotana, the well-to-do can indulge in a spot of shopping at the Afra Mall, an ultramodern, California-inspired Turkish mall stuffed with Western goodies. Only the 4x4s of the World Food Program lined up in the parking lot served to remind us where we were.

As the world focuses its attention on Darfur, the Sudanese capital, spurred on by Chinese and Arab investment, is undergoing an economic boom. The beggars and refugees who line the streets must make way for the many luxury cars that glide around, ferrying the nouveaux riches from one place to another. At the Ozone Café, an ice cream parlor famous for its gardens and outdoor air conditioning, the wealthy youth of Khartoum flirt over grapefruit-and-grenadine cocktails. In 2006, Sudan received the second largest amount of foreign investment of any African country. That year it got $5 billion, fueling a growth rate that leapt from 9 to 13 percent just a year later.

$\cdots$

The next morning the hotel lobby was once again crowded with unlikely figures, this time French pilots flanked by their technicians, all of them acutely uncomfortable coming face-to-face with French-speaking journalists. They weren't happy about speaking at all while we were within earshot, let alone answer questions, but we managed to elicit a rough outline of their mission. They had come to carry out aerial reconnaissance of the Merowe site, the African version of the Three Gorges Dam built two hundred kilometers north of Khartoum by the Chinese, in conjunction with the French firm Alstom, the German Lahmeyer, and the Swiss-Swedish ABB.

The Merowe Dam has been nothing more than a dream since it was first conceived of in 1943, when Sudan was under Anglo-Egyptian control. The project hobbled along going nowhere fast until independence, and it was then shelved while the country tore itself to bits over three decades of civil war, coups, and clan infighting. The plans were dusted off in 1992 when al-Tourabi came to power, but the World Bank refused to provide the necessary funding, citing environmental reasons. Then, in 1997, the first round of sanctions against Sudan seemed likely to kill the dam once and for all, until China offered to build it and even to pay for most of it.[3] The China Water Resources and Hydropower Construction Group (Sinohydro) proposed a structure two hundred feet high and nearly a mile long capable of generating 1.25 gigawatts, or half the country's total power demand. Work began in 2000 and—thanks to the 5,000 Chinese workers—opening ceremonies took place on March 4, 2009.

The road north to Merowe is also the one leading to Port Sudan, running alongside the pipeline and the Nile. Not far down this road from Khartoum, the landscape becomes parched, endless sands strewn with mounds of rock blackened as if charred by the sun. The journey is not entirely void of curiosities, however, such as the imposing pyramids of the famous black pharaohs of the Upper Nile or, indeed, the road itself, which was planned and laid out by the world's most sought-after man. A refugee in Sudan in 1993, Osama Bin Laden, who went by the title "The Engineer," wanted to thank President al-Tourabi for his hospitality by building a new road that would link the capital and Port Sudan and would be 250 miles shorter than the existing 750-mile road. Hang a left off the highway to al-Matig and you get to the village where the man lived in hiding. While he was there, one of the very few visitors he received was the British journalist Robert Fisk,[4] to whom he confided his ambition to build a whole network of roads in Sudan. When he fled with his three wives to Afghanistan in 1996 after organizing attacks on U.S. bases in Saudi Arabia, the road was far from complete, but Chinese companies moved in, finishing the job and even now planning a railway to run alongside it for a cool $1.2 billion.

Three hours' drive after the turnoff to al-Matig the road and the pipeline sheer off to the right toward Port Sudan and the Red Sea. To the left, a side road snakes toward Merowe, but those with no business there are quickly brought to a halt and turned back. Those who are allowed down the road will eventually come to the site perimeter and gates, next to which is a sign, in English and Chinese, that reads, "Thank you for your visit and support of the Merowe Dam Project." The Arabic version is annotated thus: "We're sorry for any inconvenience."

This apology is unlikely to provide comfort to the 50,000 Nubian peasants who've been dispossessed to make way for the 110-mile-long reservoir that the dam will create. One of the few independent experts to have visited the region, French researcher Jean-Gabriel Leturcq,[5] with whom we later met up in Cairo, showed us photographs he took in 2006 of villages before and after their inhabitants were evicted. The photos showed razed houses, and palm groves either uprooted or burned so as to destroy any hope of return. "After a desperate opposition, the residents came together in the Movement of the Displaced in order to obtain some meaningful compensation for their losses," Leturcq told us. "The agreement promised each family a new house, and for every acre lost, nice new ones in the resettlement zone. Owners of date palms were also promised $250 for each mature tree lost." It was a reasonable offer from the government, he told us, "but the displaced were deceived. Most of the new houses were never built, and the land offered in compensation was often barren." As for the money, only a third was actually paid out. The other two-thirds, it is said, will be paid on the dam's completion, and in Sudanese pounds, a highly volatile currency. Every time the Nubians tried to demonstrate against their treatment, the repercussions were bloody; the leader of the movement himself only narrowly survived an assassination attempt. To the authorities, the movement was a threat—several thousand men ready to fight because they had, as had been intended, nothing left for which to hope. The Chinese, however, weren't scared. What threat could 50,000 farmers pose when back home the Three Gorges Dam had displaced 1.3 million people?

Perhaps Africans are less easily subdued. Whatever the reason, sometimes just a few hundred Africans, if determined and well armed, are enough to decide the fate of nations. These men were a possible new northern front threatening Khartoum, in addition to the old fault line in the south, which could open up again at any time, and the one in the east, in Darfur. From 2006, the government and the dam authority would be on the alert, and Chinese militiamen would keep watch over the site in addition to the 7,000 already guarding the pipeline.[6]

So there are Chinese to drill the oil and then pump it into the Chinese pipeline guarded by Chinese strongmen on its way to a port built by the Chinese, where it is loaded onto Chinese tankers headed for China. Chinese laborers to build the roads and bridges and the gigantic dam that has displaced tens of thousands of smallholders; Chinese to grow Chinese food so other Chinese need eat only Chinese vegetables with their imported Chinese staples; Chinese to arm a government committing crimes against humanity; and Chinese to protect that government and stick up for it in the UN Security Council.

In December 2007, three months after we had left Sudan, we went back to Beijing. There we approached a high-level official in the Africa section at the imposing Ministry of Foreign Affairs and asked whether the Chinese presence in Sudan did not betray by its very scale the Chinese principle of noninterference in the domestic affairs of another country. We asked if China would not end up making enemies in places like Sudan and its neighbors, against whom China will one day have to defend its interests.

"Not a bit," the official replied. "We apply our principle of noninterference very strictly, and in the context of mutually beneficial cooperation and with the greatest respect for the local populations. And if we use our great influence, it is with the best of intentions."

• • •

Less than a year later we had proof to the contrary. As 2008 came to a close, as we were preparing the U.S. edition of this book, the UNAMID forces in Darfur numbered barely 10,000 soldiers, and the force was struggling to assemble the essential military and logistical contributions. Under attack, these soldiers were taking casualties, and it was fast becoming clear that they were underequipped for the great scale of the Darfur disaster. The same was true of the European force (EUFOR). On January 28, 2008, the European Union's foreign ministers had approved the sending of 3,700 men, of which 2,100 were French, for Operation EUFOR CHAD/RCA. They were to be deployed for a year as a supplement to the UN-AU force and to protect "endangered civilians" in the refugee camps. But even this, the biggest military contingent ever coordinated by the EU, was to be delayed by a new assault; Chadian rebels crossed the border from Darfur and arrived in N'Djamena on February 2.

Over the period stretching from June 2007 to October 2008, the various peace initiatives had, essentially, little effect. On top of the attack on N'Djamena came an offensive launched from Darfur on Khartoum itself. On May 10, 2008, fifteen hundred men from the Justice and Equality Movement, having covered hundreds of miles in 150 vehicles, seized the city of Omdurman, which is as close to Khartoum as Newark, New Jersey, is to New York City. They captured the airport and the suburbs, and they were moving on toward the center in order to overthrow the regime entirely before they were finally brought to a halt. The scare, rather than provoking a rethinking by the al-Bashir government, provoked instead a ferociously bloody counterattack.

On July 14, 2008, the prosecutor of the International Criminal Court (ICC), Luis Moreno-Ocampo, accused President al-Bashir of genocide, crimes against humanity, and war crimes. This was the first time a sitting head of state had been charged. Subsequently, three judges from the ICC set about deciding whether to issue an arrest warrant, though their deliberations were cut off by the following events.

In late July, when the Security Council's UNAMID mandate needed to be renewed, Libya and South Africa succeeded in inserting an amendment into Resolution 1828 specifying that "certain members of the African Union" were concerned about the possible consequences of legal proceedings in The Hague. These "certain members" said they thought that al-Bashir's prosecution would impede the pursuit of peace. The president of the AU at the time, the Tanzanian Jakaya Kikwete, relayed the message that his organization would support "postponing the indictment." Of course—though Kikwete's phrase seems callous, it is certainly valid—the possible consequences that so worried these "certain members" had less to do with peace in Darfur than with the prosecution's setting a worrying precedent: They didn't like the idea that heads of state might be held account-able for their actions.

Appealing to the "Olympic Spirit," China asked to be trusted by the world for the sake of the Beijing Games. For Darfur, that trust was fatal. Barely a week after the games ended, in early September, the Sudanese regime launched a major offensive in northern Darfur. In just ten days, twenty villages were razed.

That September, analysis would show that the situation in Darfur was worse than it had ever been. The United Nations Office for the Coordination of Human Affairs (OCHA) in Geneva cited 4.3 million victims in Darfur, of whom 2.4 million were internally displaced. Nearly 190 humanitarian convoys—largely from the World Food Program—had been intercepted and the drivers kidnapped. The OCHA also counted about a hundred attacks on humanitarian cen-ters, as well as dozens of dead and wounded among the UNAMID forces. The commander of those forces, a Nigerian named Martin Agwai, summed it up succinctly on CNN in July 2008. "We are a peacekeeping force," he said, "but there is no peace to keep."[7]

Adding insult to grievous injury, the British and French also col-luded in torpedoing the ICC's prosecution of al-Bashir. In early Sep-tember, Bruno Joubert, the new "Mr. Africa" to French president Nicolas Sarkozy, went to Sudan. According to the *Sudan Tribune,* Jou-bert promised to support a deferment of prosecution,[8] information that was confirmed ten days later as Paris and London prepared to have the proceedings in the ICC suspended—probably planning to re-sume lucrative Total and BP operations in Sudan. But in vain—in March 2009, the ICC ordered the arrest of Omar al-Bashir, charging him with war crimes and crimes against humanity.

Chapter 10

Oil Above All

> We must simultaneously be cautious, smart and quick to act if we are to procure the spoils of that magnificent cake, Africa.
>
> —*King Leopold II of Belgium, 1877*

It's all very well, this intrepid-reporter-braves-terrible-danger-to-discover-the-truth thing, but occasionally you have to wonder why you do it. There are many reasons. John Le Carré was fairly honest about it. "Sometimes you do it to save face," he wrote. "Other times you do it because you haven't done your job if you haven't scared yourself to death. Other times again, you go in order to remind yourself that survival is a fluke. But mostly you go because others go: for machismo; and because in order to belong you must share."[1] But even these self-deprecating reflections are calculated to convey a kind of earthy humility, of essentially human camaraderie. They can ring true upon reflection, when, glass in hand, you are seated in a comfortable chair in a familiar bar in the society of friends.

But these are not the philosophies that permeate the mind when it, along with its poor beleaguered body, is being forced out of a car by Sudanese security personnel onto an empty street in the middle of the night. Other, less lofty considerations tend to draw your attention as you find yourself marched into one of Port Sudan's derelict buildings. You don't even have the chance to think, veteran of innumerable hot spots though you may be, that "this rubble-strewn courtyard has very much the aura of one of those rubble-strewn courtyards across which your correspondent will be led to a white cell lit by a solitary, naked lightbulb."

Even if you did manage to entertain such thoughts, you would have little time to congratulate yourself because your hosts, radiating a mixture of supreme confidence and easy menace, are curious fellows and are wondering whether you would satisfy their curiosity and tell them *precisely* what you and your young Chinese accomp— sorry, *friend*—were doing in the restricted zone of the Port Sudan oil terminal. They only ask, really, because, well, you see, the oil terminal is the end of a 1,650-kilometer Chinese-built pipeline carrying oil from the heart of the south's rebel provinces, where some small unpleasantness is currently under way. Unaccountably, you find your mind empty of soul-searching questions surrounding your vocation; you find yourself unable to explain in six grandiloquent phrases quite why you're there.

And then, despite it all, you remember how great everything was just hours before, when you were dawdling over coffee in the Hotel Intercontinental, absently licking a forefinger and dabbing at the crumbs of an excellent breakfast. You had no thoughts then of restricted zones, security personnel, or white rooms in abandoned basements. No thoughts beyond the company of three Chinese men who were in excellent spirits because they had just signed a major contract for their company, Shanghai Zhenhua Port Machinery Company to install cranes at the port's container terminal.

The eldest of the trio, the leader of the delegation, didn't stay long. Another, unable to speak English, repaired upstairs to watch TV, leaving John, the Chinese accompli—sorry, *friend*—to pick over the last

AT10044061

ATG Tickets is one of the leading ticketing companies in the country, managing the ticketing needs for venues and events across the UK and internationally.

Ticket your event with ATG Tickets.
Find out more at www.atgtickets.com/ticketing

ATG AMBASSADOR THEATRE GROUP

The Ambassador Theatre Group is the largest owner/operator of theatres in the UK, an internationally recognised theatre producer and a leader in theatre ticketing services.

Find out more at www.atg.co.uk

heatre Gift Vouchers
he Perfect Gift

ccepted at all Ambassador Theatre Group venues and for all events sold on www.atgtickets.com

Buy yours today at
www.atgtickets.com/giftvouchers

SECURE TICKETS from AUTHORISED RETAILERS™

STAR

Terms and Conditions
A copy of our Terms and Conditions is available at all ATG Box Offices and from our website at www.atgtickets.com/terms

Edinburgh Playhouse, Edinburgh
EH1 3AA

ATG TICKET

Disney Presents

THE LION KING

Fri Oct 11 2013 - 7:30 PM
Balcony R 18

Please be seated by 7:25pm

Mr Robin Campbell

2013-09-12 4:13 PM   Card - Visa

GBP 30.00	Full Price
GBP 0.00	Fee
GBP 30.00	

1865181

This ticket contains a restoration levy of GBP1.00

1865181

of the watermelon slices and to do his duty by the bread and honey. He was wondering aloud, between watermelon pips, what he was going to do with the rest of the day, his last before flying back to Shanghai the following morning.

"What are your plans?" he asked us.

That was a good question. We had been trying to visit the oil terminal for several days, but it hadn't worked out, and we thought that perhaps we would have to content ourselves with a look at the pipeline itself. We had a flight booked that evening so were eager to do at least this much, and perhaps take in a small town called Suakin, which lies on the road that happens to run parallel to the pipe.

Sixty kilometers to the south of Khartoum, Suakin was a fine excuse for innocent tourists such as ourselves to take a drive: Even the irredeemably positive writers of the *Lonely Planet* guide could suggest little else worth visiting. The village itself was abandoned in the 1930s but dates back as far as the fourteenth century, when Venetian merchants recorded visiting the place. It was the major departure point for Ethiopian Christians making their pilgrimages to Jerusalem, and then also for Muslims on their way to Mecca after the Ottomans conquered Suakin in 1517. Ferries still leave from Suakin, running the ancient route across the Red Sea to Jeddah.

We proposed our plan to John. "We thought we might go to Suakin. If you're interested, we've got a driver, Saber, waiting for us in the parking lot."

We didn't have to ask twice. John was in his thirties, a prime example of that generation of Chinese men more interested in discovering what lies beyond the horizon than in conforming and following rules. This was his third voyage overseas but his first visit to Africa, so he wanted to see all he could while he had the chance.

Port Sudan is a low-rise city, an uneven plateau of flat roofs that sag under the oppressive heat atop desert-ocher and sea-green houses. As Saber threaded the car along the streets, the aromas of coffee and ginger wafted through the open windows until we reached the arterial road out of town, clogged with taxis and rickshas. The outskirts stretched interminably, for Port Sudan is rapidly becoming one large industrial sprawl. We passed through the duty-free zone, marked by the lines of tankers parked up along the shore, and then the terminal itself, al-Bashaïr 2, hidden behind dunes that run right up to the sea. We saw signposts leading to various oil facilities bearing names we'd come to think of as familiar, such as PDOC (Petrodar Operating Company), a firm that is currently prospecting for oil in the Nuba Mountains.[2] PDOC's main stockholder is the China National Petroleum Corporation (CNPC),[3] which in turn controls nearly all Sudan's oil and has invested $15 billion in the country. It was Chinese money that developed the oil fields and built the three refineries (not to mention the two pipelines that converge in Khartoum before running down to al-Bashaïr and the awaiting tankers). We had seen the pipeline from our plane on the way in, and from up there it had looked like a snake, half buried in sand, winding its way through the desert; from the ground it looked less impressive, more like a great big metal tube.

At last we arrived at our destination. Suakin is still redolent of its former prestige and boasts some of the oldest extant architecture in Africa. Its glorious history is highlighted somehow by the dilapidated state it's currently in. The coral from which the buildings are made has suffered over centuries of harsh weather, the inhabitants long gone. The only movement is from the Bedouins who have settled near the small fort, selling handmade craft works to the place's few visitors. It was easy, if only for a moment, to imagine the great adventurer Corto Maltese leaning against a pillar, puffing thoughtfully on a cigarette, contemplating the green waters of the Red Sea. In contrast to the coral ghost town and the transitory Bedouin presence were the specters on the horizon: fat-bellied oil tankers, some of the largest man-made objects on earth, crawling along in either direction, some heading up the coast toward the Suez Canal carrying Saudi crude to the Americas, others, loaded with Sudanese crude, going the other way toward the Bab el Mandeb strait between Yemen and Djibouti to continue their journey east bearing 10 percent of China's energy requirements.

Perhaps the word *contrast* isn't the right one. In many ways it was perfectly natural that the past and the present should coexist, not least because the politics surrounding the area haven't changed a great deal over time. The faded inscriptions on the fort's walls were mementos from the second half of the nineteenth century, when the colonial powers were squabbling over the few remaining morsels of "unclaimed" African territory. We told John about the 1898 fiasco when 250 French infantry under the command of Jean-Baptiste Marchand marched from Congo-Brazzaville to a fort at Fachoda in Sudan hoping to take control of the Nile Valley. They were met by the enormous mustaches of Lord H. H. Kitchener (which twitched noticeably on that stiff upper lip) and the 20,000 troops under their command. Kitchener and his mighty whiskers had just been engaged in a spot of Mahdi-army crushing at Omdourman, and the French, after a tense standoff, wisely retreated.

"European partition of Africa has always been bad for Africans," we told him.

John wasn't going to let us Europeans have the monopoly on postcolonial guilt, however. "We do it, too," he said, to our surprise. He was referring to the Chinese demand for ivory that has been behind the African elephants' demise. Somewhere between 6,000 and 12,000 of these rare giants are killed each year in Sudan, Congo-Brazzaville, Chad, and the Central African Republic.[4] "The ivory is loaded up in Port Sudan," he said with evident regret. "It's very sad."

Saber, meanwhile, was unmoved by our self-flagellation, and on our way back to Port Sudan he tried to cheer us up. "I think," he told us, "that I could get you inside the oil terminal. What would you say to that?"

As we approached the terminal he slowed the car and honked a couple of times at the guards. To our great surprise, the guards duly raised the barriers, and we drove straight in. We parked and got out, stepping immediately into an acrid puddle of raw crude that had dripped down from a leak in the pipe. We shuffled about trying to get the stuff off our shoes, muttering to one another that despite the increase in price—and this in the face of the planned rise in Sudanese production from 500,000 barrels a day to 600,000—we would at least be taking some home with us free of charge.

We were still scuffing about when one of the guards approached, not for our immediate arrest but in order to greet his friend, Saber. The man, it turned out, was an engineer at the terminal. He was about fifty years old and was wearing a few days' stubble. He didn't seem particularly curious about our presence and didn't ask any questions. He was even happy to answer some of our own as we snapped away with our cameras. We could hardly ignore the thirty or so tanks nearby. "Each one holds 10,000 tons of oil," he said.

This oil is only a fraction of what's produced in Sudan. The rest is loaded straight onto the tankers about a kilometer to the south of where we were standing, where the pipeline raises its head from the sand and runs out to sea to the tankers anchored in the deep water. As we walked around, we found on one of the redbrick buildings a faded sign, the yellow Shell logo still visible. This British-Dutch company was one of the many that bowed to Western public opinion at the end of the 1980s and early 1990s and packed its bags, leaving the Chinese with a clear run at the target.

That evening, back in the hotel, we were chatting with John while we waited for Saber, who was going to drive us to the airport. When he arrived, he wasn't alone. He had a small but very sinister entourage of security personnel in tow. The hotel staff looked away as the newcomers approached us, finding that they suddenly had a great deal of urgent work to attend to. John, too, understood what was going on.

"Follow us," said the man in charge of the detail. "Don't make a scene." He told us we'd be taken to the police station, a building less than five minutes away. We weren't wholly surprised when we drove straight past it, on the opposite side of the road. We pointed out the station to the chief and asked again where we were headed. He started yelling frantically at us through a translator, who employed a more placatory tone, to the effect that it was all OK and that we weren't to worry.

If you've ever been sailing close to the wind regarding the locals and are unlucky enough to merit attention from the authorities, the best you can hope for is to be handed over to someone of military bearing who'll work himself up into such a fury that he'll quite forget who he is, who you are, and how much money he wants you to hand over. Such men, being military men, are usually prohibited from doing anything too rash because they'll inevitably have superiors somewhere down the hall who'll want to know the reason why. What you *don't* want to see peering at you across the table in such situations is anyone with even a passing resemblance to Dr. No.

The man asking the questions fell into the second category. He was dressed in white from head to toe and exuded a supreme confidence. He wanted to know who we were, where we came from, and whom we worked for. We did our best to explain why we had entered the country on visitors'—as opposed to journalists'—visas, and why we seemed in such a hurry to leave. As we blustered, he took his time inspecting our possessions: cameras, laptops, tape recorders, and phones.

Then John spoke up. He held out his business card, hands outstretched and with a slight bow in the Chinese fashion. His card was accepted and inspected, and our interrogator's expression—much to our surprise—softened a little. The white-clad gentleman couldn't help but know of the Shanghai Zhenhua Port Machinery Company's contract signing the day before. Pressing home his advantage, John simply told the man the truth about our expedition: that we had been killing time in Port Sudan and had visited Suakin, and on the way back our driver had suggested a visit to the terminal; that we had had no idea this driver had been an employee of the company; that we had not befriended him especially; and that he, the driver, had simply wanted to accommodate the wishes of foreign visitors. Dr. No accepted the story. He thanked John for his fulsome and succinct explanation. Case closed.

John's case, that was. Dr. No turned his attention to his captive Westerners.

We looked at him as he weighed us up, hoping we would not be found wanting. There was no way of telling what he would decide.

"We will destroy your photographs," he said. But then he smiled and handed back our passports. "You are always welcome in Sudan," he concluded. A gift horse. A strange and unnerving one, but a gift horse nonetheless. No veterinary dentistry for us. We were quite obsequious in our gratitude, not least for the proffered lift to the airport so that we might catch the flight that all parties knew we had already missed. "I'll come with you," John told us.

It is useless to speculate about what our fate would have been had John not been with us. One thing we knew for certain, though, was that the "special relationship" between the Sudanese and the Chinese had proved wholly beneficial. Beneficial to us, at least.

· · ·

And on this subject, it is very difficult to say for sure which side of the China-Sudan relationship gets the most out of it. In 1995, when Sudan was still harboring Osama Bin Laden, it was labeled by the Clinton administration a "rogue state." The White House ordered the bombing of a factory north of Khartoum that was suspected by the Americans of being involved in the manufacture of chemical weapons. It turned out to have been precisely what it purported to be: a pharmaceutical plant. Making the most of this bad blood, China introduced itself as Sudan's savior, investing heavily in the country, supplying it with weapons, and defending it tirelessly in the UN Security Council whenever the subject of Darfur raised its ugly head.

China is indebted to Sudan, too, however. Sudan is the only place in Africa in which China has been allowed to develop its own oil facilities, a state of affairs about which it is so happy that all of CNPC's managers have been promoted within the Communist Party ranks back in Beijing. China knows that its oil security cannot be left to the whims of foreign governments and speculators: It must be able to *produce* oil overseas rather than simply to *buy* it. Oil security is something that China, like many other powers, takes very seriously.

In 1996, China was the second biggest exporter of oil in the whole of Asia. Only nine years later, however, it had become the second largest importer of oil in the world after the United States. The reason was partly the meteoric rise in the number of cars on Chinese roads. In 1999, there were 3 million cars in the whole country, but nearly three times that number were sold in 2007 alone; some expect car ownership to hit the 100-million mark by 2015. Oil consumption projections are, of course, similarly staggering: By 2020, China expects to have to import between 10 and 15 million barrels per day—twice Saudi Arabia's current total production, and equal to production figures for the whole of Africa.

But spare a thought for the Chinese. When you're at the back of the line when the oil companies are dividing up Africa, getting your fair share can be difficult, particularly when you have no former colonial ties on which to draw. Shell, for example, dug in in Nigeria as long ago as 1938 and raked in a tidy sum from its monopoly there, which lasted until independence in 1960. The French company BRP (Bureau de Recherche de Pétrol) struck oil in Gabon in 1956; this company would develop into the more familiar Elf, which itself later merged with Total, which itself had merged with Fina. The United States wasn't to be left out either, as evidenced by Texaco's presence in Angola, a presence deemed so valuable that Cuban soldiers were sent to protect the company's facilities during the civil war in the 1970s, despite Cuba's having fallen into the Soviet Union's sphere of influence: a highly unusual case of communist soldiers defending the interests of a capitalist multinational. And Africa's importance to the West has only increased in the twenty-first century.

In summarizing this enthusiasm for African oil, John Ghazvinian has noted that "African oil is less expensive and better quality, is more accessible and less dangerous to drill than anywhere else in the world, and every day it looks like there could be more of it."[5] The estimates for African reserves increased 56 percent between 1996 and 2006 compared to a 12 percent rise throughout the rest of the world. Another important point is that the oil fields of exporters such as Saudi Arabia and Russia are closed to outsiders, which is hardly the case in Africa; 30 percent of Total's reserves are there, so Africa is more important to Total than even the North Sea.

All in all, it seems that in the scramble for Africa's oil China is bringing up the rear. One of the things it will have to address if it is to turn this situation around is its lack of expertise when it comes to offshore drilling, something that is particularly important in the deep waters of the Gulf of Guinea. Those in the know consider this to be one of the most promising areas of exploration in the world, one that could replace the Persian Gulf and that might one day account for a quarter of all American imports. The Center for International Policy, an American think tank, has estimated that if the price of a barrel of oil stays around the fifty-dollar mark, then over a trillion dollars in revenues—twice the amount that Africa has received in Western aid in the past fifteen years—could make its way into the coffers of countries along the Gulf of Guinea.[6]

With such a prize at stake, and without many options, China has chosen to use checkbook diplomacy to forge relationships with Africa. This, very broadly, entails the financing of enormous infrastructure projects that buy the goodwill of the ruling elites—sometimes in a direct swap for oil field rights. Beijing favors a unilateral approach, which has produced mixed results, and though the Chinese government claims excellent relations with forty-nine African countries, some relations are decidedly more excellent than others. The list of countries that have received Chinese investment is almost exactly the same as the list of countries that are sitting atop their own oil. Angola has received $8 billion, Nigeria $11 billion, and Sudan $15 billion, nor is it coincidence Congo-Brazzaville has received Chinese money for its dam at Imboulou or that Gabon has also been paid close financial attention by China. China's promise of $12.5 billion to the Democratic

Republic of the Congo (also called Congo-Kinshasa) in September 2007 shows nothing more than that the Chinese value their presence in Africa more than their profits.

For a long time, Angola was where the teamwork between the Chinese state and its oil companies proved most effective. In March 2004 the Exim Bank of China loaned $2 billion at a very generous rate of interest to Luanda to help rebuild the country after twenty-seven years of civil war. At the end of that year the Angolan government exercised its right of what's called *preemption* in order to halt BP's sale of half of Block 18 of the Greater Plutonio field (a block that produced 200,000 barrels a day) to the Indian Oil and Natural Gas Corporation. Angola gave that particular chunk to Sinopec, which subsequently got hold of another block when Total's license was not renewed. In Nigeria, the situation is a little different: 45 percent of the Akpo field, operated by Total and producing 225,000 barrels per day, was in line to be sold to an Indian company for $2 billion, but the Indian parliament blocked the transaction, having decided that the field would be unprofitable. The Chinese company CNOOC (China National Offshore Oil Corporation) is less concerned with profit making and so snapped up the field for $2.3 billion in January 2006.

China's advances in Africa's oil-rich regions have been viewed with concern bordering on paranoia in the United States. In recent years, countless confidential reports, U.S. Senate committees, and think tanks from both political parties have all evoked the image of the "strangulation" of the U.S. oil supply. They have worked the angle of a "war of resources" in Africa that could, it is said, deteriorate into a head-to-head clash between China and the United States, prompting the kind of open conflict that some see as inevitable by 2030. Already the United States has had to go to some lengths to obstruct CNOOC's $18.5-billion offer to buy the California-based UNOCAL, the ninth biggest company in the world. U.S. officials have dusted off the cold war rhetoric and now talk about "containment" of China. In November 2006, the U.S. assistant secretary of state for African affairs, Jendayi

Frazer, proposed a strategy that would draw on the regional powers allied with the United States, anchor states such as Nigeria, Algeria, Ethiopia, and South Africa. Frazer acknowledged that these countries could very well find reasons to align themselves with China; nevertheless, hysteria has eased a little in recent times.

"We should stop acting so alarmed," wrote Erica Downs, a researcher for a U.S. think tank called the Brookings Institution, in the summer of 2007.[7] "Chinese companies are not about to win the race for African oil," she claimed and went on to point out that China's oil portfolio in Africa is minuscule in comparison to that of the Western powers and that, apart from Sudan, China has managed to get hold of only the crumbs from the West's table, crumbs in places like Gabon and Niger or in other unstable regions. As a result, China, unable to produce oil itself, has had to buy the vast majority of its African oil at market price. This is the case even in Angola, China's biggest supplier after Saudi Arabia and Iran, a country that supplied 25 percent of China's oil at a cost of $9 billion in 2007.

Downs warns, however, that China could still have a few surprises up its sleeve, because China needs African oil much more urgently that the United States does: Africa supplies 30 percent of Chinese oil, but only 15 percent of America's. The surprise, if indeed there is a surprise in store, will probably come about on Africa's east coast. While the West was busy locking up as much of the Gulf of Guinea as possible over on the Atlantic coast, CNOOC has been getting its hands on six licenses and sole control of 28 percent of oil exploration areas in Kenya. A smaller Chinese company, Sunpec, has also secured three licenses in Madagascar. In Uganda, China has plans to finance two hydroelectric dams on the Nile in exchange for CNOOC's receipt of two oil exploration concessions. An attack on a camp full of Ethiopian oil workers in April 2007 by the United National Liberation Front—which resulted in the deaths of seventy-four people, including nine Chinese Sinopec employees—goes some way toward showing how seriously Chinese involvement in Ethiopia is taken. And just two months after this attack, CNOOC confirmed that it had signed a contract that allowed it to prospect for oil among the many battle-fields of Somalia—without the knowledge of the Somali prime minister. Somalia appears to be completely disintegrating.

• • •

Released from our basement interview with Dr. No thanks to a Chinese businessman's card, we at last caught a flight. The brakes on our Ethiopian Airlines jet were released, and it hurtled off down the runway and then up, roaring out of Sudan, its fuselage filled with the Chinese men and women whose custom the country—and the airline—values so highly. The plane, one of a fleet that boasts in its advertisements more connections with China than any other airline, devotes one of its radio channels to Chinese music, and its in-flight magazine, *Selamta,* is filled with articles about Beijing and the Great Wall of China as well as ads that display a variety of made-in-China products, from pharmaceuticals to cosmetics and clothing.

An hour after takeoff we could see the flare from the Melut oil fields, where, since 2000, CNPC has been drilling alongside the Malaysians and the Sudanese. Three years after the company arrived, its prospectors found an enormous deposit just to the east of the White Nile, a find they called their "biggest technological and scientific success." Today, CNPC extracts about 300,000 barrels of oil from the Melut fields every day.

A little to the south of Melut lies one block that in particular has become famous in petroleum circles: the innocuously named Block B. Total acquired the rights to Block B in the 1980s before having to vacate the country and has had to defend them against all comers ever since. For example, in March 2005, the authorities in south Sudan offered these rights to a British company, White Nile. On its Web site, Total goes out of its way to explain that the drilling of oil in a certain country doesn't imply the company's support of the government of that country. With this stance made abundantly clear, Total is preparing for its return to Sudan. This, as we know, is bad news for Chinese interests, since it was only the civil war, the U.S. embargo, and the pressures of public opinion that made it possible for China to compete in Sudan. Erica Downs, the aforementioned researcher, sees the "acute dilemma" that now faces Beijing: In order to improve its international reputation, China needs Khartoum's cooperation to help solve the Darfur crisis; on the other hand, it's not in China's interests to find a solution to this crisis because such a solution would encourage Western powers to return and thereby threaten CNPC's domination of Sudan's oil industry.

It felt strange, somehow, to be flying over the Horn of Africa in the company of so many Chinese, evidence, if more were needed, of their ubiquity in Africa. Soon we were flying over Ethiopia, the strategic crossroads of the entire region. China and the United States are locked in a battle for influence there, a rivalry that President Meles Zenawi has long used, in the tradition of the Great Game and the cold war, to further his power. Not only has China invested a great deal of money in Ethiopia, building roads, dams, and communication networks, but as a result it also has an eye on the oil underneath the region's deserts.

And then there's Eritrea, on the Red Sea. It finally, after thirty years of war, won its independence from Ethiopia in 1991, but ever since then the two countries have refused to give up their old habits and have been fighting sporadic wars against one another, wars that have left 100,000 people dead in just the last two years of the last century, wars made possible by over a billion dollars' worth of Chinese arms.

Further on, another strategic hub, Djibouti, looks out over the Bab el Mandeb straight between the Red Sea and the Gulf of Aden. This former French colony has made the hosting of military bases a primary source of revenue: There are 1,800 American GIs on one side and 2,900 French soldiers in white kepis on the other. The Chinese are cropping up here, too, though only on a commercial and diplomatic footing for the moment.

And beyond Djibouti, the Chinese are looking to Somalia, that diabolical cauldron of misery on the Horn itself. Toward the end of 2006, the United States encouraged Ethiopia to invade, or "liberate," Somalia, so that it might be free of its Islamic tribunals, which looked to Washington very much like something the al-Qaeda bogeyman might engage in.

The borders of all these countries are incredibly porous, of course, and geopolitics is not as precise a practice as it is elsewhere. Armed groups cross from one country to another every day, engaged in a twenty-first-century version of the old Great Game, a war that blew hot and cold and was fought between Britain and Russia for the control of Central Asia and the approaches to India. Britain's and Russia's respective spheres of influence were all-important, and the same tactics are now being employed in Africa, and this time the protagonists are the United States and China. The latter is moving its pawns forward and readying its fleet in the Pakistani port of Gwadar—at great expense—to defend itself in the Arabian Sea and the Indian Ocean. The United States is characteristically anxious not to be outmaneuvered and is seeking to secure its own foothold, with a brand-spanking-new military command center included.

The Chinese, for the moment, seem to be getting the best of it, however. It's not too flippant to posit that their mastery of the situation may owe something to their mastery of that other pursuit: go. This famous Chinese board game, equivalent in subtlety to chess (and proponents will argue that it's even more complex, more akin to an art than a game), is a contest between two players, one using black stones and the other, white. They play on a board marked with a grid, and the stones may be placed on the intersections of the grid lines. The object of the game is very gradually to mark out territory in such a way that one's opponent finds himself or herself suddenly surrounded, cut off, and with no way out.

Chapter 11

The New "Great Game"

[China and the United States] will be on a
collision course if China continues to pursue
energy deals in countries like Iran or Sudan....
The Chinese will have to decide if they want to
pay the price.

—*Robert Zoellick, deputy secretary of state,*
September 2005

According to President Obama, America is "ready to lead again." The
world's only superpower wants to remain the world's only superpower.
The question, then, that most of the world wants answered is this: Do
the ambitions of the United States and China inevitably put the two
countries on a collision course? Are their efforts to secure access to energy resources going to bring them eyeball-to-eyeball, in direct and
open confrontation, in the coming years? Some commentators reply to
such questions in terms of *when* rather than *if.*[1] Our answers, for the
purposes of this book, must also address the *where.*

When George W. Bush was still in office, our search for answers took
us to Washington, D.C., where we hoped the analysts at the National

Security Council, which advises the White House on such strategic questions, might be able to give us a few pointers. We ended up being introduced to what we later learned was the customary "background breakfast," having interrupted the NSC senior staff's regular exercise routine. We were invited to join him at the luxurious Hay-Adams Hotel on Lafayette Square, just steps from the White House, and interrogate him over toast, scrambled eggs, and Florida orange juice.

"China's progress in Africa did concern us," he admitted, "but that was a few years ago."

"And now?"

"And now?" he echoed, reaching for the coffee. "Now Africa desperately needs help, and it's not such a bad thing if China provides that help. Who's actually there, in Africa, building roads?" he asked, and then answered himself. "The Chinese."

"That doesn't worry you?"

"Well. We have to make sure that the Chinese do a little more to help than just building some roads if they're going to be getting their hands on African resources in exchange. And we have to make sure that they don't do too much environmental damage as they go about their business."

And how, we asked him, did one do that?

"We can't just sit here and worry about it. We have to talk to the Chinese. There's no great mystery. They're not unreasonable. They'll listen. I showed them photos of planes in Sudan, disguised as UN aircraft. You know, the planes that were carrying weapons to Darfur. Well, obviously I told them, 'This isn't good—it isn't good *at all*,' and they got the message. We're lucky, actually. They do have a conscience. You just have to talk to them."

By and large, Washington's China experts may be divided into two groups: The "panda huggers" are those who don't see China as much of a threat; the "dragon slayers" are all locked and loaded for World War III. Our breakfast companion appeared to fit into the former category, but he made sure we knew he was under no illusions nevertheless. He lowered his voice and leaned in over the table, more as a way of telling us that he was saying something important than of keeping the conversation private; it wasn't as if the surrounding tables weren't similarly full of other officials whispering other secrets into the ears of other journalists.

"Did you know that the Palestinian missile that hit an Israeli boat last year was made by the Chinese?" he asked, his lips barely moving. "Or that in Iraq we're constantly uncovering Chinese-made military hardware intended for Iran?" He sat back again, one eyebrow raised. "You can find Chinese weapons all over Africa. This isn't common knowledge because our African specialists tend to be more interested in humanitarian issues. What we know about Chinese activities in Africa is purely anecdotal, based solely on what our ambassadors on the ground can find on the Internet. We devote a lot more time to the War on Terror than we do to finding out what the Chinese are or aren't up to."

Nor does China loom large on the radars of the Washington think tanks. The day after our breakfast meeting we attended a conference held by the Carnegie Endowment for Peace. Josh Kurlantzick explained how China makes highly effective use of "soft power" to insinuate itself into African countries. "The United States could really learn from this model," he told his audience. The irony dripping from the lips of one conference participant was shared by all when he said, "So if I understand this correctly, China's plan in Africa is to bring peace and harmony to the continent. Surely now, these can't be *serious* plans. . . . "

It seemed that the panda huggers held sway over at the American Enterprise Institute too. This is particularly surprising because this think tank has a reputation for deep conservatism, having supported overseas military ventures including the Iraq war. Resident fellow Mauro de Lorenzo, who has written extensively on China's activities in Africa, stressed the importance of the infrastructure contracts won and completed by the Chinese and the Chinese tendency to put business interests above humanitarian issues. In doing the opposite over the past few decades, he believed, the West had actually caused considerable harm to Africa as a whole. "The fact that we favor humanitarian aid over economic opportunity is seen by Africans as a sign that we still don't take them seriously. We continue to act arrogantly, using aid as a way of controlling Africa. This is a strategy that no longer works now that we're not the only ones active there. We could," he emphasized, "learn a lot from the Chinese."

• • •

Just where such benevolent, almost indulgent attitudes toward the Chinese had come from was a mystery to us. Several weeks after our trip to D.C. we were back in Brazzaville meeting a member of the U.S. embassy staff under conditions of anonymity.

We met him in the restaurant of the Hotel Hippocampe, under ceiling fans struggling to keep the air moving fast enough to give even some slight relief from the humidity and relentless heat. The entire place, from the exclusively black hotel staff to the mosquitoes to the pink Englishmen sipping their gin and tonics on the terrace and the girls around too smiling to be honest, seemed to have been lifted from a William Boyd novel. The restaurant, owned by a French-Vietnamese couple, was a well-known hangout for the capital's expat community. There were those who worked for NGOs trying to save the gorillas. There were American engineers and architects chewing big Cuban cigars after a long day spent working on the new embassy, outfitting it with the latest security equipment. Finally, there was a smattering of the city's nouveau riche, conspicuous in their peerlessly tailored clothes, clothes so exquisitely cut that it was impossible to tell that they contained not only a very rich African man but also the three cell phones that he felt compelled to produce, as if pulled magically from a top hat, and lay deliberately, one by one, on the table in front of him. While we waited for our American friend, we spotted

André Ondele, the communications director for the Brazzaville entity in charge of major infrastructure work, a body that was deeply involved with Chinese contractors. The previous night this charming Congolese man had treated us to a guided tour of the luxurious house that the Chinese are building gratis for his boss, Jean-Jacques Bouya, in return for the contracts he has ferried their way.

The American arrived right on time. He appeared immune to the heat—a cool, unruffled individual. He exuded a sense of calm and refinement that caused the other diners to look up as he passed. As he sat down to join us, he was all business.

"You've got to understand the sheer scale of Chinese involvement here," he warned us, "and of course we want to make sure we're not eating their dust." He pulled a neatly folded sheet of paper from his jacket pocket and slid it across to us. It was a list of Congolese officials who were known to have the greatest contact with Chinese officials. As we were reading it, he produced a sheaf of papers from another pocket: copies of diplomatic cables relevant to China.

"That's just about everything we have on them. It's not much, but we take it very seriously. Anything you might have interests us."

"Look," we told him, eager to avoid any kind of misunderstanding, "we're not American agents. What we learn here we're going to publish in our book."

"Go ahead. It's no big deal. Western countries need to work together. Here's the situation. France isn't a player here anymore. You've disappointed the Africans too often and for too long. And though the Chinese might win over African minds, they'll never win African hearts. Do you ever see Congolese kids hanging out, listening to Chinese music? No. The Congolese will eventually turn to America, if only we play our cards right."

He went on to explain what this would entail. The embassy had recently tripled its staff, and the ambassador had made competing with Chinese businesses his highest priority. He wanted to fight for the rights of American businesses to bid for contracts. "We just lost out on a contract to build four locomotives," he said with evident disappointment. "But that's OK," he added, "We just need to work harder. The Congolese will show China the door when they discover just how poorly planned and organized the projects really are. A couple of days ago we went and checked out a Chinese project that's supposed to be supplying drinking water to the Bikaroua neighborhood. No surprise that the people still had to haul water to their houses from miles away."

Our diplomat clearly felt he could express himself freely, perhaps because Oliver, the owner of the hotel, was loudly spreading anti-Chinese propaganda to his companions at the next table. The diplomatic service's gain was the hotel business's loss, it turned out. We got an email from him a few months later that read: "I've a favor to ask. Do you have any Chinese contacts that might be interested in investing in a hotel or restaurant in Congo? Or any influential or important contacts in Congo? Frankly, I would like to sell our hotel to the Chinese in two or three years, and I would love to know more about who does what and who wants what among the Chinese in Brazzaville."

• • •

It's the Ethiopian capital, though, that is the true nexus of competition between America and China, and this time it was the Chinese that we were meeting in Addis Ababa. The embassy there is China's biggest after the one in New Delhi, and it seemed to us as we approached it that the only way in or out of this vast, bougainvillea-bedecked mansion was through a tiny little door in the wall.

It's as if the Chinese built their embassy on this scale to oversize the British and French ones; a great brick statement of intent telling anyone who sees it "We're here, and we've got a great deal to do and a great number of people to do it." The recent extension added on to the U.S. embassy seems to say "Me too!"[2] This architectural one-upmanship is just a sign of the Great Game once again being played out. In December 2005 the United States opened its biggest West African embassy in Abidjan, the former French stronghold. Beijing, naturally, built an even bigger one just down the road. The Americans then directed their flair for home improvement toward their embassy in Yaoundé, Cameroon, and sent their assistant secretary of state for African affairs, Jendayi Frazer, to oversee the grand opening. A year later, and Guinea got a makeover. But the battle to keep up with the Joneses has been most intense in the Horn of Africa. That the African Union elected to build its headquarters there has turned Addis Ababa into a den of diplomatic and military intrigue. It's a place that is used to being fought over, having seen France, Italy, and Britain all jostle for position at one time or another. During the cold war, the White House and the Kremlin thumbed their noses at each other through the dictators they had each imposed on it. Currently, though, it's Washington versus China.

We soon found ourselves in the official residence of Mr. Lin Lin, or "His Eminence the Ambassador Extraordinary and Plenipotentiary of the People's Republic of China," according to his full title. He looked all thirteen words of it as he sat, stony-faced, throughout these extended introductions. But then he cracked a smile and invited us to have a seat on a leather sofa in his thickly carpeted drawing-room. He hitched up the knees of his gunmetal suit as he sat down, waiting for us to make the first move. Lin's impressive résumé—he's been working in Africa for twenty-two years—is evidence not only of his suitability for the job but also of how important this particular post is considered to be by Beijing.

"In China I am considered something of an expert," he told us, smiling a bit to take the edge off such unseemly immodesty. It wasn't hard to believe. His role put him in charge of an army of diplomats with its own officials, culture, economy, and, increasingly, its own military affairs.

We wanted to move on from the general chitchat and asked him about the events of April 24, 2007, when two hundred rebels of the

Ogaden National Liberation Front (ONLF) attacked the facilities of a Sinopec subsidiary—the Zhongyuan Petroleum Exploration Bureau—near the town of Abole. Sixty-five Ethiopians and nine Chinese were killed in the raid, and seven Chinese hostages were freed after the International Red Cross negotiated their release. The ONLF subsequently declared that it was banning all foreign hydrocarbon companies from operating in Ogaden until it won independence from Ethiopia. We asked Ambassador Lin whether the incident would have a detrimental effect on Chinese activities in Ethiopia and received only an inscrutable smile in return.

"The answer is no, of course. That was an isolated incident. Chinese are in no greater danger than any other nationality. Everyone has become a target."

As the interview progressed, we learned how formidable a diplomat Ambassador Lin really was. Despite our best efforts to lure him offtrack, he stuck to Beijing's script, only once allowing himself to venture an opinion: Chinese companies needed to communicate better with the Africans around them so that the rebels might come to know that China was their friend.

As for relations between China and the United States, he had nothing but stock responses for us. It soon became apparent that our interview request had been granted so quickly not because Lin was desperate to answer our questions but because he had a few good questions he wanted us to answer for him. Only grudgingly did he provide the most basic statistics, such as the number of Chinese in Ethiopia in 2007 (5,000),[3] and we drank tea, exchanged pleasantries, and smiled until interrupted by a visit from the Iranian ambassador. We were introduced briefly, and then shepherded toward the door. "You know, of course," Ambassador Lin concluded, "that the amount of trade that my country carries out with Ethiopia is as nothing compared to the West's." But the interview confirmed one thing: Beijing was making headway in Africa even as it contrived to lower its profile there.

That said, the ambassador was certainly correct in his final assertion. The United States is just ahead of Japan at the top of the list of countries financing aid to Ethiopia;[4] China is way down the list. Statistics can be misleading, however. Most Chinese money available to Ethiopia comes in the form of loans, 85 percent of which come from the Exim Bank of China; the rest comes from the Chinese government, secured against access to natural resources or infrastructure projects. It's a system referred to by the Chinese as "the English model." The day after our interview, Ambassador Lin was interviewed by the Xinhua news agency, an article subsequently published under the headline "China: A Major Commercial Partner for Ethiopia," in which we learned that trade between the two countries quintupled between 2002 and 2006, rising from $100 million to half a billion.[5] Two years earlier, in 2005, Lin had told the agency, "Chinese contracts for projects in Ethiopia amounted to only $800 million. That number has doubled [in 2007] to $1.7 billion."[6]

There's certainly a lot of construction going on. The China Road and Bridge Group (CRBC) finished the massive perimeter highway around the capital in 2003. China built the 180-meter-high Tekeze Dam in northern Ethiopia, referred to by the Chinese press as "the biggest project that China has cooperated on with an African country."[7] Sinohydro, the Chinese company that won the contract, dubbed it "The Ethiopian Three Gorges Dam."[8] China signed an even more significant contract—worth $1.4 billion—in April 2007; it calls for ZTE, the telecommunications company, to quadruple the number of cell phones and ground lines in Ethiopia by 2010. In 2008, the Anhui Foreign Economic Construction Group Corporation finished the construction of a polytechnic in a suburb of Addis Ababa in only thirteen months and within the $10.6 million budget. These red-and-green concrete buildings were a gift from China, and will house and cater to 3,000 students when the university opens.

And that's not all. On May 25, 2007, in celebration of Africa Day, commemorating the founding of the Organization of African Unity in 1963, China set out to impress the entire continent with a $150 million contribution toward the African Union's new headquarters in Addis Ababa.

After leaving Ambassador Lin and his Iranian counterpart to their own devices, we found out for ourselves just how much China has invested in Ethiopia. The country—one of the poorest in the world—simply can't afford to turn down China's assistance. Some 95 percent of Ethiopians live on less than two dollars a day, 64 percent don't have access to clean water, and 83 percent don't have electricity. Competing with the Chinese has become more difficult since international organizations like the World Bank and the European Union have started to distance themselves from Ethiopia's dictator, Meles Zenawi. The regime instituted a reign of terror, similar to that of General Pinochet's in Chile, right after it consolidated power in the May 2005 elections. As a consequence, financial aid, which makes up 40 percent of Ethiopia's budget, has fallen off considerably, a situation that suits China. And China has not let itself be hindered by "Ethiopia's Tiananmen Square," the massacre that followed Zenawi's order to his troops to fire live rounds at citizens marching peacefully in the streets of Addis Ababa in protest against perceived election rigging. Opposition leaders were arrested, imprisoned, tortured, or assassinated or they simply "disappeared." In total, some 30,000 people were jailed without trial.

• • •

To be fair, the United States hasn't disowned Zenawi either. Its problem—and Ethiopia's—is that, with any credible opposition either in prison or otherwise unavailable, there's no one else to support. Even if there was, it's unlikely that both China and the United States would want to risk the progress they've made with the devil they know to replace him with one they don't. America, for instance, might be better off referring to its precarious progress as a "comeback," after its humiliating pullout from Somalia in 1992 and the failure of Operation Restore Hope; in the decade that followed, its involvement in Africa was virtually nil beyond formal diplomatic and humanitarian dealings. The American comeback, whatever our source at the Brazzaville embassy might have said about it, is based more on military might than straightforward business. Washington's choices when it comes to sending officials to Addis Ababa reflect this. In July 2008, George W. Bush assigned John Simon as his ambassador to the African Union. Before that, Simon had been vice president of the Overseas Private Investment Corporation, a government agency that helps U.S. businesses invest abroad and a member of the NSC. Once installed in Addis Ababa he began working closely with an African American named Cindy Courville, who had worked as a special assistant to the president, on African Affairs for the NSC, and as a senior intelligence officer for the Defense Intelligence Agency.

It is fair to assume from such appointments that Washington considers Addis Ababa a strategically important place, particularly when you consider the fact that the ambassador to Ethiopia, Donald Yamamoto, is a particularly talented, particularly senior diplomat and alumnus of the National War College. He was working in Beijing during the Tiananmen Square massacre and subsequently became a specialist on the Horn of Africa region—Eritrea, Djibouti, Ethiopia, and Somalia. He speaks Chinese, Japanese, Arabic, and French and is unquestionably a big gun.

The predominantly military aura surrounding America's image in Africa is no accident. Having risen to prominence in 2001, neoconservative politicians made the War on Terror their main focus and pursued the "terror" not just in Afghanistan and Iraq but also in Africa. The war began mezzo piano under the Clinton administration following the dual attacks on U.S. embassies in Tanzania and Kenya on August 7, 1998. The war entered a mezzo forte stage after seventeen American sailors were killed when a suicide bomber hit the destroyer USS *Cole* on October 12, 2000, in Aden, Yemen. The attacks of September 11, 2001, prompted fears that the more lawless areas of Africa were vulnerable to "Talibanization," creating safe havens for terrorists such as those in Afghanistan. The Pentagon went into action. It stepped up scheduled military exercises in North Africa, in countries on the coast of the Mediterranean where its Sixth Fleet had long been deployed. It began to work with these countries to establish military bases where officers and men of the North African countries' armed forces would receive training under the program known as IMET (International Military Education and Training). The Bush administration increased the U.S. military presence in Morocco, Tunisia, and Mauritania and entertained hopes of establishing a base in southern Algeria that would help in the fight against al-Qaeda.

In 2002, the White House also launched the Pan-Sahel initiative, later renamed the Trans-Sahara Counterterrorism Initiative (TSCTI). This partnership's aim was to prevent terrorists from gaining a foothold in Mali, Niger, Chad, and Mauritania by providing military training to both American and African soldiers and mercenaries, and to encourage cooperation between the countries. The initiative didn't confine itself to these countries, however. The initials TSCTI are emblazoned across every region of sub-Saharan Africa including Gabon, Nigeria, and Rwanda.

But America's military presence in Africa is concentrated round the Horn and in those countries along the border with the Gulf of Aden and the Indian Ocean. Toward the end of 2002, when Washington set up the Combined Joint Task Force of Africa in Djibouti, it did so with 1,800 personnel already stationed nearby at Camp Lemonier, not to mention the French base farther down the track that was teeming with 2,900 French soldiers. The task force had been given a broad and exacting mission: to improve stability in the region and to wage war on terror wherever they found it. Not content with this, the Pentagon is also hoping for a green light to build a camp on Socotra, a small archipelago belonging to Yemen, known as "the Galapagos Islands of the Indian Ocean."

Despite this increased presence, the Defense Department is, due to the Somalia debacle, understandably hesitant to involve itself directly in African affairs. Clinton's government favored action through local organizations—hence the creation of the African Crisis Response

Initiative (ACRI), today known as African Contingency Operations Training and Assistance (ACOTA). The U.S. Army also provides support for its allies in the form of supplies and logistical advice to the peacekeeping forces of both the African Union and the Economic Community of West African States (CEDEAO).

America has thus begun to subcontract some of what it calls its "preventative wars." When the radical Islamic movement known as the Union of Islamic Tribunals chased Somalian warlords from power in June 2006 and announced that it intended to "reunify" Somalia by taking back the Ogaden province in Ethiopia, Washington went ahead and encouraged the Christian Ethiopia (and President Zenawi) to handle the situation. Zenawi's forces, well armed and advised by Washington, routed the army of the tribunals and grabbed Mogadishu. Ironically, in providing Zenawi with much-needed logistical support, the United States found itself lending a hand to the very same Somali warlords responsible for the debacle of Operation Restore Hope in 1992.

Ethiopia's "liberation" of Somalia has degenerated into a humanitarian crisis as severe as the one in Ogaden after rebels attacked the Chinese in April 2007. Well provided for and well trained by the United States, the soldiers have proved indiscriminate about their victims, carrying out atrocities against villagers and nomads[9] as well as those who take up arms against them. In the Anuak region in the eastern part of the country, Ethiopian soldiers have taken to shackling their prostrate prisoners on the road and driving over them in their trucks, a practice designated by Human Rights Watch as a crime against humanity.

All this—the killing, the unrest, the suffering—has been met with various levels of concern but also with an attitude of "Well, what can you do?" for this is just the beginning of the Great Game. The ends are inevitably seen to justify the means, and the ends are usually related to oil. The Chinese have a head start when it comes to Ethiopian oil, but the wildcatters from Texas are working overtime to catch up.[10] On August 25, 2008, the Titan Resources Corporation, under the leadership of Nelson Bunker Hunt, obtained four licenses in Ogaden and five in the Abbey Basin. Oil is in Hunt's blood, it seems: His father, Haroldson Lafayette Hunt, is the founder of Hunt Oil, a company that had been active in Ogaden until it was forced to leave the region in 1995. Titan teamed up with another American company, Capitan Energy, and incorporated a business in Dubai named Ethiopian Exploration and Production Ltd., whose purpose was to prospect Ethiopian land along the Somali border.[11] Just prior to Titan's appearance in the region, the Texas company Trans-Global Petroleum obtained a license for Afar. Yet another, White Nile—run by the former cricket player and Zambian native Phil Edmonds—won exploration rights in southwestern Ethiopia along the Kenyan border. It's clearly a complex and crowded market, and that's only for Ethiopia. The scramble for oil, though, extends to every corner of Africa.

Nor are the Chinese and Americans the only ones involved, of course. Arab, European, Canadian, Malaysian, Russian, Indian, and Brazilian companies are all jockeying for position, though if they're going to be reporting large profits they'll be doing so despite the ace up the U.S. companies' sleeve—that is to say the U.S. Army, which is currently looking to secure its burgeoning influence in Africa with a unified command center: AFRICOM. Before this plan was announced by George W. Bush in February 2007, the army's responsibilities were shared between three stations: Europe (EUCOM), Pacific (PACOM), and Central Command (CENTCOM). Bush appointed General William Ward as head of the latest addition to this list. The general soon set about scouting out an African country to host his new headquarters since Africa Command was not yet in Africa at all, but rather in Stuttgart, Germany. Two years down the line, and the general is still looking. It seems that no one will have him.[12] He courted Nigeria, Algeria, and Morocco, but they all turned down his proposal; nor could he find a life partner among the countries around the Gulf of Guinea. South Africa, too, refused him, the defense minister's reasons being that South Africa opposed the idea of creating a unified command center on the continent. General Ward, thick-skinned though he may be, must surely have had his feelings hurt when this sentiment was seconded by the fourteen members of the South African Development Community. In North Africa, Libya advised its friends in the Community of Sahel–Saharan States not only to refuse the general's hand but to get their neighbors to do so, too. Nigeria wanted nothing to do with him, either. Only Liberia took a shine to Ward and his considerable fortune, but the lure of her weak, war-torn infrastructure wasn't enough for him.

Unsurprisingly, AFRICOM feels misunderstood and dejected. "There have been some misunderstandings," said Eric Elliot, a spokesman for AFRICOM on June 3, 2008. "Some countries think that the United States wants to put more soldiers in Africa and to increase our influence. It's not true. We probably didn't communicate our intentions very well from the beginning." Perhaps that's true. Perhaps the general's advances were misinterpreted, but whatever the case, it's clear that to African eyes it looks very much as if American aid comes with the warning "terms and conditions apply" and a good deal of military small print.[13] It's no secret that, as was discussed in a previous chapter, the Pentagon now controls nearly a quarter of the U.S. Agency for International Development's budget.

Even U.S. Secretary of Defense Robert Gates, who remains in his position under the new Obama administration, has expressed misgivings about the militarization of the U.S. Africa policy.[14] The military angle to the American presence in Africa has certainly caused China some misgivings, which has introduced one of its own: The arms race is well under way.[15] And it's an insidious process. First China offers troops and observers to the United Nations' peacekeeping operation, then treaties for military cooperation are signed, and then military instructors arrive. It's impossible to deny their existence when they're openly walking the streets of Harare in Zimbabwe. We've also seen them in Sudan, where several thousand Chinese soldiers guard the oil facilities; it is also worth mentioning that China plans to build an arms factory in Chad, having chased perpetual rival Taiwan out of this oil-rich country in 2006. Even without Taiwan's presence there, the Chinese will still be competing with France and the United States.

What is perhaps most striking, though, particularly in light of General Ward's difficulties, is that China has been able to establish permanent military bases on the continent. In the summer of 2008 Beijing deployed troops in the Democratic Republic of the Congo and installed a military base in Kamina, in the mining province of Katanga. Joseph Kabila, Congo-Kinshasa's president, approved this deployment just as Angola did.[16]

From this base in Katanga, China can keep a close eye on its ever-growing business interests and, should the need arise, move swiftly in their defense not only in the DRC but also in Nigeria and all the countries around the Gulf of Guinea. In fact, the place that has aroused their greatest interest recently is an archipelago in this gulf, Sao Tome and Principe, which is sitting atop enough oil to have China, Taiwan, and the United States all doing everything they can to gain its favor.[17] True to form, the United States would like to set up camp—military camp—there, and, equally true to form, China is hovering (in this case supporting the opposition party that wants to sever its ties with Taiwan). Taiwan is relying on checkbook diplomacy to retain the government's favor, handing over somewhere between $10 and $15 million in aid in 2007. But it remains to be seen whether the two bigger players won't raise the stakes in the hope of securing the loyalty of Sao Tome and Principe for themselves.

The contest for influence, military access, and resources between China and the United States is going on everywhere in Africa. While denouncing American neoimperialism, Beijing has been moving its pawns forward. An article in a 2005 edition of the *People's Daily* claimed that "U.S. hegemony and unilateralism are swelling malignantly," words that, according to researcher Joshua Eisenman, are reminiscent of the opening speech of the second ministerial meeting for China-Africa Co-operation in Addis Ababa by forum premier Wen Jiabao: "The people of the world share an aspiration for peace, stability and development," he said, "but the issue of hegemony is raising its ugly head."[18] Clearly the accusations are not entirely un-founded, but the Chinese manage to make them while engaging in precisely the activities that they so publicly deplore.

Chinese leaders definitely know the effect that words such as "im-perialism" and "hegemony" have on the collective African psyche. They've used the same language to discredit France, the former colo-nial power, with marked success—though Chinese input is hardly necessary, as France has done such a good job discrediting itself since the beginning of the 1990s. However, France's demise as a regional power did not seem foreseeable in the 1960s, when many European colonies were winning their independence.

During this time, at the height of the cold war, Paris was slowly but surely winning over the leaders of these freshly independent countries, and those who didn't see things from a French perspective had a ten-dency to wake up either dead or out of a job so that someone with more sensible, more Francophile views would take over. Indeed, many in Europe still remember the grotesque coronation of "Emperor" Jean-Bedel Bokassa of the Central African Republic, which was at-tended by President Valéry Giscard d'Estaing and a host of French of-ficials. When the man known as the Ogre of Berengo offered a gift of diamonds to these officials they could find no reason to refuse them—igniting a scandal at home that directly contributed to d'Estaing's 1981 defeat at the hand of François Mitterand. It is important to re-member that was still the time of cold war and realpolitik: They were there to show solidarity with Bokassa not because he was a cannibal but, more important, because he wasn't a communist.

Throughout this period France waged its ideological war in every corner of Africa through an elaborate system of alliances and mili-tary bases.[19] The linking of the Central African franc—known as the CFA originally after the French acronym for "Colonies Françaises d'Afrique—to the French franc helped impose France's special status. France also invested heavily in French-speaking countries and even created a special government office called the "Cellule Africaine de l'Elysée": the President's African Cell. Its purpose was to put African policy directly under the French president's purview, allowing him personally to choose which African plutocrats to support with French humanitarian aid. In return, many African leaders would make donations to the RPR, the party that dominated the right wing of the French political landscape in the 1970s and 1980s.

This complex web of insider political chicanery, designed to maintain French influence in Africa, came to be known as *Françafrique*, a term coined by Charles de Gaulle's Africa specialist, the late Jacques Foccart. Though Foccart didn't intend for the word to be used as such, it soon came to refer to the corruption, clandestine operations, and support for rebellions in which the French government engaged. Himself a highly controversial—not to mention cynical—figure, Foccart was a sort of Gallic Kissinger, serving presidents of any political persuasion. This "shadow man" had a talent for subversion and advised coup-plotters across Africa on how best to achieve their ends, from General Gnassingbé Eyadema in Togo in 1967, to General Lansana Conté in Guinea in 1984, to Blaise Campaore in Burkina Faso.[20] Campaore brought misery to a country whose motto is "The Country for Honest Men" and was implicated in the murder of the former president, Thomas Sankara. In Chad, Idriss Déby came to power, as has been mentioned elsewhere, in a coup that had France's approval. President Chirac really seemed to express the French foreign policy at the time when he said in a speech in Abidjan in 1990 that "Africa is not mature enough for democracy."[21]

But the tone of Western involvement in Africa changed after the Berlin Wall came down, because those who had seen fit to finance particular dictators began imposing conditions on their continued support, conditions such as raised standards of democracy and human rights. The World Bank began making such stipulations in 1991. The West, it seemed, now intended to use them as yet another clever tool with which to deal with Africa. Little by little, France fell in line with this approach.

The effects of France's new attitude toward Africa hit home when it announced that it would no longer allow the value of the CFA to be linked to the French franc. The value of the CFA promptly dropped by half. The French maneuver amounted to fiscal shock therapy for an Africa unprepared for global competition and brought about severe and widespread poverty. These impoverished Africans looked to emigrate, and their logical choice of destination was France. France, in turn, closed its borders to them. Paris adopted a hard-line border policy, while efforts to help those who had managed to get through to integrate into French society failed utterly. Then, on February 7, 1994, Felix Houphouet-Boigny, the president of Ivory Coast and *Françafrique* standard-bearer, died. Two months later the Rwandan genocide kicked off. France, supposedly allied to the Rwandan government, claimed to be just as surprised as everyone else, though some believe that they not only knew the genocide would happen but actually *allowed* it to happen. French courts today are trying to find the answer to these allegations.

It was at around this time—the mid-1990s—that France began to extricate itself both politically and economically from Africa. It sounds absurd, but while Africa might have been used for France's own ends during colonial times, Africa has now gained the upper hand in the relationship. Continued French condescension and neglect, which lasted well into the 1990s, gave Africans little reason to maintain good relations. On the other side, Africa's corruption and laziness and its unpredictable, solipsistic, and occasionally belligerent attitude have made the former colonies an international embarrassment. And with French-speaking Africa left to its own devices and left to suffer a decade of conflict and economic decline, there was nothing to stop it from being wooed by a less unpredictable and petulant suitor: Asia.

Beijing proposed a marriage of convenience to which Africa quickly agreed. As has already been pointed out, it wasn't as if Africa had much choice. Though the romance with China had started out as much out of pique, as a way of showing its frustration with France, it soon blossomed into something more sincere. China's pledges of loyalty and its optimism combined with Africa's economic recovery (such as it is) turned the relationship into one of genuine affection. As a result, Africans are even more unwilling to endure French arrogance and condescension, and have in effect forced France to withdraw from the field entirely. From a cultural point of view, French as a language is in decline. Politically, dictators such as Idriss Déby in Chad and Mamadou Tandja in Niger can now stand up to France because their new ally, China, has their backs. As to military issues, Africa is seriously questioning why French forces need bases there and whether Nicolas Sarkozy, who came to power in 2007, will keep his preelection promises to close some of them. It's widely assumed that he will renege on this issue and that France will renew its assault on Africa despite Sarkozy's words in a speech given at Bamako in 2006: "France's economy does not need Africa."[22]

As for America, although it may not have been a colonial power as such, it isn't always fondly remembered in Africa. Its role in the slave trade, for one thing, is not forgotten, and although it may champion human rights it is also still remembered for sitting on the sidelines, with France, during the Rwandan genocide. This latter decision is doubly injurious to the U.S. reputation because it reminds Africans of Lyndon Johnson's refusal to allow a UN peacekeeping force into Rhodesia (now Zimbabwe) in the 1960s.

America's cold-war attitude to realpolitik has also caused it to support, and in some cases to install, various African dictators. Back in the 1960s in the Democratic Republic of the Congo, for example, the United States conspired in the assassination of democratically elected president Patrice Lumumba. Lumumba was considered a Soviet ally and therefore had to be replaced by someone who wasn't—in this case Marechal Mobutu. The State Department also supported Angola's Jonas Savimbi and UNITA no matter how disgraceful their actions, and supported the apartheid regime in South Africa until well into the 1980s.

Certainly, America has had more edifying moments in Africa, such as when Jimmy Carter played a decisive role in bringing the Rhodesian conflict to a halt in the 1970s, and when Congress acted to combat widespread famine in 1985. Despite the objections of then president Reagan, that same Congress approved sanctions against South Africa that were instrumental in bringing apartheid to an end. The Clinton administration recognized the danger of an AIDS epidemic in Africa and fought more vigorously than many people thought they could or would. But still, as Raymond W. Copson has written, "despite the good things that occasionally happen in U.S.-Africa policy . . . the United States has done less that it could to fight poverty, foster peace, and promote human rights in Africa."[23]

This sentiment is felt particularly strongly around the Horn of Africa. Washington has long coveted Somalia's oil and natural gas, not to mention its rich deposits of copper, bauxite, and uranium. Even after Muhammad Siyad Barre led a coup against the government in Mogadishu and installed his Marxist regime in 1969, America managed to swallow its ideological pride and supported him, even encouraging him to invade Ogaden, that part of Ethiopia then under Mengistu's Stalinist rule. Barre's failed invasion of Ogaden led him to reject Moscow and come down on the West's side. Then in 1989 the tables were turned, and Ethiopia attacked Somalia under the pretext of helping a Somalian clan hostile to Mogadishu. Thus began one of the most brutal conflicts in Africa's history. It lasted until Barre's downfall on January 26, 1991, with the implosion of Somalia as a whole. The northwestern part declared independence and renamed itself Somaliland, while the eastern part chose to function under the name "Puntland."

Quite apart from human cost, this all caused a great deal of trouble for the big American oil companies such as Chevron, Amoco, Conoco, and Philips, which by 1986 had done a lot to secure licenses to prospect for oil in over two-thirds of Somalia. In 1992, Operation Restore Hope was initiated, with UN support, by the United States. Its aim was to aid the starving population and to bring the country's

various warlords into alignment. The resounding failure of the operation resulted in acute humiliation for America, forcing it to swap
sides and back Ethiopia because it was Zenawi's forces that eventually
brought down Mengistu.

President George W. Bush and his neoconservative administration, the same people who demanded progress on human rights and
democracy in Iraq and advocated, via the Millennium Challenge Account,[24] the principle of "transformational development," took a
more realistic attitude in Africa. Copson summarized the phenomenon thus: "In recent years, policy has come to be more and more influenced by two security interests, the Global War on Terror and the
protection of oil supplies, that are pushing the United States away
from a fair and more just relationship with Africa."[25]

It was in pursuit of these interests that Bush put together his
"dream team" for Africa, led by three strong African American
women—Secretary of State Condoleeza Rice, her old friend and director of African affairs at the State Department Jendayi Fraser, and
Arlene Render, the former ambassador to the Ivory Coast whose résumé included postings to the Democratic Republic of the Congo,
Ghana, Gambia, and Zambia. In March 2005, Paul Wolfowitz's appointment to head the World Bank was supposed to complete the
plan and put the more stubborn African leaders on alert.

The Bush administration shed even more of its ideals during its
second term in power when energy security became increasingly important. In fact, energy security and a pressing need to maintain access to Africa's natural resources brought America and China, the
world two biggest oil consumers, to enact an almost symmetrical and
possibly clashing policy on the continent.

In the last ten years, the dragon slayers in Washington have been
presenting China as a palpable threat to the United States: "The National Intelligence Council's *Global Trends 2015* study was published
in 2000 and it claimed that by 2015 China will have deployed tens to
several tens of missiles with nuclear warheads targeted against [the]

United States . . . [and] would seek to adjust regional power arrangements to its advantage, risking conflict with neighbors and some powers external to the region."[26]

On the eve of President Hu Jintao's state visit to Washington in September 2005, Assistant Secretary of State Robert Zoellick warned that the two countries would be on a collision course if China persisted in procuring energy deals with countries perceived as "troublesome" by Washington, namely Sudan and Iran.

The authors of a 2006 Council on Foreign Relations report on the need for America to increase its influence in Africa felt compelled to include a chapter specifically on China.[27] In it they accused Beijing of supporting so-called rogue states, a phrase aimed squarely at Zimbabwe and Sudan. They went on to claim that Beijing used its influence to counter Western pressure intended to improve human rights and good governance. The report also charged Beijing with unfair competitive practices toward American companies. As Barry Sautman and Yan Hairong have shown,[28] many other analysts have since expressed similar criticisms.[29]

In 1995 Henry Kissinger, the former secretary of state and still an advocate of realpolitik said: "The Great Game is still taking place. . . . It would be ironic if oil pipelines—where they are located and whom they supply—become the modern equivalent of colonial disputes in the nineteenth century."[30] It would seem that Kissinger's fears are coming true. More and more, Washington's strategists are using language borrowed from the past, increasingly from the cold war. Reports and lectures talk about containment of China because neoconservatives insisted on dealing with China as *Communist* China—that is, as an ideological enemy. In adhering to this point of view, they not only instigated an arms race with China (along with Russia and Iran), but compounded their error: They targeted the wrong ideology using the wrong methods. In practice, China is now communist only in name. Most Chinese, if they are political at all, are more nationalist than anything else.

That China is no longer communist, though, isn't to say that it poses no threat. It is still a dictatorship whose essentially authoritarian, totalitarian structure is replicated wherever China holds sway. However, the Iraq war, rendition flights, Guantanamo Bay, and America's support for Zenawi in Ethiopia have used up most of its political, and moral, capital. It is no longer in a position to lecture Africans on right and wrong.

As to America's methods and how they differ from China's, Joshua Eisenman provides a succinct summary: "Today, Mao's Red Book has been replaced by a balance sheet. Africa is now a component in China's larger strategy to cultivate political support, bolster its claims to Taiwan, acquire energy and natural resources, and secure its commercial interests. Beijing also sees the African nations as valuable backers of its claims to lead the developing world and in the struggle against American 'hegemony.'"[31]

When China does business with the outside world its successes help validate its own worldview. Advocates of the free market in America and elsewhere find themselves confronted by a system that mixes capitalism with authoritarianism to great effect, chalking up success after success. In 2006, Beijing held more than a trillion dollars in foreign currency reserves, 70 percent of which was in U.S. dollars. Beijing is also the largest holder of U.S. government bonds (Treasury bonds). In other words, China helps finance America's public debt, which, as of January 2009, stood at more than ten trillion dollars.[32]

All the same, China is indebted to the United States or, more precisely, to the American consumer. It is the world's biggest exporter and as such was cash-rich enough to buy massive amounts of T-bonds in the fall of 2008 as the world economic crisis loomed large. In so doing, Beijing is playing a crucial role in America's rescue strategy. Wallace Bello, the director of the Transnational Institute, also has the knack of succinct summarization: "Chinese production and American consumption are like prisoners who seek to break free from one another but cannot because they are chained together."[33]

Thus, in the short term, it is hard to see how the two superpowers can avoid direct confrontation. But the rivalry is likely to continue through intermediaries, particularly in Africa. Several questions are yet to be answered. Is the West, led by America, going to pack up its toys and toddle home, taking its money with it, a result of the global recession and collapse in commodity prices? If it does, will China fill the power vacuum? When Barack Obama (whose father, lest we forget, was born in Kenya) was on the U.S. Senate Committee on Foreign Relations, he often concerned himself with African issues: Darfur, stability in the DRC, war crimes trials in Liberia, and the development of a coherent strategy for stabilizing Somalia.

Since taking office, Obama has named Susan Rice, an African American who is his most trusted foreign affairs adviser, as UN representative. This has been seen as a sign that he plans to put Africa at the top of his agenda—not simply because this bold and unarguably brilliant woman was previously assistant secretary of state for African affairs, but also because she is renowned for her fervent support of what she has called *dramatic action* to end the atrocities in Darfur.

Chapter 12

The Chinese Locomotive
Begins to Lose Steam

"We say to our Angolan friends: It's great that
you're taking a little walk with the Chinese. Enjoy
yourself. But when you're ready to play in the big
leagues, pay your debts and come back and see us."
—*Western diplomat in Luanda, October 2007*

It was a miracle that the train could pull such a load. A swarming mass
of African humanity stacked itself, pushed itself, pulled itself, and generally sucked in its belly so that it managed to fit itself, if only just, onboard. Matters were complicated by the bulk and the nature of the
passengers' possessions. Bags were balanced on heads, leaving arms free
to carry everything from gas canisters to bunches of chickens, held by
their legs, which kept the children on the passengers' backs amused. The
challenge, of course, was to see how many plastic-wrapped Chinese-
made motorcycles could then be loaded into the overburdened carriages. The challenge was well met, the whole arrangement lurched as

the engine gave an impatient tug on its load, and the water sellers and sweets vendors peeled off.

The train began to pick up speed and then thought better of it, limiting itself to a sedate ten miles per hour as it sauntered through the fields that cover the coastal plain. Sometime later, as the tracks began their long uphill weave to the fertile land of the high plateau, the locomotive sucked in a breath, braced itself for a surge, and added another five miles an hour to the clock. This show of speed was no simple achievement, and the thirty-year-old South African–built wagons jolted, shook, and whined as they rattled along the rails. The disapproving whine sprang from the fact that these rails had originally been laid by the Portuguese eighty years before and had been battered by decades of civil war and strong weather. Yet despite the obstacles, somehow the whole assembly would routinely arrive at its destination, if not on time then at least in one piece, as it did three times a week, every week.

It leaves the Angolan port of Lobito at dawn on a round-trip that stretches 154 kilometers inland to Cubal. This stretch is all that is left of the thousand-kilometer Benguela-Luau line that was opened in 1928 to serve as one of colonial Africa's most vital arteries, carrying corn, wheat, sugar, coffee, cotton, and cattle from the farms on the Angolan plateau and copper from Zambia's mines all the way down to the Atlantic coast.

This Angolan section was restored in 2005 to as high a standard as limited funds allowed. If the line has lost some of its earlier grandeur, it is because it now plays the different, more modest, role of people carrier, and a great many passengers rely on it—passengers such as Laurimo, a sergeant in the Angolan army who is on his way to rejoin his regiment in Cubal. Next to him are two teachers, Angela and Milena, on their way to their school in Caimbambo. Eduardo is off to Ombe to look for charcoal, and his neighbor, Eugenio, is going there, too, to consult a doctor about the swelling in his leg. Each stop seems to have its own specialty on offer from the trackside vendors: fruit here, chickens there, charcoal at the next station.

The carriages are old and jittery, and their griping is best ignored; despite what they might sound like at fifteen miles an hour, the original line did in fact survive the War of Independence that drove the Portuguese out in 1975. It is true, though, that the twenty-seven years of civil war that followed took their toll. During this war, the National Union for the Total Independence of Angola (UNITA), a group of rebels led by one Jonas Savimbi and supported by the United States, Israel, China, and South Africa's apartheid regime, fought the Soviet- and Cuban-supported MPLA government (the Popular Movement for the Liberation of Angola), led by Augustino Neto and José Eduardo dos Santos. The railway was a vital piece of infrastructure and became the frequent target, resulting in three hundred employees of the Benguela rail company being killed by land mines and ambushes; an additional two hundred simply went unaccounted for. And of course passengers were not immune to the fighting, either. There's no record of the countless number of passengers who were caught in the crossfire.

The train had connected Lobito to Huambo, an agricultural hub in the fertile plains high in the center of the country. But when Savimbi was defeated by dos Santos in the 1992 presidential election, a multi-party election that everyone had hoped would help secure the ephemeral peace, Savimbi ended his brief flirtation with politics. He returned to guerrilla warfare, quickly overrunning 80 percent of the country and threatening the capital itself, Luanda. He set up his headquarters in Huambo, an Ovimbundu heartland—the ethnic group from which Savimbi came—from where UNITA had drawn many of its recruits. The fighting raged once more, and when forty-seven bridges and other structures had been destroyed, the railway effectively ceased to exist.

The CIA and the South Africans withdrew their support soon after, but Savimbi still had plenty in his war chest of smuggled diamonds. Dos Santos's MPLA government lost its two main sponsors, too, as the Soviet Union dissolved and Cuba fell into disarray. Though his war chest wasn't stocked with diamonds, he had the country's oil revenues to use to buy the weapons he needed, which he needed fast. His appeal to France for help in this department bore fruit in the form of Pierre

Falcone, a shady businessman and notorious arms dealer who supplied Luanda with $633 million worth of military equipment in 1993
and 1994, giving the MPLA the upper hand in the war and eventually
putting them in a position to fire fifteen rounds into Savimbi's chest
on the afternoon of February 20, 2002.

This last act was a decisive blow, for Savimbi *was* UNITA. A charis-
matic warrior, he had been born sixty-seven years earlier in Mun-
hango, one of the stops on the railway where his father had been both
a hard-line Protestant minister and also the town's stationmaster. His
death marked the MPLA victory, though their French sponsors were
never able to reap the rewards of their investment because Pierre Falcone was sent to prison in December 2000, convicted of illicit arms
dealing, tax evasion, fraudulent dealing in a company's assets, breach
of trust, and, last but not least, corruption. The prolonged pretrial
investigation ensnared many others in the process, including former
interior minister Charles Pasqua and his son Pierre, alongside Jean-
Charles Marchiani, Pasqua's right-hand man, and Jean-Christophe
Mitterand, the former president's son, as well as Jacques Attali, a former presidential counsel.

While members of the political class in Paris were blaming each
other, Angolans continued to die by the thousands. The war had left a
half-million people dead, half as many again displaced, and 80,000
maimed, of whom only one-third would ever get a prosthetic limb to
help them function. They and the other survivors were forced to live
off leaves, roots, rats, and insects.[1] Although Angola has technically
experienced peace for the past six years, it is a peace during which an
Angolan child under five dies of hunger or illness every three minutes.

During these years, however, $5 to $8 billion in oil revenue also
flooded into the country annually, but Angola had, and continues to
have, a very special talent for misappropriating such funds, a talent
known locally as "evaporation," as if corruption were as inevitable as
the weather. It condenses on the privileged few or, more precisely, the
privileged few hundred. Locals call these lucky power brokers and

plutocrats "Special Angolans," those for whom life in Luanda is a never-ending party of opulence and sparkle graced by concerts by the likes of Jay-Z and Beyoncé. These Angolan "bright young things" retreat back into their money or their vast carelessness, finding it much simpler to blow $130,000 on a 4x4 with good shock absorbers than to spend the same amount filling in the potholes.

The IMF estimates that at least $1 billion evaporates each year before it even shows up on the Finance Ministry's books. What does make it into the official figures quickly vanishes, and so by the time the state starts thinking about rebuilding schools, hospitals, and railways, it finds itself a little short of funds. With a government as corrupt as the one currently in place, one with which the United States and Europe have refused to negotiate aid as long as it continues to overextend its debt and will not submit to the IMF's principles of good governance, where could this neglected and downtrodden nation turn for help to rebuild the rest of the country beyond Luanda's nightclubs? They had little choice but to appeal to China.

China was only too happy to help. All it wanted in return was the reassurance that it would be Angola's single largest trading partner. The deal was concluded very quickly.

In November 2003 the two countries signed a treaty in which they promised to "renew economic and trade cooperation." Four months later, the Exim Bank of China extended a $2 billion line of credit to the Angolan Ministry of Finance. The ministry had lined up around fifty projects to spend the money on, in areas ranging from energy and water to health and public works. Two years later, on June 20, 2006, the bank extended Angola's credit by another $2 billion, while, at an unknown date, the Hong Kong–based China International Fund (CIF) extended a third line of credit to the National Cabinet for Reconstruction estimated at $6 billion.[2] The man in charge of the National Cabinet was a member of President dos Santos's military staff and the second most powerful man in the country, General Helder Vieira Dias, or "Kopelipa."

Thus, Beijing has apparently loaned $10 billion to Luanda, making Angola the greatest beneficiary of Chinese funds second to Sudan, which received approximately twice as much but over a longer period. This injection of cash into Angola is far greater than anything the West was prepared to offer.

The only thing that makes the Chinese money different from that of any other country is that this $10 billion, loaned at a low rate of interest, carries with it the proviso that it be spent only on infrastructure work, and that two-thirds of the contracts be given to Chinese firms, for which tens of thousands of Chinese workers would have to be found. Such firms, as one might expect, prefer to import their skilled workers rather than use local labor.

The Angolan workforce, squeezing into the shantytowns of Luanda, knows how to fight—either for UNITA or for the government—but precisely because it *had* to learn these skills, it has had little or no experience when it comes to construction. At any rate, loan repayments are made in oil, which China is buying in increasingly large quantities, spending $5.6 billion in 2005, then $9 billion in 2006, making Angola its biggest provider of crude oil, ahead of Saudi Arabia and Iran.

• • •

Back on the train, the journey was taking forever. Every time the engineers managed to coax the great brute out of a station, the conductor would weave his way through to punch tickets. "We're not as late today as we might be" was his refrain. The scheduled arrival at Cubal was 10:50 A.M., but these days, he told us, the train generally arrived around midday. "A few months ago we weren't making it in until one o'clock, but if the Chinese keep things up, we'll soon be arriving early."

The reconstruction of the Benguela-Luau line is a key project for Angolans and Chinese alike. It will allow the interior to be repopulated over time and is of course a tremendous example of Chinese technical expertise, or more specifically the ingenuity of Office 20 of the China

Railway Construction Company (CRCC), the second largest company in China, with 220,000 employees on the payroll. Since calving off from its former owner, the People's Liberation Army, the CRCC has built 14,000 kilometers of highway in China and 27,000 kilometers of railway line, including the famous one running from Beijing to Tibet, a technical marvel with tunnels at altitudes of more than 4,000 meters. For this company, throwing a few bridges over Angolan rivers will be child's play.

We wanted to meet these fabled workers in the camps at Cubal and Ganda. People we'd spoken to were amazed at the sheer size of the camps and the amount of equipment the Chinese had brought with them. Neither the Transport Ministry nor the CRCC would meet with us in Luanda, but a Chinese man we'd talked to in Lobito gave us the name of a translator, Elisa, who lived in one such camp. We decided it was worth a shot.

We had learned the hard way that gaining entry to a Chinese work site was difficult in the extreme. It takes an element of skill and a good deal of luck. Sometimes it's possible to brazen your way past the guards with a hastily concocted yarn about a meeting with their boss, but as we had again learned the hard way, the interview with the boss lasts only as long as it takes to get out your pen and notepad and admit that you're a journalist. The boss tends to be much more accommodating if you tell him that you've got twelve tons of cement to sell him, for camp bosses are, as a species, exceeded only by honey badgers in their determination to get what they're after, and the construction boom has made cement one of the most sought-after materials in the entire country.

"Chinese *non fala*," an official at the Finance Ministry told us. "The Chinese don't talk. Not even to government auditors." To us, this sounded distinctly like a dare, and we took his $1,000 bet that we'd not get a word out of a Chinese manager. We're still waiting for the check.

What he didn't know, and what we had guessed, was that we could use the Chinese translators as "wooden horses." Having attended

China, if farmers don't plant rice, they will die of hunger come the autumn. Here, though, in Africa, you can just pick fruit from the—" He was interrupted again by his telephone's muffled strains of the German group Banaroo singing "Dubi Dam Dam" in his trouser pocket, and another long conversation ensued. Again he hung up and took up where he had left off. "In China, if you don't build your house in the fall, you'll die of cold in the winter. In Africa, you can go nude all year and—"

Before we could ask anything else, the Germans surrendered to the "Pink Panther Theme." He excused himself: This call, he said, he really had to take. After a few minutes he was back with us. "Take our rivers, for example. Our rivers are wild. They flood, killing thousands every year. The rivers here look like they're asleep. And the weather! I mean, come on! In China we have cyclones, thunderstorms, tsunamis, and snow. Here, it's nothing but the most pleasant—excuse me," he said as Banaroo resumed its "Dubi Dam Dam"–ing. "True, you have to invest a lot, but the profit margins are attractive. Very attractive. Chinese businessmen here are rich. Very rich. And if—"

"Hello? Yes?" he said as he answered. "That's right . . . "

"And when I say 'rich,' I'm not talking about $1 or $2 million."

In 2003 and 2004 the massive influx of Chinese initially provoked panic among the Angolan merchants, who had been making a respectable living off the shortages created by war and corruption. The smartest of them, however, quickly realized that the newcomers could help them to get rich as well.

We found one such man, a businessman called Paulo Diarra, in his store. He told us, in perfect English honed at the finest American universities, "The Chinese brought competition and lowered prices. They're courageous, and whilst the West wastes its time lecturing us on democracy, human rights, and accountability, the Chinese are hard at work.

"They never stop. They're always working round problems, finding solutions. If they need metal for a bridge they're building, then they open a mine and just dig it out of the ground. I don't mean to offend you, but there's no way the West could ever have done so much for this country, and so fast, as the Chinese have done."

Diarra's body, from which this perfectly modulated English came, was that of an athlete encased in the clothes of an excessively elegant rapper. He had with him two cell phones and two pairs of sunglasses that would have cost the average Angolan a year's salary. His business activities include Internet provision and selling cell phones. As he told us about the many benefits of China's arrival in the country, he had his back to a team of sweat-soaked, dust-caked laborers busily unloading a truck full of Hisnese phones newly arrived from China. He saw us watching them.

"I had DHL airmail them," he said, looking over his shoulder. "It costs $10 a kilo, but there's no other way of doing it. This load we're looking at is worth $800,000. There hasn't been a charter plane available for months, and there's so much money washing about here, and so many people importing things, that the port is completely clogged. Ships have to spend three or four weeks steaming in circles just waiting for a chance to get in and unload. And it costs $25,000 for a ship to steam in a circle for a day, so what choice did I have? But don't worry," he said, turning to face us, "with a little help from the Chinese, things will soon get back to normal."

"You really think they're going to help you?"

He thought about this for a moment. "No, not really. They're here for the oil. But why are you here? The Americans and the French think they can give us lessons in ethics and transparency, but all you've done is sneak our oil out from underneath us for forty years. You corrupted everybody. You prolonged the war—especially the Americans. The Westerners swagger about preaching 'family values,' and then pile in here to Luanda, stuff their faces, and screw hookers. But the Chinese are disciplined. They're modest and respectful. If they so much as touch an Angolan woman, they get sent home."

• • •

The train to Cubal was crawling very carefully, like the youngest billy-goat gruff, across a bridge that creaked and groaned. Having made it across, it then steamed slowly past a collection of modest houses and slid into the Cubal terminus without undue fuss, as if to say to its passengers, "What? You didn't think I'd make it?"

A dozen blue trucks were outside the neglected station, waiting to be loaded with passengers and cargo alike before rumbling off toward the outlying towns that are still waiting for the railroad to reach them again. According to the last press release from the CRCC, this should have been in 2007.

We found a taxi to take us the fifteen kilometers to the Chinese camp at Chimbassi. The driver spoke as quickly as he drove, jumping from statement to statement as if they were hot coals, and expressed his frequent exclamation marks with raised eyebrows and ever-widening eyes. "Ah, the Chinese! Where there's one, there's sure to be more! Yes, yes! You'll see the ones in the camp here. And their machines!"

He turned his mind to driving for a moment, executing a flawless racing maneuver as he went wide on a corner, the wheels spitting gravel at the somber funeral procession of a local bigwig. Having raced back up through the gears on the straightaway, he approached our turn at speed, causing the car's tail to twitch as it slid neatly onto the uphill dirt road, and then continued praising the Chinese to the heavens, eyes agog.

He negotiated the final corner without taking his foot off the gas and abruptly slammed on the brakes. We looked out of the windows at the scene before us in silence as the hot metal under the hood ticked and hissed.

"Oh," he said.

The camp, he said, was gone.

"Gone?"

"It was right here. But now it isn't." That much was true. There was only a huge field, devoid of industrious Chinese, and weird sugar-loaf mountains in the far distance. "It was right here," our driver insisted. "The entrance was just here, just the other side of those baobab trees. I've seen it *with my own eyes!* It was here last week!"

At the very edge of the field we could make out the patch where the huts had been and where the cooks had grown their vegetables, all now vanished except for a clump of Chinese parsley. Save for a discarded packet of malaria pills, there was no evidence of the site's former inhabitants. We got out of the car and poked around until we found a scattering of rusty, twisted rails, remnants of the old railroad, but of its modern replacement there wasn't a sign.

"Perhaps they packed up and went to Ganda," the driver said as we kicked around in the field. "It's east of here. Not very far."

When we got to Ganda we headed for the market to ask if anyone knew where the Chinese had gone. Nobody could recall seeing anything, and the majority opinion was that they had broken camp two weeks before and gone back to their base at Alto-Catumbela, a place somewhere down the now-extinct line, and two hours' drive along bad roads, even with our rally driver. The roads, incidentally, were the responsibility of a Brazilian construction company, Odebrecht, which had won the contract but had also been unable to meet its deadlines.

We arrived at sundown. Alto-Catumbela wore the dusk badly and gave the impression of an abandoned set from a war film. The roads were plowed up, the buildings were caved in, and the shops hadn't been open for years. It looked so war-torn because it was. The town had often found itself on the shifting front line between UNITA and the MPLA. The previous year, crews from a mine-removal organization, the Halo Trust, had uncovered and removed 1,654 mines from around the nearby railway bridge alone.

But where was the camp? There was nobody out and about, if indeed there was anybody there at all. Our driver had heard that a factory not far away had been adopted by the Chinese as a new camp. He pointed the car in the direction of a distant chimney, and we carried on. Rough-cut eucalyptus and the hulls of abandoned tractors lined our way, which ended at the gates of a dilapidated paper mill. A plaque, speckled with rust and bleached by the sun, had been mounted on one of the walls when the factory had opened in 1961, and had been there ever since. It's message—"Long Live the International Proletariat!"—would no doubt have made its Chinese proprietors feel right at home. It was very nearly dark, and two guards could be seen warming themselves by a fire.

"Are the Chinese here?" we asked.

"They left," said one. "Two weeks ago," added the other. "There were a dozen of them. They had a woman with them who spoke Portuguese. Elisa, I think her name was. They were here for three months, but then they ate their dogs and left."

This singular disappearance of the Chinese from the biggest construction project in Angola is at odds not only with the ubiquity of CIF trucks in Angola but also with the official line from both Beijing and Luanda that the Benguela-Luau line is the cornerstone of the good relations between the two countries. This dogged insistence that all is well is reminiscent of the propaganda that accompanied the early operation of the Chinese-built Tam-Zam railway that opened up Zambia to the world in the 1970s.

On the way back to Lobito we came upon a Chinese worker excavating a trench with a mini digger. We pulled over to the side of the road and waved. He gunned the engine to drown out our questions. He looked up only as we turned to go. We followed the trench, and a little farther down the road we found the likely reason for his silence. A dozen Angolans, who had been digging the same trench but by hand, were standing there, leaning on their shovels.

"Are you on a break?" we inquired.

"Nope," said one. "Told to stop. Chinese guy just stepped on a mine. They're coming to get his body. Said to wait. Said not to move. Two other guys got hurt, too."

The men were employees of Huawei, the Chinese telecom giant. The trench they'd been digging was for a fiber-optic cable that would run between Benguela and Lubango. The men had already dug fifty kilometers and were paid 400 kwanzas ($5.80) a day.

This wasn't the first time something like this had happened, but such incidents were never reported in the press. A few days later, back in Luanda, we met Rebecca Thomson, a mine-clearance official with a Norwegian outfit. She confirmed the complete indifference of the Chinese to land mines. "We've got over 2 million Angolans living next to more than 3,000 areas that we know are mined. And those areas are just the ones we know about. One day I came across a crew of Chinese workers," she told us, "who were firing up their machines right in among the little red marker stones that identify a minefield. I pointed to the stones and told them what they meant. They didn't care. They just shrugged their shoulders and got on with the job."

A Chinese diplomat in the city did his best to explain his compatriots' indifference to mortal danger. "They're just not scared of dying. They know that if anything happens to them, their families will be handsomely compensated. These men are not afraid of sacrifice." He told us that the family of the Benguela victim would receive 300,000 yuan ($44,000), an astronomical sum if the relatives were from rural China. The body would be cremated in Angola because it would cost too much to transport it home, though the widow might be invited to the cremation.

Besides the Chinese attitude to sacrifice, it must be said that they've also gotten themselves caught up in the gears of an economy moving at full speed. Angola is in a hurry. The competition and the distinctly healthy profit margins encourage the companies to impose extremely— one might say insanely—long hours on their workers, so that they might finish the current contract in record time in order to move on to the next one. Their Angolan backers require such commitment because, for instance, they need houses not only to make up for those that weren't being built during the civil war but also to fuel their property speculations. And the flames have been fanned by a deluge of petro-dollars that has swept into the country since 2005. In 2007, the economy was growing at a rate of 27 percent, and the government had become one of the most courted in the world as a result—and not just by the Chinese. The advance of China seems to have lit a fire under the

Portuguese, which has in turn made the Brazilians sit up and take notice. And whatever these countries want, America and France want, too, as do former UNITA allies South Africa and Israel (all of whom simply pretend they had nothing to do with the war; they offer generous loans, such as the Israeli one that, it was hoped, would secure some right to one or two particularly fecund diamond mines).

This great rush to do business had filled Luanda's hotels with guests from all over the world and lined the pockets of those in Futungo, the presidential palace. Those who persist in advocating the best practices and good governance have been not only swept aside but positively trampled by those congregating at this new Klondike. As a result, Luanda has become the most expensive city on the planet, overtaking former title holders Oslo and Moscow.[3]

Yet there was still that Chinese worker killed near Lobito, an incident that we felt compelled to investigate further.

His Angolan coworkers didn't seem all that upset by his death, and we asked them how they tended to get along with their Chinese counterparts. There was an awkward pause and a little shuffling of feet. Eventually, one of them spoke up. "They come and measure the ditch every night. If we haven't dug at least five meters to the depth of precisely one meter, then we don't get paid. They only know two Portuguese words between them: '*Cava! Cava!*'—Dig! Dig!'"

This broke the ice. "No, they know four: '*Rapido! Rapido!*'" laughed another. "They think they need to hit us if something's not going right, like hitting us is going to help. I don't know—I reckon they think we're retarded or something, but they're the ones going 'ho-ho' like a bunch of monkeys."

The man who had spoken first piped up again. "They never listen to us. They don't care if the ground is full of rocks, or if it's too hard to dig—it just means they won't pay us."

We hadn't meant to, but we had opened a can of worms. As their confidence grew, so did the torrent of their complaints: They eat dogs . . . they don't brush their teeth . . . they spit everywhere, and so on. Stepping back, it seemed as if this fiber-optic cable, running past shantytowns that have no running water or electricity, had brought into focus the cracks in all this grand talk of "friendship between peoples."

. . .

Finding out what was going on with the railway was our top priority. In Luanda, armed with references from the Angolan Embassy in Paris, we showed up at the Ministry of Transport and requested an interview with the minister himself, or perhaps his assistant. We spent two days standing in the hall counting marble floor tiles until someone from the PR department finally put us out of our misery and threw us back out the way we had come. So we drove to Lobito and got on the phone, thinking that perhaps we might be able to get a few words with the director of the railway, or "Camino de Ferro de Benguela" (CFB), to give it its proper name. We got through immediately, and he promptly hung up on us. We played his game twice more and then gave up. So we called the man who runs the harbor because one of his nephews had told us to look him up, and he was much more helpful. Not only did he not hang up immediately, but he even offered to meet us, though he was a bit busy at present and really couldn't squeeze us in anytime in the next four months. He was really very sorry.

We tried our luck once more with the Camino de Ferro de Benguela. We managed to get through to the assistant director, José Manuel M. Vas de Carvalho, to give him *his* full name, who initially denied that we were in fact speaking to the assistant director. After a few pretty searching questions he gave in, reluctantly admitting that he was, indeed, the man we wanted to speak to and—even more reluctantly still—that he would be in his office the following morning.

Dawn saw us trooping off once again to the CFB's headquarters in downtown Lobito, a magnificent building thrown up in the 1950s and perfectly preserved ever since. A cleaning woman was polishing the marble atrium as we arrived, and two security guards were sitting

behind the kind of desk usually graced by judges. At the foot of the
broad staircase hung a gigantic map of Africa dating from colonial
times, crisscrossed with innumerable railways. Back then, you could
go first-class from Lobito to Cape Town or Dar es Salaam by steam
train. On the map, Portuguese territory was marked in red, and the
rest of the continent was simply a uniform sandy color. It had no
names of countries on it, only the towns and cities through which the
various lines ran. Local peoples were denoted pictorially: a naked,
dancing Zulu here, a Massai warrior there, a Tuareg on his camel
where the Sahara is.

No expense had been spared on these offices, and we reached out
like children to touch the leather padding on the assistant director's
waiting-room door and traced our fingers along the rich, dark wood
of the wall paneling. On the walls, carefully framed, was a series of
statistics, showing the traffic of goods and passengers rising steadily,
running from 1941 and then coming to an abrupt halt in 1974.

José Manuel M. Vas de Carvalho turned out to be a charming man.
An engineer by trade and Portuguese by nationality, he showed no
sign of the toll you'd expect would be taken on a man who had spent
twenty-eight years running a railroad whose trains barely ever moved.

"Before I retire, I hope to see the first train to run from the Congo-
Brazzaville border all the way to the Atlantic," he said. It would have
been rude to point out that, although the National Cabinet for Reconstruction had commissioned the China International Fund back in
January 2006 to build the Lobito-Luau line, the CIF had then subcontracted the job to the CRCC. It would have been rude, because pointing this out would also be drawing attention to the fact that the CRCC
had then set up sixteen camps along the line for thousands of workers,
had imported tons of construction materials and hundreds of bull-
dozers, but had yet to begin work. And that would have been rude, or
at least insensitive. But he knew what we were thinking.

"A lot of money hasn't got here yet," he said by way of explanation.
The CIF project had been canceled a few weeks before and given di-

rectly to the CRCC. "I can't tell you any more that that, because I don't know any more than that. We don't get to talk to the Chinese—everything's arranged by the Cabinet for Reconstruction."

The CIF is certainly one of the most mysterious Chinese organizations in Africa, and Angola is the only country that has merited this peculiar type of holding company. It's registered in Hong Kong and appears to perform a dual role. On one hand, it's the parent company of all the companies that receive funding from Beijing, and on the other, it receives all the oil that Angola can supply in return for these funds. The list of projects on the company's Web site is staggering and includes 215,000 council houses, three railway lines, bridges, airports, factories, roads, and administrative buildings—as well as the new capital city, all 780 square kilometers of it. It's fitted out the new city with marinas, lagoons, and enough artificial islands to make Dubai look positively medieval. Don't, however, hope for a telephone directory by name from the "Contact Us" section of the site.

The Ministry of Finance is a whopping chunk of a building made of marble, glass, and metal, and looks like it's been parachuted in, right in the center of Luanda's epic traffic jams. It's the nerve center of Angola, the place where billions of Chinese dollars in oil revenue end up. Even if you manage to get through the heavily guarded entrance, you're left looking pretty silly when you discover that the office doors are all fitted with fingerprint-recognition systems. Luckily for us, we had an invitation from a vice minister, Bastos Elmeida, who had told us that that he would be happy to see us in person if only to give credence to his assertion that nothing untoward had happened to the $4 billion that his department had received from the Exim Bank. He also took the opportunity to distance himself from the CIF. "I've no idea how much they've given out in loans, and I don't know anyone at the CIF. I don't," he added, "even know where their Luanda offices are."

His ignorance of the mysterious workings of the CIF is, to tell the truth, shared to some extent by the Chinese themselves. We spoke to one diplomat from their Luanda embassy, who wished to remain anonymous, who told us, "Nobody at the embassy even knows how to get in touch with them. We don't know what they do to earn their privileges, by which I mean, for example, the fact that they're the only ones who seem to be preapproved for Angolan visas. And they have direct access to leaders both here and in Beijing. One thing I *do* know, though: Those thirty projects they're talking about? Lies. All lies. The ones that they started have been stopped, and the others will never get off the drawing board.

"They're responsible for all the misunderstandings between the two countries, and they're the reason that we're currently [at the end of 2007] having to use every diplomatic trick in the book to restore good relations with Angola."

The passengers waiting for the train that never comes are not the only ones waiting on Chinese promises. Stockbrokers at the Shanghai exchange have also been on the edge of their seats, keeping a close eye on the CIF's operation in Angola ever since one of the company's suppliers pulled a fast one. On February 15, 2007, Zhejiang Hangxiao Steel Structure Company, Ltd., a previously unknown company, announced that it had won a $4 billion contract—a sum fifteen times larger than its total revenues from the previous year. It was no surprise, therefore, when its share price shot up 500 percent, especially after a second announcement a month later to the effect that the CIF had bought from them all the steel needed for its many public housing projects in the Cabinda Province of northern Angola. The stock market got Africa fever for several weeks on the back of the news.

The trouble started when it came to light that in advance of the first announcement, Hangxiao Steel board members had been busy buying up stock in the company. This flagrant breach of regulations put Shanghai's reputation in danger, and so the authorities came down swiftly on those involved, arresting the guilty parties for insider trading. Nevertheless, the share price continued to rise until July, when it was suspected that the CIF wouldn't complete the projects for which it had ordered so much steel. Trading in Hangxiao Steel stock was twice suspended before it finally dropped through the floor, ruining hundreds of investors.

· · ·

The National Cabinet for Reconstruction, the CIF's only partner in Angola, doesn't enjoy a much better reputation for transparency. General Kopelipa had been keeping a watchful eye on José Eduardo dos Santos's position in case there should ever be a vacancy for the top job. But in the event of such a vacancy, he wouldn't enjoy a free run at the target. He is already a powerful man, and powerful men tend to have powerful enemies. One of those enemies, General Fernando Garcia Miala, had been the director of the Foreign Secret Service until Kopelipa accused him of plotting against the president. The judge at Miala's trial in 2007 handed down a four-year jail sentence. During the trial, Miala's relatives had testified against Kopelipa, asserting he had "evaporated" $2 billion of China's money, prompting the Finance Ministry, under pressure from every governmental quarter, to publish details regarding Chinese loans for the first time. Regarding the $4 billion given to the Ministry of Finance, the numbers were explicit and precise to the point of absurdity, but regarding the sums that had gone directly from the CIF to the National Cabinet for Reconstruction, the Ministry of Finance was keen to plead noninvolvement, merely confirming that the total was $2.9 billion.

Interestingly enough, six months earlier, Angola's finance minister, José Pedro de Marais, told a meeting of the African Bank for Development in Shanghai that the CIF had supplied $6 billion in funding. The question, of course, was what became of the missing $3 billion. Had it been siphoned off by the country's rulers? Or had the CIF never actually handed it over? The answer, regrettably, is likely to remain a secret, along with many other aspects of this so-called win-win cooperation.

We left the railway's extravagant headquarters and hit a beach bar called Zulu, where the expatriate community congregates. We ordered drinks and sat down, noticing as we did so a Chinese man at the next table, hunched over a laptop, fussing so busily over a spreadsheet that the cigarette that jutted out of the corner of his mouth seemed like a factory chimney, lit from the inside. We gave the CIF another call, more out of superstition than anything else, and a secretary hung up on us before we'd gotten six words out. The gods did not seem to be smiling on us.

Figuring we had nothing to lose, we cast a line over the man next door. "We're trying to find out about the CIF," we explained. "There isn't the remotest possibility that you work there, is there?"

Such is the CIF's reputation that we wouldn't have been surprised had he snapped his computer shut and fled.

"Not anymore," he said, and introduced himself. Zhou Zhenhong was a smallish, thick-set engineer, and apparently happy to be distracted from the figures that swam about the screen in front of him. He leaned back, stubbed out his cigarette, and then immediately lit another. "I came to Africa with the CIF two years ago, but my bosses there encouraged me to open up on my own. They said that it would help Angola more than if I stayed with CIF, and they even invested in my construction company."

"And how is life treating you now? How's business?"

He took a moment, pulling thoughtfully on his smoke. "Never," he concluded, "have I seen anything like it. I went in fifty-fifty with an Angolan general, and we managed to scrape together a million dollars to buy equipment and bid on contracts. In the last twelve months we've got $10 million worth of contracts and a profit of around a million. Angola's different, you see."

"In what way, exactly?"

"The authorities want everything done yesterday. They want to transform the whole country, they want to do it immediately, and they're willing to pay. Look at Mozambique or Zambia: Nothing's changed in those places for a decade."

Zhou Zhenhong's story is a fine example. Over a pack of cigarettes, he told us more about himself. He started off working in China for a company that sent him to South Africa for five years, from where his work often took him to Zambia. Then, in 2005, the CIF hired him to work in Angola, and just three years later he started out on his own. His company, Kaituo, employs thirty Chinese and a hundred Angolans and has built two schools, a hospital, and a fire station as well as several apartment buildings, all in the Benguela Province.

• • •

The tensions between the CIF and the National Cabinet for Reconstruction and the question of the missing $3 billion keep roughly twenty Western diplomats in Luanda busy around the clock. They spend their time sending coded cables back to their various foreign offices, exuberantly (or as exuberantly as diplomatic vocabulary allows) proclaiming that the Chinese have come to the end of their period of grace in Angola, that the CIF projects are dead in the water, and that their sources are all agreed that General Kopelipa—China's go-to man—is no longer the odds-on favorite to succeed President dos Santos. As a result, Western leaders are clearing space in their diaries for official visits to the country, and business-class tickets on Luanda-bound flights are at a premium.[4] We managed to catch a few minutes with one such diplomat.

"The only person who could figure the relationship between the CIF and the Cabinet for Reconstruction is Al Capone's bookkeeper," he laughed. "The Chinese don't have enough experience in Africa to stay on top forever; they'll disappoint the Angolans before long."

Another Western diplomat agreed. "Even the Chinese are beginning to feel disappointed. They didn't realize the kickbacks would cost so much!"

Yet another summed up his colleagues' comments: "We say to our Angolan friends: It's great that you're taking a little walk with the Chinese. Enjoy yourself. But when you're ready to play in the big leagues, pay your debts and come back and see us."

Nevertheless, the success of the chain-smoking engineer from the Zulu bar and those like him suggests that this complacency may be ill-founded; the Chinese might well stay ahead of the pack in Angola. Their strategy appears to be taken directly from Sun Tzu's *Art of War*. They finance enormous projects in Africa, sometimes at a loss, which guarantees access to natural resources while granting Chinese companies a probation period that allows them to prepare for other overseas markets such as Australasia, Latin America, and perhaps even Europe and the United States. Some of these companies, like the CIF, provide capital to certain of their managers to encourage them to start up their own businesses, thus expanding the Chinese presence in the country regardless of the original company losing market share. If we are to believe what our man from Shanghai told us, around twenty companies like his have been started in Angola in just the past few months. We asked him whether all of them have been started by former CIF employees. It was the only question he refused to answer.

"Your former employer seems to have had a little difficulty meeting its deadline for the railway. Does your company meet its deadlines?"

"Of course. Speed is what it's all about; it's what the Angolans care about above all. So we work seven days a week, and that gives us the edge over the Brazilians and the Portuguese."

"But what about your Angolan employees? Don't they mind this kind of workload?"

"At least half of them are happy with it. But then again, I pay very well."

"Don't you lose time with all the mine removal?"

He was remarkably philosophical when it came to buried high explosives. "Yes, we do. But you can't wait for the Angolan army to remove them, and even if you do, then the certificate you get from them isn't worth a damn. So we do it ourselves. With a bulldozer. The trick is to depress the trigger and release it very quickly so that the mine explodes without wounding the driver. It's an expensive way of driving a bulldozer, and it's cost us a few, but it's better than delaying the project."

Chapter 13

A Friendship Between Peoples—of the Bittersweet Kind

> Zambia is becoming a province—make that a
> *district*—of China.
> —*Michael Sata, leader of Zambia's opposition party*

China's penetration of Zambia had never particularly thrilled Vivien Kalunga. True, she has in the past spoken well of the Chinese immigrants, praising their zeal and good intentions; in a southern African country such as this, when 5.5 million out of 11 million are unemployed and life expectancy is just thirty-eight, such attributes are sorely needed. But zeal and good intentions weren't enough for Vivien after July 13, 2004, when her second child was born with distinctly almond-shaped eyes.

"I never should have worked in that Chinese restaurant in Kitwe," she told us.

The restaurant manager in question, Cheng Yu, skipped town soon after the boy, Jonathan, was born, leaving behind nothing but a Sansui television. The Chinese embassy in Lusaka never responded to

Vivien's pleas for help, and her husband, of course, wasn't disposed to look kindly on his illegitimate son, refusing not only to school him but even to have him sleep under the same roof. Jonathan was therefore sent to live with his grandparents in a remote village atop a swamp, where the infant soon caught malaria. He sees his mother once a month.

• • •

China has long considered Zambia a kind of showcase for its kindness and generosity toward Africa and its people. In 1970, six years after the country won its independence from Great Britain, Chairman Mao sent 25,000 men over to Zambia to build what would become known as the Tam-Zam, the great railway line that linked Dar es Salaam in Tanzania and Lusaka in Zambia. This 1,870-kilometer line opened Zambia up to the rest of the world, allowing it to export cotton without having to depend on apartheid South Africa. The line was opened with due pomp and ceremony in 1976, whereupon the Chinese packed up and went home, not to be seen again for twenty years. When toward the end of the century they did return, they were less concerned with socialist ideology and showing the Soviets how helpful they could be. They came instead to oversee their rather more capitalist interests in agriculture, business, and, of course, the copper mines of Chambishi in the Copperbelt Province.

At present, the Zambian government claims to have 3,500 Chinese living within its borders, although the opposition party, the Patriotic Front, puts the figure far higher, closer to 80,000. What is certain, however, is that for the Chinese in Zambia, things are not as good as they could be: Anti-Chinese sentiment is running strong, stronger than in any other part of Africa.

Ma Jong, a forty-year-old engineer, found this out for himself in June 2008. He was in the dock of a Chambishi courtroom, accused of severely beating a miner, who happened also to be a union representative. The plaintiff, Richard Sinkala, claimed that he was beaten after he accused the company that owned the mine, China Nonferrous Metal Mining, and its African subsidiary, NFC Mining Africa, PLC, of failing to pay out the requisite compensation following the death of a miner. From the bewildered look on Ma Jong's face as he stood before the judge, listening to the translation, it was apparent that he thought that this whole incident was a private affair. Ma Jong cut a lonely figure in the assembled court, as nearly a hundred miners and other locals exuded a distinct sense of menace, whistling their disapproval as the defendant asked Sinkala if he had any witnesses to back up his allegations. Sinkala said that yes, he did indeed have a witness, who had seen Ma Jong grab Sinkala by the belt as he got off the bus to work. This witness was willing to testify that Sinkala was then led into Ma's office, where they would be left undisturbed: At this time in the evening, all the other offices would be empty.

According to Sinkala, once in the office Ma Jong sat him down, lit a cigarette, and asked, "Do you know who I am?"

"No," came the reply.

"Well, you're about to find out."

But Sinkala's luck was out: Despite the summons, his witness failed to appear. As the clerk of the court appealed both inside and outside (where those unable to squeeze into the courthouse were assembled in the blazing sun) for the witness to come forward, he was met with nothing but groans of despair and resignation. "It's the usual Chinese intimidation tactics," muttered one of their number, a fellow miner called Gilan. "Richard is the first person with the guts to say anything, but the Chinese have beaten all of us at one time or another. The Chinese think we're lazy, and they've got very short tempers."

Sinkala's account was evidence of this bravery. "NFC Mining offered me money in return for my silence," he had told us in private, "but I turned it down. I don't want money; I just want Mr. Ma to be sent back to China."

In the absence of witnesses prepared to testify, the only evidence that Sinkala could produce was the report from a medical examination he received on the night of the assault. As Ma Jong began once again to deny any of the charges, the judge cut his testimony short because he still had a dozen or so divorces and a handful of other assaults on the day's docket. But the judge then added a dramatic twist to the proceedings: He ordered that Ma Jong be remanded to ensure that the Chinese man would be available for the next hearing. The decision was, at long last, something for those present to cheer about. For the first time, someone from China would see the inside of the local jail.

The decision of the judge, Davy Simfukwe, betrays a subtle understanding of Chinese-Zambian relations, an understanding born of experience. When asked if he had been pressured into detaining Ma Jong, he just smiled and said nothing. The following week would see him trying six of his fellow countrymen, all now former employees of Chinese Copper Smelting (CCS). They stood accused of burning a truck and causing $200,000 worth of further damage to CCS facilities during a March 2008 strike in which five hundred Zambian workers, who were paid $100 for twenty-nine days' work a month, threw rocks at their Chinese supervisors and even took a CCS manager hostage, albeit briefly. The workers were fired but after protracted and intense negotiations were all taken back by their employer, apart from the dozen or so whom CCS saw as ringleaders. Six of these men were to stand trial, the prosecution and the CCS calling for harsh sentences to make an example of them.

However, this was by no means the biggest event of its kind. In fact, the biggest never even got before a Chambishi court. It was China's original sin in the Copper Belt. In April 2005, 250 miles north of Lusaka, the Bgrimm Explosives Plant, owned by NFC Mining Africa, PLC (for whom both Ma Jong and Sinkala worked), blew itself apart, killing all fifty-two Zambian workers inside. Many of the bodies were torn to shreds by the force of the explosion, and it seemed as if everyone in Chambishi, from the manager of the Lion restaurant to the owner of the Cholynda furniture store, had lost a father, a brother, or a son. The father of one of those killed, an electrician called Bill Sinyangwa, opened his door to us and said, "The president has sold our country to the Chinese. He's sold *us* to them, too." All that's left of the explosives plant is a rusted sign that stands by the road that once led there—"Bgrimm turns your rocks to gold"—and a small memorial amid the victims' graves.

When you begin to piece together the events that led up to the disaster, the question soon becomes not "How did this happen?" but "How did this not happen sooner?" The workforce was selected, if that is the word, from the crowd that would gather outside the plant's gates each morning. None of the chosen few had any training in handling dangerous materials, and fifty of them were crammed into a workshop designed to accommodate fewer than one-third that number. The workers were not made to surrender their cigarettes, lighters, or cell phones on their way in, and, most important, there were no separate areas for those making dynamite and those making the detonators. Yet despite these breaches, the investigation into the company's liability soon petered out, and the company paid 48 million kwacha ($9,750) in compensation for each man killed. Emmanuel Kasongo, the president of the group representing the families, told us, when we mentioned the compensation, that the families wanted to reopen the case, and that "all [they] needed was a little bit of money and some good lawyers."

Since they had neither lawyers nor the money with which to pay them, the relatives of those in the blast took to the streets. They organized protest marches and strikes, and they blocked the roads along which hundreds of trucks laden with copper travel every day on their way out of the country to Durban, South Africa. On at least one occasion, the Zambian police opened fire on the crowds, creating still more victims.

The Zambian government, like its police force, has given its full support to the Chinese and their business interests, even as its people's hostility increases. We managed to track down Felix Mutati, the Zambian minister of commerce, trade, and industry, who was doing his monthly tour of the area to inspect the progress of certain Chinese business projects. We asked him about the events of April 2005. He had the politician's knack of answering the question he wished he had been asked. As he sat in his luxury SUV, he told us, "What caused the explosion is still a mystery, but what we really need is a change in our mentality. We need to work 24/7. We need to make sacrifices if we're going to improve our country. Unemployment has been crippling us for a decade, and now, when the Chinese arrive and offer jobs, the first thing everybody does is go on strike!"

These rather callous words need some exegesis. Under British colonial rule, the country's copper mines were run along what could be called "paternalistic capitalist" lines: The miners were paid what they'd been promised and were represented by union officials who annually renegotiated the pay and benefits with the mines' owners. The owners would provide everything necessary for the workforce, including schools, hospitals, and sports facilities, developing a system that would—at least in theory—keep the mines up and running when they were eventually nationalized following independence. As the industry developed, so too did the country, until the discovery of significant copper deposits in South America caused the value of the metal to plummet. On top of this, the inexperienced government managed the mines into bankruptcy by the end of the 1980s, and so, obeying the instructions of the World Bank and the IMF to the letter, it privatized most of its remaining mining operations, which were immediately snapped up by "investors" who sacked the workforce and sold off the assets piecemeal.

Such was the state of affairs when NFC Africa Mining came to Chambishi in 1998. It found a mine that had been closed for several years, but there was little doubt that the company had grandiose plans and the money to realize them and was greeted at first as a savior. It soon became apparent, though, that the savior would operate only under certain conditions: visas for Chinese workers and managers, low wages for the local workforce, no unionization, only token taxation, and the stipulation that any negotiation of these conditions must be carried out directly with the umbrella company in Beijing or, at the very least, with the Zambian president.

After a few years and numerous problems, however, even the Chinese were eventually forced to negotiate, this time across the table from one of the biggest unions in Zambia. The talks were fraught. "I've never seen such difficult negotiations," said Agnes Bwalya, a member of both the union and the Chambishi City Council. "The Chinese like to keep changing the makeup of the delegation. It's a stalling tactic: They send people who don't have the authority to make decisions, and then replace them with *more* people with no decision-making power. And then, if we do make any gains, they split up companies so that those gains no longer apply to most of the workers in them. But they don't have to do this much, as they never really concede anything anyway," she pointed out. "If they start to feel put-upon, then they just lay off a load of people and turn to ununionized temporary workers." These protracted negotiations were once again suspended when the violence exploded at the CCS facilities in March 2008—the very same facilities that President Hu Jintao had planned to visit on his African tour in early 2007 but had been forced to bypass due to the fomenting unrest, the biggest insult endured by a Chinese official in Africa.

Like most union leaders, Agnes Bwalya had tried to negotiate wage and vacation increases for workers, but she had also been trying to persuade NFC Africa Mining to make a gesture of reconciliation to the people of Chambishi. She pointed out to the management that whereas around a thousand Chinese workers lived in comfortable, well-supplied camps, the locals had to make do with corrugated-iron shacks. The only solid buildings in the place were the missionary-built churches. "We asked the Chinese to build a shelter so that their Zambian workers would be protected from the rain when they waited for the bus to work," Bwalya said. "Even that took four years to negotiate!" In the ten years since they arrived, the mine's owners have managed to build only a playground and a single kilometer-long road that leads to its own camp.

"The Chinese have made an enormous effort," Maxwell Kabanda told us, with no apparent trace of irony. Kabanda is a Chambishi official who is considered a friend by the Chinese bosses whose cause he pleads to all and sundry. They even take him, he said, out to dinner from time to time to one of those luxurious Chinese restaurants in Kitwe. They are very nice to him. "And you know," he admonished us, "it's not very polite to ask people who have come to help you for even more help."

Nevertheless, the fourfold rise in the price of copper (the same as the increase in oil) has meant that *some* companies are finding a little more change burning holes in their pockets. Thirty miles south of Chambishi, in Luanshya, a British company called ENYA Holdings has built an Olympic-size swimming pool and cricket and rugby playing fields (naturally), and sponsors a football (that would be "soccer," old chap) club. It provides free health care at company-built clinics, has built schools stocked with books and computers, and offers scholarships to talented students.

One of the problems the Chinese face is that in Zambia they find themselves operating in a country far more democratic than their own. The Lusaka press is comparatively free, and the opposition party was able to put forward a presidential candidate that came close to winning the last election under the slogan "China Go Home!" Michael Sata, the opposition candidate, having led in the polls, lost the election due, he claimed, to the ruling party's rigging the ballot—with Chinese help.

Zambian media, on the other hand, have certainly been influenced by China for some time. When we perused the June 9, 2008, edition of the *Post*, Zambia's largest independent newspaper, we noticed that a great deal of the reports came from Xinhua, the Chinese official press agency. Page 9, for example, had a long jeremiad against the Dalai Lama under the headline "Why Does the Dalai Lama Feel Helpless?" The angle from which the piece was written, and its ideological emphasis, hardly corresponds to your average Zambian's interest in the affair:

Why is he going nowhere? Why did he acknowledge that he felt helpless? The real reason is that he has been trying to return to feudal serfdom, a social system that has long been discarded . . . even at the price of splitting China. Such a move goes totally against historical trends. The era with which the Dalai Lama is reluctant to part is one of the darkest in Tibetan history, when serfs and slaves, who accounted for 95% of the population, could not enjoy basic personal freedoms under ruthless economic exploitation, political oppression, and spiritual control. They were even denied the right to live.

The same edition of the *Post* featured twenty-nine other Xinhua articles. In fact, the Chinese agency seemed to be the newspaper's only source; if Xinhua was the prism through which the *Post*'s readers viewed the world, it was one that refracted world affairs so as to make China appear on the border of Zambia. Next to the Dalai Lama piece was another, this one celebrating China's world-leading efforts to encourage sustainable economic growth and to combat climate change. Page 12 was given over to the May 2008 earthquake and how the disaster had made the Chinese more philosophical as a people. This particular silver lining was backed up with scientific data: The quake had inspired 82.1 percent of Chinese youths to appreciate life more. "I am going to follow my heart," said one of those polled. "I am going to give money to good causes," said another. Yet another had been so inspired by the vast scale of the destruction and his government's lightning-fast reaction to it that he pledged to "save energy." Another was so affected by the death of 70,000 of his compatriots that he had resolved to "buy a better brand of cigarettes." The article then cited another young Chinese's intention to become a vegetarian as evidence that the earthquake really wasn't *all* bad.

Other news sources—Reuters, the Associated Press, Agence France-Presse—were nowhere to be found. If Arthur Miller was right when he said that "a good newspaper . . . is a country talking to itself," then either the *Post* was an appalling newspaper or Zambia had somehow become detached from Africa and shifted a long way to the east. If, however, Miller had meant to imply that talking to yourself was a sign of mental weakness, then perhaps the *Post* wasn't so bad after all. Hence the Xinhua-supplied article about the wheelchair user who had been robbed by a young drug addict near an ATM in Pennsylvania.

Xinhua's journalists have long been considered spies who write top-secret reports for officials in Beijing, though so subtle are the operatives' covers that they seem to spend a good deal of their time dealing in Western celebrity gossip. Among the pieces covering the U.S. election and Senegalese president Abdoulaye Wade's remarks thereon, there was speculation on what the author called a "romance" between David Beckham's son and Kate Beckinsale's daughter; another article dealt with the latest escapades of a Colombian drug baron.

• • •

Though the Chinese may be making ground when it comes to business in Chambishi, their image is, as has already been mentioned, sorely in need of a boost. One of the reasons for this might be illustrated by the following story.

Because not a single Chinese official in the region would agree to meet us, we set off again on one of those aimless but not altogether fruitless pokes about town. Before long, we came across a very pretty young girl and her half-Chinese daughter.

The mother's name was one that was recognized all over town at the beginning of the new millennium, when the eighteen-year-old Betha Mulanga had been crowned "Miss Chambishi 2001." But her moment of triumph also marked the beginning of her downfall. The title was accompanied by a prize of 300,000 kwacha (roughly $60), a few nice dresses, and a few new friends. One of these new friends was Mr. Wang, who quickly asked the young Miss Mulanga out for a drink. He pulled a few kung-fu moves, told great stories, and generally made her laugh. She agreed to meet again. This went on for some time, with the generous Mr. Wang giving her money for clothes and buying her a cell phone. When Betha became pregnant, however, a couple of years later, the genial kung-fu king Wang was nowhere to be seen.

Betha's parents, who had both put in twenty years at the copper mines, were at first stunned by the news of the pregnancy, though they came to think of the child as a "gift from God," and gave her that name in their language: *Tawanda*. Nevertheless, Betha's previous life was over. The days spent flitting between the workers' club and the church where her friends married local boys were long gone: She had been branded as "easy," "loose," a "fallen woman." Lovers came and went, each looking with undisguised disgust at her baby's Asiatic features.

As the general attitude toward Chambishi's Asian guests became more hostile, Betha took her child out with her less and less often. The jibes and half-whispered insults that greeted her as she walked through the market were bad enough before another Chinese gentleman caller, Mr. Chang, arrived on the scene and started courting the disgraced young mother. A year after this Mr. Chang arrived, he disappeared without warning, leaving in his wake another child, whose mixed heritage was even more pronounced.

This time her parents threw the girl out. In the meantime, the catastrophe at the explosives plant had blown apart the last vestiges of Sino-Zambian good relations. In desperation, Betha sought help at the Chinese camp. The official slammed the door in her face, insisting as he did so that she must be lying, that the boy's father could not be Chinese because all the workers there had been given fertility-blocking pills. When we met Betha, her son, Bupa, was three years old and never left the house: There was nowhere for him to go, since his mother didn't have the money to send him to school.

• • •

It would be wrong to claim that the Chinese did nothing to salvage their reputation after the Bgrimm plant claimed those fifty-two local lives. A month after the accident, Beijing responded to what it referred to as Zambia's "legitimate questions" by making a "win-win" proposal: China would designate six special economic zones in Africa, the first of which would include Chambishi. These zones, like the ones created in the 1970s in Shenzhen and elsewhere on the Chinese east coast, would be tax havens and bring prosperity wherever they fell, just as they did in China. The Chambishi zone, for example, would attract 150 Chinese companies, take in $800 million in investment, and create 6,000 Zambian jobs.

In the three years since this generous proposal was made, the only progress has been the forcing of Zambian farmers off their land to make way for the zone. And the zone definitely exists; there are signs up along the nearby roads that prove it. The officials working on the zone are all so busy that they were unable to respond to a single interview request from a foreign or Zambian journalist. Nobody knows quite how big this gold-plated zone is, and—apart from the CCS, which had been planning to invest in the area anyway—no Chinese company has invested in it.

In June 2008 Luo Xingeng and Gao Chang, respectively the CEO and his deputy of NFC Africa Mining, the company that runs the Chambishi mine, hosted two very different visits. The first was a slick affair, as is the way with all such visits that include Zambian government ministers. Felix Mutati, the minister of commerce, trade, and industry, had already been over to China to do a great deal of smiling and handshaking. He arrived in Chambishi, inspected the copper-smelting facilities, told everybody how happy he was that the Chinese were investing so much in his country, and hopped back in his shiny new 4x4 with Luo and Gao to go and find a bite to eat in the finest of the area's many Chinese restaurants.

The two Chinese might not have found much of an appetite had they the faintest idea what lay in store for the second visit to the zone. This one consisted of a Zambian parliamentary commission, which made an inauspicious start in a yellow Chinese-made bus that broke down several times over the twenty-five-kilometer journey from

Kitwe to Chambishi. The visitors were willing to put up with the delays and inconveniences, though, because, in the words of Given Lubinda, a member of the opposition Patriotic Front and the leader of the group, "We wanted to check out this economic zone we've been hearing so much about."

For us, as well as for Lubinda, this was an excellent opportunity to get inside NFC Africa Mining's compound; the China Nonferrous Metal Mining subsidiary had been turning down our interview requests for two weeks. We had tried to sneak our way in on Mutati's visit, but the guards saw us coming; they sent a pickup truck to intercept our car, which we had—unobtrusively, we thought—tagged on to the back of the minister's cavalcade. The truck drew up alongside us and forced us off the road, where we sat, wheels spinning in the dust until the minister's entourage had been admitted and the gates slammed shut behind them. This time, though, the Zambian officials were so pleased to see foreign journalists taking an interest in their cause that they left the Chinese little choice but to let us in.

Luo Xingeng and Gao Chang were there to greet the party, but seemed hesitant as to how to handle the visitors. After a brief discussion, they decided to begin with a tour of the facilities of two subsidiaries, Sino-Metals Leach Zambia and Sino-Acid Products Zambia, which process the copper extracted by the parent company. The meeting with the two companies' boss, Xie Kaishou, was a peculiar spectacle. The atmosphere was one far removed from that applauded so unanimously at the Beijing Summit.

Given Lubinda was positively blunt. "Are you," he asked Xie Kaishou, "going to raise the salaries of your 321 Zambian workers?"

"My workers are like my own sons and daughters," the businessman explained, "because harmony is the trademark of my companies."

Lubinda tried a different, more oblique, approach: "How many Zambians have risen to management rank?"

It was hard to decide whether his answer was any more—or any less—relevant than the previous one: "It goes without saying, of course, that both Chinese and Zambian alike loves to work hard, and that the long-standing friendship between our two peoples has brought mutual prosperity."

The reply to Lubinda's third question—"Are you happy with the Zambian workers?"—could have been highly complimentary, highly insulting, or, more likely, entirely beside the point.

"We expect," the beaming official explained, "employees of Sino-Metals and Sino-Acid to demonstrate loyalty, diligence, self-improvement, and self-restraint."

And on this note, the meeting was concluded. The visitors were then led into an imposing conference room to be greeted—perhaps "met" would be more accurate—by the stony faces of Luo Xingeng and Gao Chang, who went on to deliver a slick and well-rehearsed presentation. As they concluded the talk they invited questions but were typically opaque when it came to any that demanded answers any more concrete than the usual "mutually beneficial," "great friendship between peoples" mantra. They weren't to be pushed on the subject of profit margins. Or investment. Or the development of this new economic wonder zone.

Perhaps one reason for the stonewalling was economic. At the end of 2006, Zambia attempted to reform the rules that governed foreign mining companies so that they might at least partially index-link the taxes to the price of copper on the London Metal Exchange. British, Australian, and South African companies circled the wagons and worked together to find ways of avoiding as much of this new tax as possible. The Chinese companies went their own way, however. One Zambian member of Parliament had told us that "they thought their privileged relationship with the government and their pseudoeconomic zone would mean they could avoid paying full tax or even the market price on our copper." No doubt the relationship was under some strain, despite the amiable rhetoric.

Eventually, the impertinent visitors and their incessant questions about what exactly was going on in their own country were halted by an announcement—somewhat more accurate and informative than the presentation itself—that grilled chicken was about to be served.

While the lowly politicians were thus distracted, we discovered that we had been singled out to receive precise and unequivocal information from the management: We were invited into an office and told that we had entered NFC Mining property illegally and had five minutes to get out.

Lubinda later recounted for us the hourlong postchicken meeting that we'd missed. "They couldn't name a single one of the 150 companies that are supposed to be investing in this special economic zone. I hope we can be forgiven for being just the littlest bit suspicious that nothing will ever be developed here, and that the whole plan is just an elaborate scheme to protect the profits of those China Nonferrous Metal Mining subsidiaries that already have a foothold in Zambia."

Back in Lusaka, the visitors' report of their trip provoked outrage from the opposition leader, Michael Sata, when we saw him in his office. "Zambia," he raved, "is becoming a province—make that a *district*—of China. There's nothing any minister can do when confronted by China's amoral scheming. The president controls everything."

On August 19, 2008, a few weeks after this conversation took place, fifty-nine-year-old president Levy Mwanawasa suffered a stroke and died in a Paris hospital. The election to decide his successor took place two months later, and once again the opposition lost by a narrow margin—though the tension emanating from the Chinese embassy in Lusaka was palpable in the days before the result was announced.

Ultimately, the inauguration day of another pliant president would provide more good news for those Chinese firms digging the country's copper. The Chambishi court that was trying Ma Jong, the man accused of beating Richard Sinkala, was forced to release the accused due to a lack of evidence to support the charges. Sinkala was summarily sacked. We spoke to him on the phone, and he told us that he'd lost everything; that he, his wife, and his children had lost their home; that there was no prospect of his finding work. He'd been blacklisted by all the Chinese companies, and, as he pointed out, "All the companies here are Chinese."

Conclusion

Countries don't have friends, they have interests.
—*President Abdoulaye Wade of Senegal in a*
letter to Taiwan explaining his decision to ally
his country with China, October 2005

Outside the Grand Hotel in Taipei, a long line of limousines drew up to the sidewalk and disgorged their cargo of foreign dignitaries. In stark contrast to the dark, conservative suits and the black limos, a row of brightly colored flags waved in the breeze above the men's heads, a riot of color strung out to welcome Taiwan's few remaining African allies—allies like King Mswati III of Swaziland, who has held absolute power over his subjects and his thirteen wives for the last thirty-seven years. One such wife trailed behind His Majesty, wearing a pink silk suit, mother-of-pearl heels, and a white hat. Attire suitable for the horse races at Paris's Longchamp race track.

The king was ushered onto a red carpet lined by seminude Taiwanese dancers, dressed, such as they were, with feathers in what was supposed to be traditional aboriginal garb. As he made his way toward the hotel entrance the dancers came alive, swirling around him and the Swaziland TV crew that were sure to capture every moment. The dance came to an end and the dancers were once again motionless, waiting for another king to set them off. Mswati waved his appreciation and followed the red carpet all the way to the elevator, which he rode up to the luxury suite on the fifteenth floor and the opening ceremony of the first Taiwan-Africa summit. When the doors opened he found himself in rare company; also in attendance were Blaise Campoare, the president of Burkina Faso, President Fradique Bandeira Melo de Menezes from Sao Tome and Principe, Isatou Njie Saidy—a lowly vice president—of Gambia, and finally, Bingu wa Mutharika, representing Malawi, a country that owed everything to Taiwanese financial assistance but that just a few months later would turn its coat and join forces with the People's Republic of China.

The pomp that accompanied this microsummit of microstates was the very least that the host nation could provide, for these were important allies. All five countries represented in the room were members of the UN, from which Taiwan had been expelled in 1971 and whose place had been taken by communist China. Ever since, Chinese officials had taken great pains to assure the world that the little fishbowl in which Taiwan was swimming had sprung a leak. Quite apart from the larger implications of this reputation, it made life for Taiwan's then-president Chen Shui-bian very inconvenient, and life for his pilot almost impossible: To this day, every time the president's business takes him to Africa or South America, the pilot has to plot a zigzag course that avoids airspace belonging to China's allies.

Still, Taiwan helps its allies as much as it can. It prefers a more "holistic" approach to helping out and considers development as an end in itself rather than a means to one, such as access to natural resources. In fact, Taiwan's involvement in Africa has been a model for how donor countries should conduct themselves, especially when it comes to health care and hospitals. Taiwan's financial contributions to the continent are dwarfed by China's, though, for it invests half a billion dollars a year there in comparison to China, which, according to the Exim Bank, plans to invest $20 billion for the years 2008–2010, and that's not taking into account the private-sector investments.

Back outside the Grand Hotel, we watched as the dancers were herded off while we waited for the opening ceremony to end and for the six Taiwanese diplomats who had agreed to speak to us. They were eager to vent their spleen about the decline of Taiwan's influence in Africa. Some had had postings in Senegal or Chad that they had had to abandon virtually overnight when their hosts decided to fall in line behind China.

"Of course what hurt," said Chi-Chih Shin, "was not only what they did but the way they did it." Chi-Chih Shin had been Taiwan's ambassador to Senegal. In May 2005, he had signed a $120-million contract with Dakar to cooperate on a five-year project. Five months later Senegalese foreign minister Cheikh Tidiane Gadio signed a pact that gave exclusive diplomatic recognition to mainland China. Taiwan's money stayed in Senegal; its ambassador was sent home. Breaking off relations with Taiwan, President Abdoulaye Wade affirmed in a letter to his Taiwanese counterpart Chen Shui-bian that "countries have no friends, they only have interests." The former ambassador spoke for all his diplomatic colleagues seated round the table when he said, "After everything we had done for him, that letter was unspeakably rude."

Unspeakably rude it may have been, but the same thing happened ten months later in Chad, where Chinese machinations were more evident. First, it contrived to gain a footing for its oil giant CNPC there, which settled down to business with an air of reluctant tolerance of the Taiwanese presence. China predicted that time would tell, and it did. In April 2006 President Idriss Déby faced a rebellion that he managed to quell only with Sudanese and Chinese help. Tzy-Yjeng Soong, Taiwan's ambassador in N'Djamena, took off round the capital taking photographs of the rebels' Chinese-made weapons and vehicles to prove to Déby that, although he might enjoy Chinese support, so did his enemies. The president was unmoved, and that summer he informed Taiwan that unless he received $2 billion in aid he would have no choice but to break off relations and cozy up to China. "But we're a democracy," Chi-Chih Shin explained to us. "We can't come up with that kind of money at the drop of a hat. We have to answer to the taxpayer!" The president remained unmoved.

Until, that is, the Chinese put an arm around his shoulder and asked why on earth he hadn't come to them. They'd do anything to help out a friend. That's what friends were. And they *were* friends, no? In which case the president wouldn't mind signing this special "we're best friends" thing? Because they've got $1.4 trillion sloshing about, and the taxpayer would be more than happy—not that they planned on asking the taxpayer—to let their Chadian comrades have a wedge of it to tide them over.

As we have seen, China doesn't just rely on images of dollars spinning around in African leaders' heads. It can also offer to call up thousands of workers, send them wherever they're needed, and have them build whatever is wanted at an unbeatable price. It has developed simple, robust technologies that are perfect for use in Africa and is also refreshingly disinterested in human rights and good governance. To hamper the Chinese image, the dragon slayers and some NGOs have spread the rumor that most Chinese workers in Africa are actually prisoners. But in all our travels we have not met a single one and feel free to assert that this is anti-Chinese propaganda. More important, China is prepared to take risks and to stick with a project for as long as it takes.

Looking to the future, if nothing checks China's momentum, its infrastructure work alone will help unify the continent. There will be a coast-to-coast railroad, electricity and water networks, oil pipelines running across national borders, and even freedom to travel between nations for the Africans.

In order to accomplish this, China needs an Africa that is at peace, an Africa that is aware of and working toward a common goal. It needs the "Pax Sinica" in place. China's strong relationships in Egypt and Sudan surely contributed to the slackening of tensions that arose between the two countries over the usage of the Nile's water. China's investment in the eastern regions of the DRC has helped curb the power of the militias there and frustrated Rwanda's halfhearted attempts to intervene. In Uganda, thanks to Chinese infrastructure projects and oil exploration, the influence of rebel groups such as the Lord's Resistance Army and the People's Redemption Army has weakened considerably. More such examples can be found in Xinhua's "Africa Moving Forward" section, a meticulous account of the positive aspects of China's presence in Africa that is updated daily.

For these kinds of reasons it isn't hard to believe that China will succeed where the West, despite all its Institutes for African Studies, its academics, its libraries and museums devoted to African art and culture, has failed. One American diplomat in Brazzaville put it bluntly but accurately when we asked him about his competitors. "God bless the Chinese. They build roads and dams, and quite frankly we don't have what it takes to do those things any more. All we can do is give English classes and try to sell our technology."

On the other hand, there is also the distinct possibility that China's incursion into Africa carries the seeds of its own failure. Africa as a whole has never exhibited a great deal of enthusiasm for the grand visions of foreign do-gooders—whether it's Dr. Livingstone in the nineteenth century or the Irish minstrel duo of Geldof and Bono in the twenty-first. China is no exception and is beginning to encounter some resistance; in some cases it seems this resistance is strongest in the very places in which China has worked the hardest to gain favor.

This isn't just because workers grumble over pay or their bosses are prone to corporal punishment or because of any of the wild rumors that are spread so eagerly around Central Africa. One such rumor that hit Brazzaville suggested that 2,000 Chinese prostitutes were about to arrive in the city. Husbands all over the place used the "news" to their advantage, cutting their wives' allowances and generally threatening that they might just go find out for themselves whether there was any truth behind the tale that Chinese women were both more affectionate *and* more economical. In Douala, another rumor had it that China's goal was to repopulate the area, bringing in 10,000 men armed with powerful aphrodisiacs that would allow them to maintain an erection for three days; as proof we were shown the Chinese-made stimulant in question, called Cavalier de Rue, which listed among other charming ingredients sealskin, buffalo penis, powdered deer antler, seahorse, yak testicles, and turtle shell. And in the Central African Republic of Bangui a story went around that the Chinese were building a whole railroad *in secret* that would allow them to transport all the country's natural resources all the way to Port Sudan and then off to China, never to be seen again.

On a more serious note, in South Africa, which is host to the biggest Chinese population in Africa, President Thabo Mbeki's own brother, Moeletsi, wrote this in 2005: "Africa sells its natural resources to China and China sells the well-manufactured products back to Africa. This dangerous system reproduces Africa's past relationships with colonial powers. Not only must Africa hold on to its own resources for its own industrialization but China must also contribute to the deindustrialization of countries that are relatively developed."

The word "colonization" is taboo when discussing relations between China and Africa, and its use by such a high-profile individual provoked outrage in Beijing. There was further jumping up and down when President Mbeki didn't hesitate to back his brother. At a conference with South African students in 2006 Mbeki said that Africa must not allow itself to get trapped in what he called "an unequal relationship with China like its previous relationships with colonial powers." China is taking a devoutly Leninist line, though, insisting that imperialism is the ultimate stage of capitalism—not communism, even if the social inequalities and triumphant materialism of modern China would set Mao spinning in his grave.

In a bid to forestall criticism, the Chinese government passed a law, just in time for the 2006 China-Africa summit, which introduced nine principles to the code of ethics governing companies operating overseas as adhering to local laws, handling bids with transparency, respecting local labor laws and protecting the environment.

Martyn Davis, the director of the Centre for Chinese Studies at South Africa's Stellenbosch University, brushes off the accusations of Chinese neocolonialism in Africa, saying that if there is such talk it has more to do with the insecurities of Africans than the behavior of the Chinese. "There are 2,000 Chinese companies in Singapore, but no one in Singapore talks about Chinese colonization, or of an economic takeover of the country. Quite the contrary, Singapore encourages Chinese investment. Then there are the 900 Chinese companies scattered all over Africa—the second biggest continent in the world, and people want to talk about neocolonialism there? This is an African problem, not a Chinese one."

Still, on the ground, the positive effects of China's presence in Africa are at times late in coming. For example, China has developed technologies that have improved agriculture, commerce, industry, and mineral extraction in Zambia, but the side effects are even more evident: Anti-Chinese feeling there came within an inch of bringing down its president. And as we've seen in the chapter about Zambia, China's wholly inadequate response to the workers killed at the Chiambishi explosives plant has caused its public standing to plummet. That's not all, either. Some of the Chinese-built factories in the copper belt were outfitted to process minerals from mines in the neighboring Democratic Republic of the Congo, and when the DRC unilaterally closed its border to Zambia to prevent illegal mining, several Chinese projects were brought to the brink of collapse. Beijing pressured both governments to resolve the situation, though without success, which is yet more evidence of how its influence in the region is diminishing.

Furthermore, in September 2007 China announced two lines of credit totaling $11.3 billion for the Democratic Republic of the Congo, intended for the revival of the country's mining industry. The DRC has a third of the world's cobalt reserves, a quarter of the world's diamond reserves, and considerable amounts of gold and coltan, an essential mineral in the production of telephones and laptops.

Less than a year later, fighting broke out in the provinces of North and South Kivu in the eastern part of the country. A rebel called Laurent Nkunda, with Rwandan help, managed to deliver a sound thrashing to the government troops while the UN looked on, unable to intervene. More than 250,000 people were forced to flee the violence, causing concern that another humanitarian crisis was looming in the very region that has seen the deaths of five million in the last decade. When General Nkunda's forces threatened the town of Goma, the UN sent one of its most senior emissaries to negotiate with him: Olusegun Obasanjo, the former president of Nigeria. Nkunda presented Obasanjo with a list of eight demands, one of which was a surprise to the seasoned politician. The general wanted the DRC to revise its contracts with China "so that our natural resources are not sold off on the cheap." Some experts felt that Nkunda was trying simply to broaden his support by trading on anti-Chinese sentiment. If he was, it didn't prevent a spectacular reversal of fortune—he was arrested by Rwandan forces in January 2009.[1]

Another example of the growing dissatisfaction with the Chinese among Africans (and of African unpredictability) can be found in Angola. Between 2004 and 2006 this country, under the leadership of José Eduardo dos Santos, benefited from massive loans at incredibly low interest rates and is China's biggest trade partner in Africa thanks to the vast quantities of oil it sells. And then, seemingly out of the blue, Luanda canceled Sinopec's contract to build a $3 billion refinery in Lobito. There was precious little explanation, just that the refinery would produce derivatives for export to China and did not address the domestic needs of Angola. As explanations go, it seemed not unreasonable, but in the months that followed Angolan officials noted (some say "caused") the cancellation of other Chinese projects such as the new Luanda airport and the overhaul of the railroads. Again, the Angolan authorities were reluctant to explain their decisions apart from mentioning something about problems between the Chinese contractors and the local subcontractors. And again, it's a reasonable explanation but hardly disguises the wholesale change of Angola's attitude toward China. And what of those grandiloquent declarations of undying friendship between peoples; what of the hymns to mutual interests when the contracts were being signed?

"In 2003 we didn't have a choice," we were told by one high-level official at the Ministry of Finance in Luanda. "Only the Chinese would help us back then. Today, it's different." One difference he might have been referring to is Angola's vast newfound wealth. Between 2001 and 2006 the price of a barrel of crude oil rose from $26 to $66, and Angolan production of it doubled from 740,000 barrels to 1.5 million. Thus the Chinese loan of $6 to 7 million that was once such a useful bargaining chip was drowned in a slick of petroleum dollars—34 billion in 2006 and nearly 45 billion in 2007.

Even tiny Guinea, whose finances are barely comparable to Angola's, although it is the third largest bauxite producer in the world, was able to turn down a Chinese package deal for an aluminum processing plant and a hydroelectric dam project worth a billion dollars in 2007. An official at the Ministry for Mines had spoken to us with a good deal of enthusiasm, but it appeared that, in the end, the guarantees demanded by the Exim Bank went beyond what Guinea was willing to put up. Events took an even more surprising turn in Equatorial Guinea when, in the spring of 2008, *Chinese* workers went on strike in the home village of dictator Teodoro Obiang Nguema. The police crackdown was ruthless, shooting into the crowds and killing two Chinese. A few days later, 400 workers were sent back to China on specially chartered flights.

"We asked China to send some other workers," an anonymous official told Reuters. "We don't need Chinese strikers, just workers."

The way things have gone it seems that many countries have taken the advice Professor Chris Alden gave in his 2005 essay, "Leveraging the Dragon." He recommended that Africa learn to say no to China, and that if it couldn't do that, then it should at least start negotiating conditions favorable to its own development, just as China has done to the Western companies that want to build factories in its special economic zones.

It seems, too, that it never occurred to China that Africa might not always be such a compliant partner. He Wemping, a research fellow at the Institute for West Asian and African Studies in Beijing, openly admitted that China lacks the experience necessary for working effectively and efficiently in Africa. "We have been overwhelmed in the last two years by companies coming to us, asking for risk assessments of such-and-such a country," she said. "We are the only institute in China that can provide such assessments, and we've only got twenty researchers."

As a result, conglomerates such as the telecom giant Huawei sometimes have to approach French or British consultants and employ them to lead negotiating teams or advise them on strategic decisions concerning their business in Africa. We spoke to several Chinese executives who all expressed dismay at the lack of expertise available in their embassies despite their being "reliably overstaffed." For too long the African experience of Chinese diplomats has been limited to airports' red carpets. Some give the impression that they haven't really been keeping up with the news, haven't heard of certain rebel groups until one of their fellow citizens is kidnapped (as happened in Nigeria) or killed (as happened in Ethiopia, and more recently, in Sudan, where four Chinese workers were kidnapped and subsequently murdered by a rebel group in November 2008).

Problems and attitudes such as these make you wonder whether China's Africa project might just founder. Some analysts emphasize how recent and how fragile China's commitment actually is and how competition, particularly from less threatening countries like Brazil, India, and South Korea, is still heating up.

Other skeptics will tell you that China has taken on too many risky, ill-considered positions at the same time. They will speculate that a number of major and unconnected incidents could be enough to force a Chinese withdrawal—incidents such as the defection of an ally like Zambia or Angola, a kidnapping in Ethiopia or Nigeria, a lethal terrorist attack in Algeria, an outbreak of disease, an ecological disaster, or even a Chinese-built dam bursting just as the water was rising behind it.

German engineers who inspected the Imboulou Dam in Congo-Brazzaville found that low-grade cement had been used and that the dam itself had been built on a pocket of water that went undetected during the geological testing that preceded its construction. But this talk of Chinese failure is for the moment nothing but talk, either excessively optimistic or excessively pessimistic depending on who's doing the talking. As we traveled through the Chinese Africa we understood that China's only real failure, if indeed it is a failure, is that it set out with a kind of messianic zeal—as a heaven-sent and fraternal partner that could cure all woes and bring prosperity. But then, the need for security guards wherever the Chinese go, the corruption scandals, and no matter how often Beijing may claim otherwise, the contempt for the locals, made it in some respects come to resemble other players past and present.

In the end, China has met Africa's needs head-on and at last established a sound basis for development. If China hadn't built the infrastructure, especially the communications and electricity networks, no one would have. China's involvement in Africa has awoken it to the fact that it is not condemned to everlasting stagnation. China is obviously there at the pursuit of its own interests, and although Chinese talk of friendship is now often derided, it has offered Africa a future—or at least a *vision* of the future—that would have been inconceivable just a decade ago. In the end, China's arrival has been a boon for a continent adrift, a continent forgotten for too long by the rest of the world.

So China has achieved something very important. It has given Africa a real sense of worth, as much in the eyes of Africans themselves as in the eyes of foreigners. The West has never been more interested in Africa than it is now that China has attempted to conquer it. Americans, Europeans, Japanese, and Australians are just some of those who have gotten the message loud and clear: If China has bothered to invest so much time, money, and energy in Africa, then there must be an opportunity there that's been overlooked by the West.

Clearly Africa has "value," however one chooses to interpret the word. The rush to discover and develop it has just begun. The ball, however, is firmly in the African leaders' court; they now have the means to see their ambitions through to fulfillment. International organizations have never offered them such huge unconditional loans as China is now

CHINA'S "GREAT LEAP" IN AFRICA

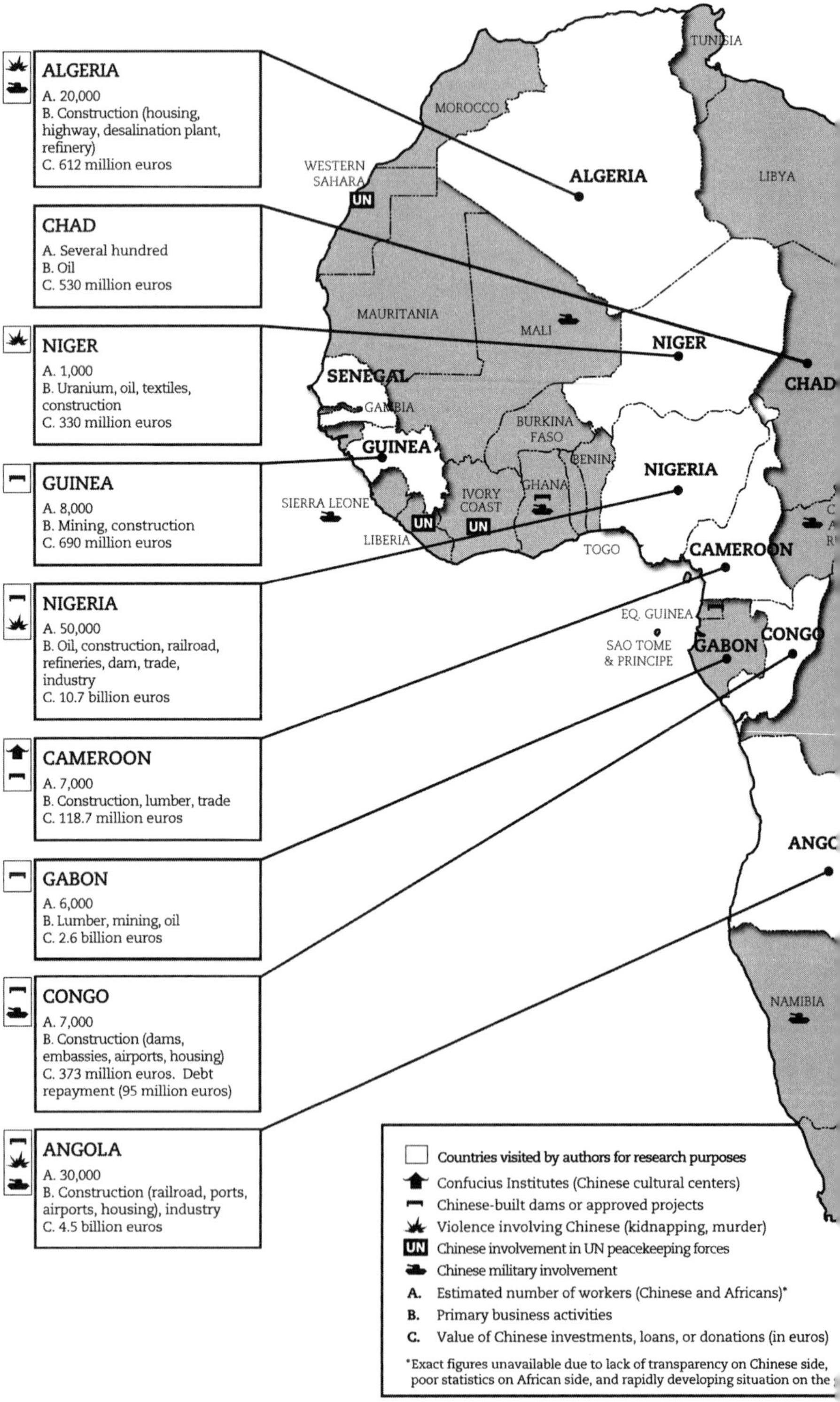

ALGERIA
A. 20,000
B. Construction (housing, highway, desalination plant, refinery)
C. 612 million euros

CHAD
A. Several hundred
B. Oil
C. 530 million euros

NIGER
A. 1,000
B. Uranium, oil, textiles, construction
C. 330 million euros

GUINEA
A. 8,000
B. Mining, construction
C. 690 million euros

NIGERIA
A. 50,000
B. Oil, construction, railroad, refineries, dam, trade, industry
C. 10.7 billion euros

CAMEROON
A. 7,000
B. Construction, lumber, trade
C. 118.7 million euros

GABON
A. 6,000
B. Lumber, mining, oil
C. 2.6 billion euros

CONGO
A. 7,000
B. Construction (dams, embassies, airports, housing)
C. 373 million euros. Debt repayment (95 million euros)

ANGOLA
A. 30,000
B. Construction (railroad, ports, airports, housing), industry
C. 4.5 billion euros

Map labels: TUNISIA, MOROCCO, ALGERIA, LIBYA, WESTERN SAHARA, UN, MAURITANIA, MALI, NIGER, CHAD, SENEGAL, GAMBIA, BURKINA FASO, BENIN, NIGERIA, GUINEA, SIERRA LEONE, IVORY COAST, GHANA, UN, UN, LIBERIA, TOGO, CAMEROON, EQ. GUINEA, SAO TOME & PRINCIPE, GABON, CONGO, ANGOLA, NAMIBIA

Legend:
☐ Countries visited by authors for research purposes
Confucius Institutes (Chinese cultural centers)
Chinese-built dams or approved projects
Violence involving Chinese (kidnapping, murder)
UN Chinese involvement in UN peacekeeping forces
Chinese military involvement
A. Estimated number of workers (Chinese and Africans)*
B. Primary business activities
C. Value of Chinese investments, loans, or donations (in euros)

*Exact figures unavailable due to lack of transparency on Chinese side, poor statistics on African side, and rapidly developing situation on the

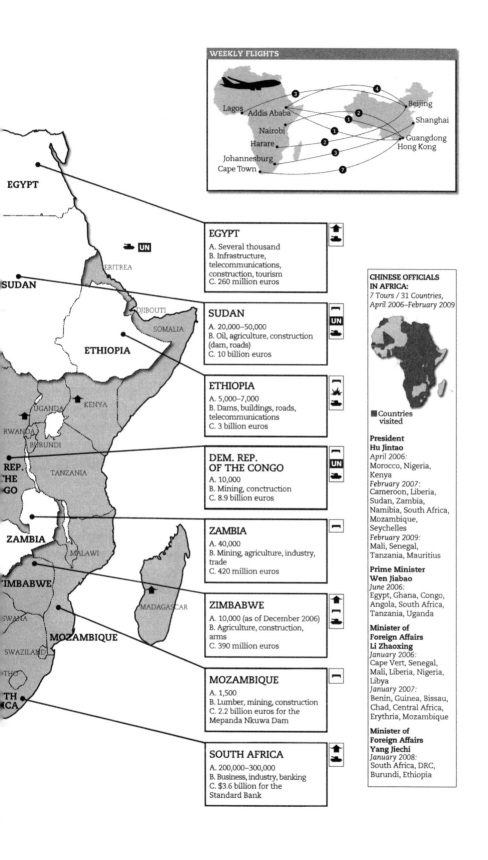

WEEKLY FLIGHTS

Lagos
Addis Ababa
Nairobi
Harare
Johannesburg
Cape Town
Beijing
Shanghai
Guangdong
Hong Kong

EGYPT

SUDAN

ETHIOPIA

ERITREA
DJIBOUTI
SOMALIA

UGANDA
KENYA
RWANDA
BURUNDI
REP.
THE
GO
TANZANIA
ZAMBIA
MALAWI
IMBABWE
MADAGASCAR
SWANA
MOZAMBIQUE
SWAZILAND
THO
TH
CA

EGYPT

A. Several thousand
B. Infrastructure, telecommunications, construction, tourism
C. 260 million euros

SUDAN

A. 20,000–50,000
B. Oil, agriculture, construction (dam, roads)
C. 10 billion euros

ETHIOPIA

A. 5,000–7,000
B. Dams, buildings, roads, telecommunications
C. 3 billion euros

DEM. REP. OF THE CONGO

A. 10,000
B. Mining, conctruction
C. 8.9 billion euros

ZAMBIA

A. 40,000
B. Mining, agriculture, industry, trade
C. 420 million euros

ZIMBABWE

A. 10,000 (as of December 2006)
B. Agriculture, construction, arms
C. 390 million euros

MOZAMBIQUE

A. 1,500
B. Lumber, mining, construction
C. 2.2 billion euros for the Mepanda Nkuwa Dam

SOUTH AFRICA

A. 200,000–300,000
B. Business, industry, banking
C. $3.6 billion for the Standard Bank

CHINESE OFFICIALS IN AFRICA:
7 Tours / 31 Countries, April 2006–February 2009

■ Countries visited

President Hu Jintao
April 2006:
Morocco, Nigeria, Kenya
February 2007:
Cameroon, Liberia, Sudan, Zambia, Namibia, South Africa, Mozambique, Seychelles
February 2009:
Mali, Senegal, Tanzania, Mauritius

Prime Minister Wen Jiabao
June 2006:
Egypt, Ghana, Congo, Angola, South Africa, Tanzania, Uganda

Minister of Foreign Affairs Li Zhaoxing
January 2006:
Cape Vert, Senegal, Mali, Liberia, Nigeria, Libya
January 2007:
Benin, Guinea, Bissau, Chad, Central Africa, Erythria, Mozambique

Minister of Foreign Affairs Yang Jiechi
January 2008:
South Africa, DRC, Burundi, Ethiopia

ACKNOWLEDGMENTS

This book would never have seen the light of day if not for the help of many, many people from Paris to Luanda, Lausanne to Beijing, and dozens more cities and villages in Africa and China; we hope we haven't missed anyone here. Certain individuals put themselves at personal risk to help us or to talk to us without official authorization. Their names do not appear here, but if they read these words we hope they know how grateful we are to them, and that without their courage, our work would simply not be possible.

Our first thoughts go to our spouses, who encouraged and supported us during the entire yearlong project. Sophia Procofieff in Geneva and Gabriela Bejan in Lausanne, as well as Sabali Meschi in Florence. Lou Rossi, in Paris, was a loyal helper. We thank too the editors who believed in us: Anne Sastourné at Le Seuil, Olivier Nora, Manuel Carcassonne and Heidi Warneke at Grasset, and Carl Bromley and Sandra Beris at Nation Books.

This book was translated into English by Raymond Valley, but James Pryor gave it its final form, which we hope is clear and convincing!

The publications we work for gave us the time and some of the financial means we needed to make our way through China and Africa: Alain Jeannet at *L'Hebdo*, Rémy Ourdan and Marie-Pierre Subtil at *Le Monde*. Those who published our reports during our travels did the rest: Marco Moussanet and Chiara Somajni at *Sole 24*

Ore, Paul Steenhuis at *M* magazine from NRC Handelsblatt in Amsterdam, Jamie Welford at *Newsweek,* Alice Gabriner at *Time,* Monica Allende and Cathy Galvin at the *Sunday Times,* Renata Ferri at *Lo Donna*, Eric Meyer and Nicolas Ancellin at *Geo,* Will Dobson at *Foreign Policy,* Hikaru Takayama at *Courrier Japon,* and last but not least Eleonora Monti in Milan, Regina Anzenberger and Waltraud Sommer in Vienna, and Marco Delogu in Rome.

Our thanks also go to Chantal Colle and Mouctar Bah at Conakry; Chen Shun and Liu Weiwei in Dakar; Gorel Harouna and Wendy in Niamey; Gislain Amba in Douala; Samuel Bogny, Charles Ndongo, and Jean-Marie Mbega in Yaoundé; Chriss Nwobu, Roy Chang, and Amy Wood in Lagos; Philippe Zhang, Jessica and Philippe Ye in Pointe Noire; Marie-Chantal Codia, Claude Alphonse N'Silou, Eric Forni, Mark Biedlingmaier, and the lovely André Ondele in Brazzaville; Fayçal Métaoui, Ghania Oukazi, and Saïd Djaafer in Algiers; Gérard Prunier in Ziyad. We thank Qin Daoqing in Addis Abeba; Mohamed Moawia and Ms. Lin in Khartoum; "Jack," who we will never forget meeting in Port-Sudan; Jean-Gabriel Leturcq and Gao Feng in Cairo; Philippe Dahinden in Luanda; Fundulu in Lobito; Chris Alden in London; Guy Dinmore and Gabriella Bianchi in Washington, D.C., and then in Rome; Gene Stone, Jason Tougaw, David Driver, and Anna Lopriore in New York; and Gail Wagman in Sauve, France.

Manuela Parrino and Paolo Longo in Beijing offered their hospitality and friendship, and Lindsey Hilsum, Caroline Puel, Azzedin Haddaoui, and Dr. Xinghua offered their advice. Jade Charles deserves special mention for her critical African contact. We thank Amélie in Chengdu for her amazing efficiency; Mireille in Chongqing, Mrs. Ni in Yiwu, and Hungdah Su in Taipei, as well as Bruno Shen and Mr. Shu, who served as our support staff. Jacky Pugin, Mursheed, and Lyushun Shen in Geneva, and Catherine Morand and Florence Duarte in Lausanne provided expert assistance.

The book benefited greatly from the critical suggestions of Francine Sacco and Laurent Dubuis in Yverdon, and Marc Wolfensberger in Lausanne, who read earlier versions of the manuscript.

Of course, there were a handful of officials in Algiers, Khartoum, and Brazzaville who did all they could to block our work—those who refused to answer our phone calls, left us for hours in a prison cell in a Congolese airport, or kicked us out of an Angolan ministry. If by thanking them we might convince them to provide better treatment to future journalists, then we offer a thank-you to them as well.

NOTES

Prologue

1. Wherever it appears, "ton" refers to a metric ton, a measurement of mass equal to 1,000 kilograms, or 2,204.6226 pounds.

2. Robert Fisk, *The Great War for Civilisation* (London: Vintage, 2007).

3. He died in December 2008.

4. Ian Taylor, "China's Relations with Sub-Saharan Africa in the Post-Maoist Era, 1978–1999," in Frank Columbus (ed.), *Politics and Economics of Africa*, Vol. 1 (New York: Nova Science, 2001).

5. *China Business Journal* (Zhong guo mao yi bao), February 15, 2007.

6. Pierre Picquart, *L'Empire chinois* (Lausanne: Favre, 2004).

7. François Hauter, "Psychanalyse d'une vie dure," *Le Figaro*, August 7, 2007.

8. Julia Lovell, *The Great Wall: China Against the World* (New York: Grove Press, 2006).

9. UN Conference on Trade and Development, Africa report, September 26, 2007.

10. Stephen Smith, *Négrologie* (Paris: Calmann-Lévy, 2003).

Chapter 1

1. Swaziland, Sao Tome and Principe, Gambia, Burkina Faso, and Malawi. Later, on January 14, 2008, Malawi announced that it would break relations with Taiwan in favor of China.

2. See "Beijing Summit & Third Ministerial Conference of Forum on China-Africa Cooperation," November 3–5, 2006 (http://english.focacsummit .org), for quotes from the summit.

3. In November 2001 negotiations broke down that would have provided developing countries access to Western markets, especially to agricultural markets.

4. NEPAD is a project inaugurated in July 2001 by Thabo Mbeki (South Africa), Abdelaziz Bouteflika (Algeria), Abdoulaye Wade (Senegal), Olusegun Obasanjo (Nigeria), and Hosni Mubarak (Egypt).

5. With the goal of fully integrating the European Free-Trade Zone by 2012. The treaty with the United States went into effect on January 1, 2006.

6. A loan of $3 billion and credit worth an additional $2 billion for export purposes, both at preferential interest rates, for the years 2006–2009.

Chapter 2

1. All Chinese names with Western surnames in this and the following chapters are shown in the Western order: first name first, last name second.

2. Harry Broadman, *Africa's Silk Road* (Washington, DC: World Bank, 2007).

3. All Chinese names in this and the following chapters are shown in the traditional Chinese manner: last name first, first name second.

Chapter 3

1. The country's name is the Republic of the Congo; it's capital is Brazzaville. It is often referred to as Congo-Brazzaville in order to differentiate it from the Democratic Republic of the Congo, itself called Congo-Kinshasa.

2. The moabi tree (*Baillonella toxisperma*) was listed as "vulnerable" on the 2007 Red List of the IUCN (International Union for Conservation of Nature and Natural Resources). The tree's bark has medicinal uses, as does oil extracted from the seeds of its fruits.

3. Associated Press, "Giant Nation's Appetite for Resources Stirs Other Growth," September 4, 2007.

4. *Trends in Wood Products, 1961–2003* (Rome: UN Food and Agriculture Organization, 2005).

5. Forêts tropicales humides du Bassin du Congo, Sylvain Angerand.

6. Reuters, "Two-Thirds of Congo Basin Forests Could Disappear," December 15, 2006.

7. Nadine Laporte, *Science*, June 8, 2007.

8. In 2000, 660 kilometers of roads were built in Congo-Brazzaville, more than four times the 155 kilometers per year built in the 1980s.

9. *Nouvelles de Brazzaville,* December 29, 2006.

10. Arnaud Labrousse, "La Conquête de Conkouati," *Congopage.com,* May 23, 2007.

11. Considerable scientific information on the mushroom fungus (*Hepialus Amoricanus Ober*) and its host (*Cordyceps sinensis*) can be found on the Web.

Chapter 4

1. Commemorative stones found in China have made it possible to date the first five voyages precisely: 1405–1407, 1407–1409, 1409–1411, 1413–1415, and 1417–1419.

2. Jérôme Kerlouégan, "Si la Chine avait découvert l'Amérique . . . ," *Les Collections de l'Histoire,* no. 38 (January 3, 2008).

3. Yuan Wu, *China and Africa, 1956–2006* (Beijing: China Intercontinental Press, 2006).

4. Books were published by his second in command and by his interpreter, as well as by a solider on board: *The Countries of the Western World* (1434), *The Wonders Seen from a Ship on the Seas* (1436), and *The Wonders of the Coasts of the World* (1451). These books are not in print. See http://en .wikipedia.org/wiki/Zheng_He.

5. Yuan, *China and Africa,* 24.

6. Ibid., 38.

7. Ibid., 47.

8. Ibid., 51–52.

9. Roland Marchal, *Afrique-Asie: Une Autre mondialisation?* (Paris: Presses de Sciences-Po, 2008).

10. Yuan, *China and Africa,* 40, 46.

Chapter 5

1. The official unemployment rate varies, ranging from 25.6 percent in northern countries of Africa to 18.6 percent in sub-Saharan Africa. These figures, however, do not reflect the true extent of the problem because many unemployed people simply aren't counted.

2. They weren't able to do so because the materials were stuck in Pointe-Noire. The railway between Pointe-Noire and Brazzaville is fragile and overused.

3. Claude-Alphonse N'Silou was elected to the assembly as a representative from Bacongo in the second round of voting on August 5, 2007.

4. The CFA franc (in French: *franc CFA,* "cé éfa," or just *franc* colloquially) is a currency used in twelve formerly French-ruled African countries, as well as in Guinea-Bissau (a former Portuguese colony) and in Equatorial Guinea (a former Spanish colony). See http://en.wikipedia.org/wiki/CFA_franc (accessed February 5, 2009).

5. "L'Actuel DG de l'AADL accusé de corruption," *Le Soir d'Algérie,* February 13, 2007.

Chapter 6

1. *IRIN*, February 9, 2007.

2. *Le Républicain,* February 9, 2007.

3. This figure comes from a statement by Chinese prime minister Wen Jiabao in August 2003 during a visit to his Nigerian equivalent, Hama Amadou (*People Daily, Beijing,* August 8, 2003). Official trade figures list Niger's main trade partner as Nigeria, followed by France.

4. In the summer of 2007, it reached a peak of $270 a kilo on the spot (cash) market.

5. The three Chinese companies were Trendfield Holdings, based in Hong Kong, which had Guy Duport, a senior employee of Areva, as a signatory; the state-owned company China National Nuclear Corporation (CNNC); and ZXJOY Invest, a subsidiary of the giant Chinese telecommunications company ZTE.

6. The first zone held 1,953 square kilometers of proven reserves of 12,764 tons of uranium.

7. The second zone held 1,872 square kilometers of proven reserves of 6,191 tons.

8. Rue89.com, July 28, 2007.

9. "La Fin des rentes politiques," *La Lettre du Continent,* no. 523 (August 30, 2007).

10. *The Impact of China on Sub-Saharan Africa* (Brighton, UK: Institute of Development Studies, November 2007).

11. See the impassioned study published by Mohamadou Abdoul, Karim Dahou, and Marie Trémolières, "Le Cas Maradi-Katsina-Kano: Couloir de développement?" in *Les Dynamiques transfrontalières en Afrique de l'Ouest* (Paris: Karthala, 2007).

12. The term *Washington Consensus* was initially coined in 1989 by John Williamson to describe a set of ten specific economic-policy prescriptions that he regarded as constituting a "standard" reform package for crisis-wracked developing countries by Washington, D.C.–based institutions, such as the International Monetary Fund, the World Bank, and the U.S. Treasury Department. Subsequently, as Williamson himself has pointed out, the term has come to be used in a different and broader sense, as a synonym for market fundamentalism; in this broader sense, Williamson states, it has been criticized by writers such as George Soros and Nobel Laureate Joseph E. Stiglitz, and also by others, such as some Latin American politicians and heterodox economists. The term has become associated with neoliberal policies in general and has been drawn into the broader debate over the expanding role of the free market, constraints on the state, and U.S. influence on other countries' national sovereignty.

13. *Perspectives économiques en Afrique* (Paris: Banque Africaine de Développement/Organization for Economic Cooperation and Development, 2006–2007); *Perspectives économiques régionales, Afrique subsaharienne* (Washington, DC: International Monetary Fund, April 2007); *Niger,* FMI report No. 17/13 (Washington, DC: International Monetary Fund, July 2007).

14. In 2007, the price of a kilo of uranium hit $270, though it had fallen to $100 by September 2008, largely as a result of the U.S. government's putting up for sale two hundred tons from its strategic reserves.

Chapter 7

1. Swiss pharmaceutical giant Novartis has already developed a commercial drug combination on the basis of artemisia, named Coartem, so the price is about to soar.

2. David Zweig is quoted in William Foreman, "Why a 'Peacefully Rising China' Wields Power Around the World," Associated Press, September 3, 2007.

3. "Guerre du sexe à Douala," *Jeune Afrique*, January 6, 2008.

4. *La Lettre du Continent*, no. 512 (February 22, 2007).

5. This figure (700,000 visa applications) provoked countless responses on Cameroonian blogs, responses occasionally marked by xenophobia. See lavoixducamer.com.

6. Ousmane Sy Ndiaye, permanent secretary of UNACOIS, quoted in "Sénégal, pour ou contre les commerçants chinois," www.afrik.com, August 13, 2004.

7. "Conflits entre commerçants: L'UNACOIS menace de faire une descente chez les chinois," *Wal Fadjri,* July 2, 2004.

8. This very controversial incident could have constituted blackmail of Taiwan on the part of President Wade, according to the Senegalese press. Wade was said to have pocketed a commission of $7 million.

9. This was confirmed in Beijing. Work visas to Senegal are among the hardest to get for the Chinese. As a result, they have become some of the most expensive visas on the black market. The Chinese who do get to Dakar usually sneak through Guinea and survive in Senegal only by bribing immigration officials.

10. Xinhua, Chen Shun, "Les Sénégalais prennent d'assaut le marché chinois," October 29, 2007.

Chapter 8

1. Sebastian Junger, "Enter China, the Giant," *Vanity Fair,* June 2007.

2. www.izf.net, Bangui, January 5, 2007 (accessed March 18, 2008).

3. *People's Republic of China: Sustaining Conflict and Human Rights Abuses; The Flow of Arms Accelerates* (London: Amnesty International, June 2006).

4. Ian Taylor, "China's Arms Sales in Africa: Beijing's Reputation at Risk," *China in Brief* (Jamestown Foundation) 7, no. 7 (April 5, 2007).

5. Xinhua, "Chinese Expert Refutes Amnesty International's Slams on Arms Trade," June 12, 2006.

6. www.transarms.org (accessed March 18, 2008). TransArms is a database on the arms trade, based on both Chinese and American sources.

7. www.fas.org/sgp/crs/index.html, the Web site of the Congressional Research Service, Washington, DC (accessed March 18, 2008).

8. *Small Arms Survey, 2005: Weapons at War* (Geneva: Graduate Institute of International Studies, 2006), 98.

9. A French acronym for UN forces in the Democratic Republic of the Congo.

10. *RIA Novosti*, March 13, 2007.

11. "Russia Pushing Ban on Illegal Production of Kalachnikov Rifles," *Novosti*, April 28, 2006.

12. "Le Génocide de 1994: La Responsabilité des bailleurs de fonds," *Global Research* (November 1996).

13. Taylor, "China's Arms Sales."

14. If people killed by Foday Sankoh's Revolutionary United Front (RUF) in Sierra Leone—with the support of Charles Taylor—are included.

15. *Annual Report, Liberia* (London: Amnesty International, 2004).

16. Made by the Harbin Dongan Engine Manufacturing Company.

17. Amnesty International, "Soudan: Les Armes continuent de favoriser des atteintes graves aux droits humains au Darfour," press release, May 8, 2007.

18. *Conventional Arms Transfers to the Developing Nations* (Washington, DC: Congressional Research Service, October 23, 2006).

19. *Bloomberg Report*, September 30, 2008.

20. New America Foundation, "U.S. Arms Recipients, 2006/07: Africa," December 2008.

21. Stephanie McCrummen, "U.S. Africa Aid Is Increasingly Military," *Washington Post*, July 18, 2008.

22. Bill Lipton, "U.S. Arms Climbing Rapidly," *New York Times*, September 13, 2008.

23. Gerald LeMelle, "Africa Policy Outlook," *Foreign Policy in Focus* (February 2008).

Chapter 9

1. Gérard Prunier, *Darfour: Un Génocide ambigu* (Paris: La Table Ronde, 2007).

2. Ronan Farrow and Mia Farrow, "The Genocide Olympics," *Wall Street Journal*, March 28, 2007.

3. With Saudi Arabia, Kuwait, Abu Dhabi (one of the seven United Arab Emirates), and the sultan of Oman.

4. Fisk, *Great War for Civilisation*.

5. Jean-Gabriel Leturcq, a Cairo-based French researcher for CEDEJ (Centre d'études et de documentation économiques, juridiques et sociales).

6. Cleophas Lado has made reference to 20,000 Chinese security men: *The Political Economy of Oil Discovery and Mining in the Sudan: Constraints*

and Prospects on Development (Cape Town: University of the Western Cape, 2000). Available at www.dur.ac.uk/justin.willis/lado.htm.

7. "Le Darfour s'enfonce dans un désastre sécuritaire et humanitaire," *Le Temps*, July 12, 2008.

8. *Sudan Tribune*, September 2, 2008.

Chapter 10

1. John Le Carré, *The Honourable Schoolboy* (London: Hodder & Stoughton, 1977).

2. The stockholders are CNPC (China) with 41 percent, Sinopec (China) with 6 percent, Petronas (Malaysia) with 40 percent, the Sudanese state-owned company Sudan Petroleum Company with 8 percent, and al-Thani (United Arab Emirates) with 5 percent.

3. CNPC holds 40 percent of the Greater Nile Petroleum Operation Company, the most important consortium in Sudan, formed in 1997 to develop Blocks 1, 2, and 4 located southwest of the Nuba Mountains. It also holds 95 percent of Block 6 in southern Darfur and 35 percent of the Red Sea Petroleum Company, which owns Block 15, located partially offshore in the Red Sea.

4. According to the British nongovernmental organization Care for the Wild International, quoted in Agence France-Presse, "L'Armée soudanaise, accusée de tuer des éléphants pour le marché chinois," www.chine-informations .com/actualite/chine-larmee-soudanaise-accusee-de-tuer-des-elephants -pour-le-marche_3165.html, March 14, 2005.

5. John Ghazvinian, *Untapped: The Scramble for Africa's Oil* (San Diego/New York: Harcourt Books, 2007).

6. Quoted in Alex Perry, "Africa's Oil Dream," *Time*, May 31, 2007, www.time.com/time/nation/article/0,8599,1626751,00.html (accessed March 18, 2008).

7. Erica Downs, "The Fact and Fiction of Sino-African Energy Relations," *China Security* 3, no. 3 (Summer 2007): 42–68.

Chapter 11

1. See especially Ted Galen Carpenter, *America's Coming War with China* (New York: Palgrave Macmillan, 2006) or Robert Kaplan's "How We Would Fight China," *Atlantic Monthly*, June 2005.

2. "US to Build Largest Embassy Structure in Addis," *Addis Fortune,* January 4, 2008.

3. Another source has estimated the number as between 6,000 and 8,000. See *China's Engagement of Africa: Preliminary Scoping of African Case Studies* (Stellenbosch, South Africa: Centre for Chinese Studies, University of Stellenbosch, November 2007).

4. *How China Delivers Development Assistance to Africa by Dr. Martyn Davies and Aliquot* (Stellenbosch, South Africa: Centre for Chinese Studies, Department for International Development [DFID], University of Stellenbosch, February 2008).

5. Xinhua, "China: A Major Commercial Partner for Ethiopia," June 7, 2007.

6. Xinhua, "A Road Symbolizing China-Ethiopia Friendship," May 14, 2007.

7. *Le Quotidien du Peuple,* May 31, 2002.

8. The other companies that competed for the contract were Strabag (Germany), Salini et Impregilo (Italy), Kajima (Japan), Enka (Turkey), Group 5 (Austria), and Satcon (Ethiopia).

9. Jeffrey Gettleman, "In Ethiopia, Fear and Cries of Army Brutality," *New York Times,* June 18, 2007.

10. "Ethiopie: Les Dynasties Texanes à l'offensive," *Africa Energy Intelligence,* no. 587, September 3, 2008.

11. Reuters, "Capitan Energy Companies, LLC, and Titan Resources Corporation Jointly Announce the Signing of Multiple Production Sharing Agreements with the Minister of Mining and Energy for Ethiopia," August 25, 2008.

12. Laurent Zecchini, "Washington rénonce à transférer son quartier général Africom en Afrique," *Le Monde,* June 7, 2008.

13. Stephanie McCummen, "U.S. Africa Aid Is Increasingly Military," *Washington Post,* July 18, 2008.

14. Gerald LaMelle, "Africa Policy Outlook 2008," *Foreign Policy in Focus,* www.fpif.org, February 7, 2008.

15. Over the last decade, its defense budget has seen yearly double-digit increases.

16. "Base militaire chinoise au Congo-K," *La Lettre du Continent,* no. 543, June 19, 2008.

17. Mercenaries from South Africa were implicated in the failed 2003 coup that also carried traces of oil-company involvement.

18. Joshua Eisenman, "China's Post–Cold War Strategy in Africa: Examining Beijing's Methods and Objectives," in Joshua Eisenman, Eric Heginbotham, and Derek Mitchell (eds.), *China and the Developing World: Beijing's Strategy for the 21st Century* (New York: East Gate Books/M. E. Sharpe, 2007).

19. France still has 8,000 soldiers in Chad, Ivory Coast, Gabon, Senegal, and Djibouti.

20. This is according to the only biography to appear on Jacques Foccart (Pierre Pean, *L'homme de l'ombre* [Paris: Fayard, 1990]). Another publication, *Foccart parle*, is a 1,000-page collection of Foccart's interviews with Phillipe Gaillard (Paris: Fayard-Jeune Afrique, vol. 1 in 1995 and vol. 2 in 1997).

21. Richard Banégas, Roland Marchal, and Julien Meimon, "La Fin du pacte colonial?" *Politique Africaine,* no. 105 (March 2007): 23.

22. Radio France International, May 18, 2006.

23. Raymond W. Copson, *The United States of Africa* (London: Zed Books, 2007).

24. Conditions set on the receipt of U.S. aid, democratic progress, and governmental transparency.

25. Copson, *United States of Africa.*

26. Horace Campbell, "China in Africa: Challenging U.S. Global Economy," in Firoze Manji and Stephen Marks (eds.), *African Perspectives on China in Africa* (Oxford: Fahamu, 2007).

27. Anthony Lake, Christine Todd Withman, and Princeton N. Lyman, *More Than Humanitarianism*, task force report by the Council on Foreign Relations, January 2006, 49–52, www.cfr.org/publication/9302/more_than _humanitarianism.html?breadcrumb=%2Fregion%2Fpublication_list%3F groupby%3D3%26id%3D143%26filter%3D2006%26page%3D7.

28. Barry Sautman and Yan Hairong, "Friends and Interests: China's Distinctive Links with Africa," in Dorothy Grace Guerrero and Firoze Manji (eds.), *China's New Role in Africa and the South* (Oxford: Fahamu, 2008).

29. Christopher Smith (R-NJ), statement in "China's Influence in Africa," hearing, House Subcommittee on Africa (Washington, DC: GPO, July 28, 2005); Joshua Eisenman and Joshua Kurlantzick, "China's Africa Strategy," *Current History* (May 2006): 219–224.

30. Caroline Daniel, "Energy Resources: The Great Game-2 Is Coming?" *Financial Times*, June 2, 2005.

31. Eisenman, "China's Post–Cold War Strategy in Africa."

32. See www.treasurydirect.gov.

33. Paper presented at the seminar "China's New Role in Africa and the South: A Search for a New Perspective," Shanghai, May 25, 2007, www.tni .org/detail_page.phtml?act_id=16957.

Chapter 12

1. "Rat-Hunting Regulators Battle Insider Trading," *Caijin Magazine*, May 28, 2007.

2. AFX Asia News Agency, "Angola Minister Confirms China International Fund Deal but Some Delays Seen," May 18, 2007.

3. ECA International, "Enquête mondiale sur le coût de la vie," November 26, 2007.

4. The price of a business-class Air France ticket from Paris to Luanda in the spring of 2008 was $10,091. The least-expensive tickets on the "Houston Express," the flight used by Texas oilmen to fly nonstop to Angola, cost double.

Conclusion

1. Agence France-Presse, "DR Congo's Nkunda Attacks China to Boost Political Kudos," November 19, 2008.

BIBLIOGRAPHY

Books

Abdoul, Mohamadou, Karim Dahou, and Marie Trémolières. "Le Cas Maradi-Katsina-Kano: Couloir de développement." In *Les Dynamiques transfrontalières en Afrique de l'Ouest*. Paris: Karthala, 2007.

African Economic Outlook. Paris: Organization for Economic Cooperation and Development and the African Bank of Development, May 2007.

African Mineral Production, 2001–2005. Keyworth Nottingham, UK: British Geological Survey, 2007.

Afrique subsaharienne: Perspectives économiques régionales. Washington, DC: International Monetary Fund, April 2007.

Alden, Chris. *China in Africa.* London: Zed Books, 2007.

Bates, Gill, Huang Chin-hao, and Morrison J. Stephen. *China's Expanding Role in Africa: Implication for the United States.* Washington, DC: Center for Strategic and International Studies, January 2007.

Broadman, Harry. *Africa's Silk Road.* Washington, DC: World Bank, 2007.

Bruckner, Pascal. *Le Sanglot de l'homme blanc.* Paris: Seuil, 1983.

Carving Up the Congo. Amsterdam: Greenpeace International, 2007.

China's Interest and Activity in Africa's Construction and Infrastructure Sectors. Stellenbosch, South Africa: Center for Chinese Studies, University of Stellenbosch, 2007.

Darfur: Revitalizing the Peace Process. Africa Report No. 125. Nairobi and Brussels: International Crisis Group, April 2007.

Les Entreprises chinoises à la conquête du monde. Paris: HEC (Haute Ecole de Commerce), in partnership with the Commission Asie Pacifique des Conseillers du Commerce Extérieur de la France, October 2007.

Gaye, Adama. *Chine-Afrique: Le Dragon et l'autruche.* Paris: L'Harmattan, 2006.

Gestion de la rente pétrolière au Congo Brazzaville: Mal gouvernance et violations des droits de l'homme. Paris: International Federation for Human Rights, May 17, 2004.

Ghazvinian, John. *Untapped: The Scramble for Africa's Oil.* San Diego/New York: Harcourt Books, 2007.

Glaser, Antoine, and Stephen Smith. *Comment la France à perdu l'Afrique.* Paris: Calmann-Lévy, 2005.

Hembery, Rachel, Anna Jenkins, George White, and Beatrix Richards. *Illegal Logging: Cut It Out! The UK's Role in the Trade in Illegal Timber and Wood Products.* Godalming, UK: WWF, January 2007.

Herel, Xavier. *Afrique, pillage à huis clos: Comment une poignée d'initiés siphonnent le pétrole africain.* Paris: Fayard, 2006.

Hery, Jennifer. *Le Soudan: Entre pétrole et guerre civile.* Paris: Harmattan, 2003.

Hugeux, Vincent. *Les Sorciers blancs: Enquête sur les faux amis français de l'Afrique.* Paris: Fayard, 2007.

Hurst, Cindy. *China's Oil Rush in Africa.* Washington, DC: Institute for the Analysis of Global Security, July 2006.

Kynge, James. *China Shakes the World: The Rise of a Hungry Nation.* Chatham, Kent, UK: Phoenix, 2007.

Levathes, Louise. *When China Ruled the Seas: The Treasure Fleet of the Dragon Throne, 1405–1433.* New York: Oxford University Press, 1997.

Manji, Firoze, and Stephen Marks, eds. *African Perspectives on China in Africa.* Oxford: Fahamu, 2007.

Marchal, Roland. *Afrique-Asie: Une Autre mondialisation?* Paris: Presses de Sciences-Po, 2008.

Menzies, Gavin. *1421: The Year China Discovered the World.* London: Bantam Press, 2002.

Ngoupandé, Jean-Paul. *L'Afrique sans la France.* Paris: Albin Michel, 2002.

Niger. IMF report no. 07/13. Washington, DC: International Monetary Fund, July 2007.

Oil Revenue Transparency. London and Washington, DC: Global Witness, March 2007.

People's Republic of China: Sustaining Conflict and Human Rights Abuses; The Flow of Arms Accelerates. London: Amnesty International, June 2006.

Perret, Christophe. "L'Afrique et la Chine." *Atlas on Regional Integration in East Africa.* Paris: Economic Community of West African States/Sahel West Africa Club and the Organization for Economic Cooperation and Development, December 2006.

Picquart, Pierre. *L'Empire chinois*. Lausanne: Favre, 2004.

Prunier, Gérard. *Darfour: Un Génocide ambigu*. Paris: La Table Ronde, 2007.

Roughneen, Simon. *Influence Anxiety: China's Role in Africa*. Zurich: International Relations and Security Network, May 2006.

Shaxson, Nicolas. *Poisoned Wells: The Dirty Politics of African Oil*. New York: Palgrave Macmillan, 2007.

SIPRI Yearbook. Oxford: Stockholm International Peace Research Institute, Oxford University Press, 2007.

Smith, Stephen. *Négrologie*. Paris: Calmann-Lévy, 2003.

Taylor, Ian. "China's Relations with Sub-Saharan Africa in the Post-Maoist Era, 1978–1999." In Frank Columbus (ed.), *Politics and Economics of Africa*. Vol. 1. New York: Nova Science, 2001.

Ten Hoove, Lotte. *La Chine à la conquête du continent noir*. Paris: Centre d'Études et de Recherche de l'École Militaire, January 2006.

Van de Looy, Judith. *Africa and China: A Strategic Partnership?* African Studies Center Working Paper 67. Leiden, Netherlands: African Studies Center, July–September 2006.

Yuan Wu. *China and Africa, 1956–2006*. Beijing: China Intercontinental Press, 2006.

Journal and Magazine Articles

"Africa Economy: Eastern Promise?" *Economist Intelligence Unit* (October 2, 2007).

"Afrique: Les Blancs y ont-ils encore une place?" *Courrier International*, no. 850 (February 15–21, 2007).

"L'Afrique courtisée: Chine, Inde, Brésil, les nouveaux conquérants." *L'État de l'Afrique*, special series, no. 15, *Jeune Afrique* (2007).

"L'Aide militaire chinoise à l'Afrique vue du Quai d'Orsay." *La Lettre du Continent*, no. 497 (June 29, 2006).

Alden, Chris. "Leveraging the Dragon: Toward an Africa That Can Say No." *YaleGlobal*, March 1, 2005.

"Areva Won't Hand over Madaouela Data." *Africa Intelligence*, no. 157 (June 6, 2007).

Beuret, Michel. "Chine-Taiwan: Combat de dragons pour l'Afrique." *L'Hebdo*, September 20, 2007.

———. "Comment la Chine a conquis les Africains." *L'Hebdo*, January 25, 2007.

———. "Le Drapeau chinois flotte sur l'Afrique." *L'Hebdo*, January 27, 2005.

———. "Le Far West des Chinois." *L'Hebdo*, May 15, 2008

———. "Faut-il changer ses dollars et partir vivre en Chine?" *Allez Savoir*, no. 42 (September 2008).

Bloomfield, Steve. "Chinese Cheques." *Monocle*, no. 1 (March 2007).

Braud, Pierre-Antoine. "La Chine en Afrique: Anatomie d'une nouvelle stratégie chinoise." *Institute for Security Studies* (October 2005).

"Un 'Brillant' mariage au palais." *La Lettre du Continent*, no. 498 (July 13, 2006).

Brookes, Peter. "Into Africa: China's Grab for Influence and Oil." Heritage Lectures, no. 885. Washington, DC: Heritage Foundation, February 2007.

Brookes, Peter, and Ji Hye Shin. "China's Influence in Africa: Implications for the United States." Heritage Lectures, no. 1916. Washington, DC: Heritage Foundation, February 2006.

Cabral, Luís Pedro. "Nouveaux riches et pauvres de toujours: Luanda côté jet-set." *Courrier International*, no. 885 (October 18, 2007).

"China's Honeymoon in Africa Turns Sour." *Economist*, April 1, 2007.

"Chine, Inde, Brésil: Pourquoi ils misent sur l'Afrique." *Ecofinance*, no. 48 (October 2004).

"Chine-Afrique: Une Équipe à double commande." *La Lettre du Continent*, no. 1202 (November 18, 2006).

"Chine-Afrique: Que des gagnants, vraiment?" *Jeune Afrique* (February 11–17, 2007).

"La Chine et Taiwan cohabitent dans le pétrole du Tchad!" *La Lettre du Continent*, no. 493 (April 27, 2006).

"Chirac, grand chinois d'Afrique." *La Lettre du Continent*, no. 503 (October 12, 2006).

Coussy, Jean. "Idéologies, diplomaties et intérêts dans les relations économiques afro-asiatiques." *Politique Africaine*, no. 76 (December 1999).

"La Déferlante chinoise." *Continental*, special report, no. 54 (November 2006).

De Laurenzo, Mauro. "China and Africa: A New Scramble?" *China Brief* (Jamestown Foundation) 7 (April 5, 2007).

"La Diplomatie du yuan." *Jeune Afrique* (February 4–10, 2007).

"Dividendes africains: Malgré un environnement difficile, les sociétés françaises implantées sur le continent se portent bien." *Jeune Afrique* (January 14–20, 2007).

Downs, Erica S. "The Fact and Fiction of Sino-African Energy Relations." *China Security* 3, no. 3 (Summer 2007): 42–68.

"Exportations: Pourquoi ils aiment l'Afrique." *Jeune Afrique* (December 24, 2006–January 6, 2007).

"Les Fantassins de la Chinafrique." *Jeune Afrique* (February 4–10, 2007).

"La Fin d'une époque." *Jeune Afrique* (February 11–17, 2007).

Fleshman, Michael. "Niger: Une Famine annoncée." *Afrique Renouveau* 19 (October 2005).

Ford, Neil. "Abuja Promises Rail Revolution." *African Business,* November 1, 2006.

Girard, Patrick. "Histoire Chine-Afrique: Un Partenariat très ancien." *Marianne,* January 19, 2006.

"Le Grand enjeu gazier du Golfe de guinée." *La Lettre du Continent,* no. 547 (December 13, 2006).

"La Guerre du Soudan, aussi une histoire de pétrole?" *La Lettre du Continent,* no. 505 (November 9, 2006).

Hilsum, Lindsey. "We Love China." *Granta,* no. 92 (January 15, 2006).

Hoh, Anne-Valérie, and Barbara Vignaux. "L'Afrique n'est plus l'eldorado des entreprises françaises." *Le Monde Diplomatique* (February 2006).

Holslag, Jonathan. "China's New Mercantilism in Central Africa." *African and Asian Studies* 5, no. 2 (June 2006): 133–169.

"L'Homme de l'ombre des services secrets chinois en Afrique." *La Lettre du Continent,* no. 502 (September 28, 2006).

"Hu Jintao: La Révolution silencieuse." *Jeune Afrique* (December 24, 2006–January 6, 2007).

"Insécurité au Nord: La 5ème République, l'uranium et la rebellion." *Le Canard Déchaîné,* February 12–19, 2007.

"Jeu dangereux avec les frontières: Comment les dirigeants africains jouent Pékin contre Washington ou Pretoria." *Courrier International,* no. 413 (October 1, 1998).

Jiang Chung-lian. "Pékin et Taïpeh: Les Enjeux africains." *Géopolitique Africaine,* no. 1 (2003).

———. "Le Pétrole, nouvelle dimension des relations sino-africaines." *Géopolitique Africaine,* no. 14 (2004).

———. "Les Relations de la Chine avec l'Afrique: Fondements, réalités et perspectives." *Monde Chinois* (Choiseul), no. 8 (Summer–Autumn 2006).

Kerlouégan, Jérôme. "Si la Chine avait découvert l'Amérique . . . " *Les Collections de l'Histoire,* no. 38 (January 3, 2008).

Lafargue, François. "La Chine: Stratégie d'influence en Côte d'Ivoire." *Monde Chinois* (Choiseul), no. 8 (Summer–Autumn 2006).

———. "La Chine et l'Afrique: Un Mariage de raison." *Diplomatie* (September–October 2005).

———. "La Chine et l'Algérie: Entre amitié et Realpolitik." *Monde Chinois* (Choiseul), no. 8 (Summer–Autumn 2006).

———. "Coopération et consequences." *Continental,* no. 54 (November 2006).

————. "Kriegspiel pétrolier en Afrique." *Politique Internationale,* no. 112 (November 7, 2006).

"Lobbying: Des VRP sino-africains." *La Lettre du Continent,* no. 1202 (November 18, 2006).

Ma Mung, Emmanuel. "La Diaspora chinoise, géographie d'une migration." *Perspectives Chinoises,* no. 79 (September–October 2003).

"Miala a-t-il voulu être calife?" *La Lettre du Continent,* no. 525 (September 27, 2007).

"Mines: Le Grand retour (de la Chine)." *Jeune Afrique* (December 24, 2006–January 6, 2007).

Mooney, Paul. "China's African Safari." *YaleGlobal,* January 3, 2005.

Neumann, Benjamin. "La France rate le coche du réveil algérien." *L Expansion* 1 (July 1, 2006).

"Never Too Late to Scramble: China in Africa." *Economist,* October 28, 2006.

Niger. FMI report no. 07/13 (July 2007).

Niquet, Valérie. "La Stratégie africaine de la Chine." *Politique Etrangère* 2 (June 2006): 361–374.

"L'Onde de choc de l'affaire Miala." *La Lettre du Continent,* no. 490 (March 16, 2006).

"Pétrole tchadien: Voilà les Chinois!" *Jeune Afrique* (January 21–27, 2007).

Robert, Anne-Cécile. "Du cauchemar à l'espoir? Rêve d'une seconde indépendance sur le continent africain." *Le Monde Diplomatique* (November 2006).

Russell, Thomas. "Shanghai Show Sees Brisk Activity." *Furniture Today,* October 29, 2007.

"Sarkozy et nous: Ce que l'Afrique et le monde arabe doivent attendre du nouveau président." *Jeune Afrique,* special report (May 13–19, 2007).

Servant, Jean-Christophe. "La Chine à l'assaut du marché africain." *Le Monde Diplomatique* (May 2005).

Taylor, Ian. "Arms Sales to Africa: Beijing's Reputation at Risk." *China in Brief* (Jamestown Foundation) 7 (April 5, 2007).

Thompson, Drew. "China's Emerging Interests in Africa: Opportunities and Challenges for Africa and the United States." *African Renaissance Journal* (July–August 2005).

————. "Economic Growth and Soft Power: China's Africa Strategy." *China Brief* (Jamestown Foundation) 4, no. 24 (December 2004): 1–4.

"23 sommets au crible: Tout ce qu'il faut savoir sur les rencontres au plus haut niveau entre le continent et l'ex-métropole." *Jeune Afrique* (January 28–February 3, 2007): 30–31.

Vescovacci, Nicolas. "Le Soudan veut briser l'isolement." *Le Monde Diplomatique* (March 2000).

Vircoulon, Thierry. "Chinois d'Afrique, Chinois en Afrique et Afro-Chinois: Les Multiples visages de la communauté." *Monde Chinois* (Choiseul), no. 8 (Summer–Autumn 2006).

Viviano, Frank. "China's Great Armada." *National Geographic,* June 2005.

Walt, Vivienne. "China's African Safari." *Fortune,* February 7, 2006.

Zambelis, Chris. "Public Diplomacy in Sino-Egyptian Relations." *China Brief* (Jamestown Foundation) 7 (April 5, 2007).

Zheng, Ruolin, and Béchir Ben Yahmed. "De la Françafrique à la Chinafrique." *La Revue (Jeune Afrique)* (November–December 2006).

Newspaper Articles and Newswires

"L'Actuel DG de l'AADL soupçonné d'avoir empoché 7.5 millions de dinars de commission." *Le Soir d'Algérie,* February 13, 2007.

"Africa Should Not Be Denied Business Opportunities with China: Zambian Minister." Xinhua, October 27, 2007. (Interview with Felix Mutati)

"Africa Welcomes Chinese Investors: Zambian Minister." Xinhua, September 8, 2007. (Interview with Felix Mutati)

"African Jobs Spur Village's Economy." *Beijing Times,* January 4, 2007.

"Afrique: La France s'enlise." Interview with Jean-François Bayart. *Le Nouvel Observateur,* May 12, 2005.

"Afrique, nouvel horizon chinois." Interview of Pierre-Antoine Braud. *Le Monde,* December 10, 2006.

"Afrique-France: Exister dans un monde en mutation." *Le Pays* (Burkina Faso), February 9, 2007.

Agunbiade, Tayo. "China: Friends or Foes?" *This Day,* February 16, 2007.

Akosile, Abimbola. "Chinese Investment in Nigeria: What Motives?" *This Day,* February 28, 2007.

Amosu, Akwe. "China in Africa: It's (Still) the Governance, Stupid." *All Africa,* March 15, 2007.

"Angola Minister Confirms China International Fund Deal but Some Delays Seen." AFX News Asia, May 18, 2007.

Ayad, Christophe. "L'Ombre de Pékin sur le conflit Tchad-Soudan." *Libération,* April 25, 2006.

Ayad, Christophe, and Thomas Hoffman. "La France craint Pékin sur son pré carré africain." *Libération,* April 27, 2006.

Barjonet, Claude. "Comment le BTP français tente de préserver sa place en Afrique." *Les Echos,* April 2, 2007.

Bernard, Philippe, and Bruno Philip. "Relation Chine-Afrique: La Montée en puissance." *Le Monde,* February 3, 2007.

Besada, Hany. "China in Africa: A Reliable Friend?" *Taipei Times,* March 25, 2007.

Bezat, Jean Michel. "L'Afrique devient la première zone de production de Total." *Le Monde,* June 12, 2007.

———. "Babel-en-Mer au large de l'Angola." *Le Monde,* July 29, 2007.

"Bouteflika et Hu Jintao signent un accord stratégique." *La Tribune* (Algérie), November 7, 2006.

Bristow, Michael. "China Trade Threatens Tropical Trees." BBC News (Beijing), July 6, 2007.

Cadu, Clotilde. "La Déforestation touche l'Afrique." *Le Monde,* June 14, 2007.

Camara, Alpha. "Guinée Conakry: De plus en plus de Chinois arpentent les rues pour vanter les vertus de leurs médicaments en langue locales." *Syfia,* April 26, 2006.

"Chambishi Copper Smelter Workers Go on Strike." *American Metal Market,* January 4, 2008.

"La Chanteuse américaine Amerie attendue en Angola." *Angola Press,* November 6, 2007.

Chen, Stephen. "Landless Farmers Urged to Migrate to Africa." *South China Morning Post,* September 19, 2007.

Cheng, Allen T. and Karl Maier, "Hu's Natural Resource Safari." *Bloomberg Report,* February 6, 2007.

Chilabi, Haggai. "Zambia, China to Sign Free Zone Deal." *Reuters,* March 4, 2008. (Interview with Felix Mutati)

"China Intl Fund Angola Deals Cancelled or under Renegotiation: Report." Xinhua Financial Network, July 9, 2007.

Chimangeni, Isabel. "China's Growing Presence Met with Resistance." *IPS Lusaka,* October 18, 2006.

"China Opens Another Copper Mine in Zambia." Xinhua News Agency, October 27, 2007.

"China, Zambia Sign 200 Mln USD Contracts." Xinhua News Agency, February 26, 2008.

"China's Weapons Exportation 'Righteous.'" Xinhua News Agency, July 29, 2007.

"China to Encourage Smaller Companies to Invest in Africa." South African Press Association, Voice of Africa Media Foundation, May 16, 2007.

"Chinese President Welcomes Election of Banda As Zambian President." Dow Jones Newswire, November 7, 2008.

"CNMC to Double Chambishi Copper Mine Capacity." Interfax China, April 15, 2008.

"Les Chinois à la manœuvre en Afrique: Les Ouvriers venus de Chine concurrencent les Africains. Exemple au Gabon." *Libération,* May 15, 2006.

"Cold Reception for China's President." *UN Integrated Regional Information Networks,* February 6, 2007.

Delaporte, Renaud. "La Chine a lancé une OPA amicale sur l'Afrique." *Agora Vox,* November 2006.

"De quinze à vingt mille ouvriers et maçons chinois travaillent en Algérie." *Le Figaro,* June 28, 2006.

"Des règles du jeu très opaques." *La Tribune,* January 4, 2007.

"Deux cents mille maisons seront construites en Angola jusqu'en 2008." *Angola Press,* March 7, 2006.

"DJ China Railway Builder, Nigeria Sign $8.3 Billion Deal." Dow Jones Commodities Service, November 6, 2006.

Durand, Paul. "Les Ouvriers dénoncent le travail à la chinoise." *Syfia,* November 2, 2006.

Eisenstein, Zoe. "Angola Seeks Investment in Lobito Port." Reuters, August 22, 2007.

"Environnement: Les Chinois dévastent le Gabon." *Le Point,* October 19, 2006.

"L'Ex-chef des SIE condamné pour crime d'insubordination." *Angola Press,* September 21, 2007.

"Foire import-export de Canton: Afflux des hommes d'affaires zambiens." Xinhua, April 11, 2007.

"La France célèbre la vitalité du lien traditionnel avec l'Afrique." *Le Monde,* February 15, 2007.

French, Howard. "China in Africa: All Trade, with No Political Baggage." *New York Times,* August 8, 2004.

French, Howard, and Lydia Polgreen. "China's Trade in Africa Carries a Price Tag." *New York Times,* August 21, 2007.

———. "New Power in Africa: Entrepreneurs from China Flourish in Africa." *New York Times,* August 18, 2007.

Goodman, Peter S. "China Invests Heavily in Sudan's Oil." *Washington Post,* December 23, 2004.

"Government Cancels Pact with China." *Africa Mining Intelligence,* March 7, 2007.

"Ground-Breaking Ceremony of China-Built Railway Launched in Nigeria." Xinhua News Agency, November 28, 2006.

Guemache, Hamid. "Autoroute est-ouest: La Proposition chinoise qui choque." *Le Quotidien d'Oran,* March 12, 2007.

Guemache, Hamid, and Pascale Braun. "Les Français en première ligne." *La Tribune,* December 12, 2005.

Guerra, João Paulo. "Caminho-de-Ferro de Benguela reconstruído até 2007." *Diário Económico,* February 22, 2006.

"Hangxiao Steel Structure Defends Handling of 4.4 Bln USD Angolan Contracts." Xinhua's China Economic Information Service, March 26, 2007.

Haski Pierre. "La Chine fait sa cour à l'Afrique." *Libération,* January 5, 2007.

Hauter, François. "Safari et lune de miel en Afrique." "Pillages chinois en forêt tropicale." "Bal lugubre dans les monarchies africaines." Series in *Le Figaro,* August 2007.

He Wenping. "China's Loans to Africaque Won't Cause Debt Crisis." *China Daily,* June 6, 2007.

Ihsane, El Kadi. "Autoroute Est-Ouest: Le Compte à rebours des 40 mois n'a pas commence." *El Watan,* July 3, 2006.

"Insécurité au Nord: La 5ème République, l'uranium et la rebellion." *Le Canard Déchaîné,* February 12–19, 2007.

Issa, O. "Rehaussement du prix de l'uranium: La Manne profitera-t-elle aux populations?" *Le Républicain,* August 8, 2007.

Joannidis, Marie. "Onu: Vers une nouvelle solidarité afro-asiatique?" *MFI,* October 27, 2006.

———. "Le Pauvre Sahel rêve d'or noir." *MFI,* August 5, 2005.

———. "Pétrole: Les Petits producteurs d'Afrique sont courtisés." *MFI,* February 18, 2005.

Keita, Oumarou. "Insécurité au Nord: Les FARS menacent les Chinois." *Le Républicain,* February 8, 2007.

Kennedy, Paul. "China Returns to Africa." *Khaleej Times,* October 16, 2006.

Labertit, Guy. "A qui profite l'uranium nigérien?" *Le Monde,* August 18, 2007.

Leplaideur, Marie Agnès. "L'Afrique de l'Ouest, troisième exportateur mondial de cotton." *Syfia,* November 17, 2006.

Lubumbashi-Mulenga, Cecilia. "Commemorating China-Africa Summit 1st Anniversary." *Times of Zambia,* November 15, 2007.

Lumisa, Godefroid Bwiti. "Ruée des Chinois sur les forêts africaines." *Infosud/ Syfia,* February 15, 2004.

McGreal, Chris. "Thanks China, Now Go Home: Buy-Up of Zambia Revives Old Colonial Fears." *The Guardian,* February 5, 2007.

McGregor, Richard. "Angola Deal Sparks China Shares Probe." *Financial Times,* April 8, 2007.

Mehdaoui, Z. "Les Entrepreneurs algériens veulent s'unir contre les Chinois." *Le Quotidien d'Oran,* January 29, 2007.

Melville, Christopher. "Chinese to Commence Rehabilitation of Key Angolan Rail Link." *Global Insight Daily Analysis,* January 11, 2006.

Mével, Jean-Jacques. "Les Réserves de change de la Chine: Un Casse-tête à 1000 milliards de dollars." *Le Figaro,* September 16, 2006.

Michel, Serge. "Reconstruire vite l'Angola, quitte à sauter sur une mine." *Le Monde,* October 27, 2007.

Mouawad, Jad. "Nowadays, Angola Is Oil's Topic A." *New York Times,* March 20, 2007.

Muanza, Manuel. "L'Angola salue le rôle de la Chine qui comprend la réalité africaine." Agence France-Presse, June 20, 2006.

Muller, Michel. "La Planète croule à nouveau sous les dépenses d'armement." *L'Humanité,* June 28, 2007.

"Le Niger et ses relations avec la Chine." *Le Quotidien du Peuple,* August 8, 2003.

"Niger Leader Denies Hunger Claims." BBC News, August 9, 2005.

Nivelle, Pascale. "La Ruée vers Canton des commerçants africains." *Libération,* November 3, 2006.

"Northern Nigerian Businessmen Debate Effects of China Investments." *U.S. Fed News,* February 22, 2007.

Okoroma, Louis. "The China Threat." *This Day,* December 13, 2006.

Oster, Shai. "China: New Dam Builder for the World." *Wall Street Journal,* December 28, 2007.

"Overseas Investment: The Myth and the Reality." *Petroleum Review,* September 30, 2007.

Puska, Susan. "Military Backs China's Africa Adventure." *Asia Times,* June 8, 2007.

Rémy, Jean-Philippe. "Bonne gouvernance: Fort de son pétrole, l'Angola se tourne vers la Chine pour échapper aux exigences du FMI." *Le Monde,* July 6, 2005.

Rodier, Arnaud. "L'Algérie privatise tous azimuts." *Le Figaro,* May 30, 2006.

———. "Déferlante chinoise sur les grands chantiers." *Le Figaro,* June 28, 2006.

———. "De quinze mille à vingt mille ouvriers et maçons chinois travaillent en Algérie." *Le Figaro,* June 28, 2006.

Russell, Alec. "Angolan Loan Casts Light on Ties with China." *Financial Times,* October 19, 2007.

———. "Angola Starts to Show It Will Not Be Beijing's Puppet." *Financial Times,* August 27, 2007.

———. "Angola Turns into Investors' Hot Spot." *Financial Times,* August 23, 2007.

———. "Infrastructure: Big Projects Fall Behind Schedule." *Financial Times,* January 23, 2008.

———. "Sky-High Rents in Rundown Luanda Fuelled by Oil Boom." *Financial Times,* October 9, 2007.

Russell, Alec, and Matthew Green. "Africa's Rresponse: Big Push to Be More Assertive." *Financial Times,* January 23, 2008.

Santiso, Javier. "Pourquoi l'Afrique intéresse de plus en plus les marchés financiers?" *Le Temps,* September 13, 2007.

Shacinda, Shapi. "Zambia Sees Foreign Investment Doubling in 2008." *Reuters,* May 23, 2008.

———. "Zambia and China to Spend $28 Million in Power Project." *Reuters,* August 31, 2007.

———. "Chinese Labour Policies Mar African Welcome." *Reuters,* August 9, 2006.

———. "Workers Shot During Zambia Copper Mine Riots." *Reuters,* July 26, 2006.

"Tchad-Chine: Un Rapprochement stratégique." *Syfia,* November 2, 2006.

Timberg, Craig. "The China Effect Hits Nigeria." *Miami Herald,* January 8, 2007.

Traub, James. "China's African Adventure." *New York Times Magazine,* November 19, 2006.

Tuquoi, Jean-Pierre. "La Chine pose ses pions en Afrique." *Le Monde,* January 12, 2006.

———. "Razzia sur le trésor du Katanga." *Le Monde,* June 11–12, 2006.

Walker, Andrew. "World's Forests Plundered as China Feeds Global Demand." *Sunday Independent,* April 8, 2007.

Wallis, William. "China to Eclipse Donors with Dollars: 20bn for Africa." *Financial Times,* May 18, 2007.

"Wolves in Africa: Chinese Banks Should Lend Responsibly in Developing Nations." *Financial Times,* October 25, 2006.

Yacoub, Hasna. "10,720 logements livrés d'ici la fin 2007." *La Tribune,* August 12, 2007.

"Zambia: Copper-Bottomed." *Economist Intelligence Unit,* April 16, 2008.

"Zambia NFC Africa Wants More Expatriate Work Permits." *Dow Jones International News,* June 16, 2008.

"Zambia NFC Mining Relieved by Banda's Election As President." *Dow Jones Newswire,* November 2, 2008.

"Zambian Government Condemns Strike at Chinese Copper Smelter." *Xinhua News Agency,* March 14, 2008.

"Zambian Opposition Leader Condemns Chinese Investment." *BBC Monitoring Africa*, July 5, 2007.

Zinsou, Lionel. "L'Afrique vous salue bien." *Le Monde,* September 30, 2007.

Online Journals

Clark, Stephen. "China Builds and Launches Satellite for Nigeria." *SpaceflightNow.com*, May 14, 2007.

Delaporte, Renaud. "La Chine a lancé une OPA amicale sur l'Afrique." *Agora Vox.fr* (November 2006).

Elraz, Khaled. "Coup d'état au Tchad: La Chine impliquée." *Afrik.com*, April 23, 2006.

"L'Embourgeoisement par les fonds politiques." *Nigerportal.com,* October 27, 2006.

Engdahl, F. William. "Darfur? It's the Oil, Stupid . . . " *GlobalResearch.ca*, May 20, 2007.

Finch, James. "Niger Rebels Interfere with Uranium Mining Plans." *Market Oracle.co.uk,* July 10, 2007.

Godwin, Nanna. "The New Face of Nigeria's Oil Industry." *ChinaDialogue .net*, November 15, 2006.

"Travail forcé des prisonniers chinois dans le BTP en Afrique: L'Omerta internationale." *Infoguerre.com*, March 17, 2006.

Violence, "Godfathers" and Corruption in Nigeria. New York: Human Rights Watch, October 11, 2007.

Yang, Cheng. "Les Fermiers chinois en Afrique." *Chinafrique.com*, September 2005.

Miscellaneous

The AK-47, the World's Favorite Killing Machine. Amnesty International, the International Action Network on Small Arms, and Oxfam International, June 26, 2006. www.amnesty.org/en/library/info/ACT30/011/2006.

Angola: "They Pushed Down the House": Forced Evictions and Insecure Land Tenure for Luanda's Urban Poor. Human Rights Watch, May 2007. www .hrw.org/africa/angola.

Arms Continuing to Fuel Serious Human Rights Violation in Darfur. Amnesty International, May 2007. www.amnesty.org/en/library/info/AFR54/019/2007.

"Chinese Involvement in African Illegal Logging and Timber Trade." Testimony of Allan Thornton, president for the Environmental Investigation Agency at the U.S. House of Representatives, Committee of International Relations, July 28. http://wwwa.house.gov/international_relations/109/tho072805.pdf.

Kaplinsky, Raphael, Dorothy McCormick, and Morris Mike. *The Impact of China on Sub-Saharian Africa*, University of Sussex, University of Nairobi, University of Cape Town, May 2006. www.uneca.org/eca_programmes/acgd/Overview_Report.pdf.

Mohan, Giles. *The Invisible Hand of South-South Globalisation: Chinese Migrants in Africa*: Rockefeller Foundation, Open University, October 2007.

Moncrieff, Richard. *French Development Aid and the Reforms of 1998–2002.* Doctoral thesis, University of Southampton Research Repository, e-Prints Soton, December 2004. http://eprints.soton.ac.uk/46178.

Pan, Esther. "China, Africa and Oil." *Council on Foreign Relations,* January 26, 2007. www.cfr.org/publication/9557.

Swan, James. "China's Expanding Role in Africa: Implications for the United States." Speech given at the Center for Strategic and International Studies, Washington, DC, February 8, 2007. www.csis.org/component/option,com_csis_pubs/task,view/id,3714.

UN Arms Embargoes: An Overview of the Last Ten Years. Control Arms Campaign, Amnesty International, the International Action on Small Arms and Oxfam International, March 2006. www.oxfamamerica.org/news andpublications/publications/briefing_papers/un_arms_embargoes.

"World Bank Group Finances Company Involved in the Illegal Destruction of the Congo Rainforest." Greenpeace International, August 29, 2007. www.greenpeace.org/international/press/releases/world-bank-group -finances-comp.

INDEX

SERGE MICHEL is deputy editor of the Swiss daily *Le Temps* in Geneva. He has worked as a correspondent in Iran and in Africa and is the founder, with Michel Beuret, of the Bondy Blog, one of France's most influential blogs, in the suburbs of Paris. Michel has written for *Fortune, Foreign Policy,* and *The Independent.* He was until recently the West Africa correspondent for *Le Monde.* He won the Albert Londres Prize, France's most prestigious journalistic award, for his work in Iran.

MICHEL BEURET is a reporter for Swiss television. He has been writing on China and Africa for over fifteen years. He first went to China in 1993 and has written extensively on migration and human trafficking in both China and Europe. He has been the foreign editor of Switzerland's *L'Hebdo* magazine.

PAOLO WOODS is an award-winning photographer dedicated to long-term projects that blend documentary photography with investigative journalism. Dutch-Canadian, he grew up in Italy and is now based in Paris. His work is regularly published in *Time, Newsweek, Le Monde, Geo,* and many other international publications. He has published four books with Serge Michel and is working on a new project on Iran. Woods has had solo exhibitions in France, the United States, Italy, China, Spain, Holland, and Austria, and numerous group shows around the world. His pictures are in the French National Library, the FNAC collection, and the collection of the Sheik Saud Al-Thani in Qatar. Various awards include a World Press Photo for his work in Iraq, the Alstom Prize for Journalism, the GRIN Prize in Italy, and the Open Society Institute's Moving Walls. His website is www.paolowoods.com.